HIGHLY PARALLEL COMPUTERS

IFIP WG 10.3 Working Conference on
Highly Parallel Computers for Numerical
and Signal Processing Applications
Sophia Antipolis, France, 24-26 March, 1986

NORTH-HOLLAND
AMSTERDAM · NEW YORK · OXFORD · TOKYO

HIGHLY PARALLEL COMPUTERS

Proceedings of the IFIP WG 10.3 Working Conference on
Highly Parallel Computers for Numerical
and Signal Processing Applications
Sophia Antipolis, France, 24-26 March, 1986

edited by

Gerard L. REIJNS
Delft University of Technology
The Netherlands

Michael H. BARTON
University of Bristol
United Kingdom

1987

NORTH-HOLLAND
AMSTERDAM · NEW YORK · OXFORD · TOKYO

ISBN: 0 444 70131 1

Published by:

ELSEVIER SCIENCE PUBLISHERS B.V.
P.O. Box 1991
1000 BZ Amsterdam
The Netherlands

Sole distributors for the U.S.A. and Canada:

ELSEVIER SCIENCE PUBLISHING COMPANY, INC.
52 Vanderbilt Avenue
New York, N.Y. 10017
U.S.A.

Library of Congress Cataloging-in-Publication Data

IFIP WG 10.3 Working Conference on Highly Parallel
   Computers for Numerical & Signal Processing
   Applications (1986 : Sophia-Antipolis, France)
   Highly parallel computers for numerical and signal
processing applications.

   Includes index.
   1. Parallel processing (Electronic computers)--
Congresses. I. Reijns, G. L. (Gerard Louis), 1930-
II. Barton, Michael H. III. International Federation for
Information Processing. Working Group 10.3. IV. Title.
QA76.5.I278 1986   004'.35   86-24001
ISBN 0-444-70131-1 (U.S.)

PRINTED IN THE NETHERLANDS

PREFACE

The papers in these Proceedings were presented at an International Working conference held from 24 to 26 March, 1986, in the pleasant surroundings of the Sophia Antipolis Research Park, near Nice, France. The conference was organised by Working Group 10.3 of the International Federation for Information Processing (IFIP).

The theme of the Working Conference, Highly Parallel Computers for Numerical and Signal Processing Applications, covers a rapidly growing field. This is caused on the one hand by the ever increasing processing requirements of more and more complex problems such as image enhancement, pattern recognition, and numerical processing of large amounts of data. Applications can be found in areas such as robotics, structural design, medicine etc. On the other hand there is the rapid development of micro-electronics, which offers solutions to the processing speed requirements in a variety of ways.

However, except for certain specific applications like image processing, parallel processing still poses many problems. We mention the need for suitable languages and compilers to express and exploit parallelism and the problem of utilising in an efficient manner the hardware resources present in a parallel structure. Many parallel computers suffer from the fact that for a large percentage of time, processing elements are waiting for the results to be provided by other processing elements.

In the past years, we have seen the success of some types of supercomputers. In order to obtain maximum computational speed, the algorithms and the architectures have to be matched more closely in the new generation of parallel computers.

The contents of these proceedings can be divided into four parts, viz:

Part I   Architectures and algorithms for parallel computers
The first 8 papers of the proceedings deal with this field. Data-flow, reduction, vector type machines and, in addition, memory structures for SIMD and MIMD architectures are discussed. Attention is also given to performance aspects of parallel processing.

Part II   Algorithms and mappings onto systolic arrays
Papers 9-14 are concerned with this subject.

Part III   Connections and communications between processors
> Papers 15 and 16 deal with the subject specifically, although other papers also touch upon this problem.

Part IV   Architectures for special applications
> Papers 17, 18 and 19 belong to this category.

As Programme Chairman, I would like to thank the members of the Programme Committee for their efforts in evaluating the submitted papers; and Mme Sonia Chakhoff, Mme Corinne Lefranc, Prof. F. Boeri and Dr. M. Auguin of the Local Organising Committee for their organisational work, and the Centre National de Recherche Scientifique (CNRS) for its support in bringing this conference to a success.

Programme Chairman
Prof. Gerard L. Reijns

PROGRAMME COMMITTEE

Prof. G.L. Reijns, Chairman, IFIP WG10.3, Delft University of Technology, The Netherlands.

Prof. F. Boeri, Université de Nice, France.

Prof. D.J. Evans, University of Technology, Loughborough, UK.

Prof. W.K. Giloi, GMD, Berlin, FRG.

Prof. C. Girault, Université Pierre et Marie Curie, Paris, France.

Prof. J.R. Gurd, University of Manchester, UK.

Prof. H.T. Kung, Carnegie-Mellon University, USA.

Dr. M.H. Barton, Secretary, IFIP WG10.3, University of Bristol, UK.

TABLE OF CONTENTS

Preface   v

Programme Committee   vii

I. Architectures and Algorithms for Parallel Computers

Rationale and Concepts for the SUPRENUM Supercomputer Architecture
P.M. Behr, W.K. Giloi and H. Mühlenbein   1

A Highly Parallel Architecture Based on a Distributed Shared Memory
A. Bode, G. Fritsch, W. Händler, W. Henning and J. Volkert   19

Parallel Programs for Numerical and Signal Processing on the
   Multiprocessor System DIRMU 25
E. Maehle and K. Wirl   29

A Parallel Reduction Architecture
T.D. Burnett   41

A Pipelined Code Mapping Scheme for Tridiagonal Linear Equation Systems
G.R. Gao   59

The Structure and Application of RPA — A Highly Parallel Adaptive
   Architecture
C. Jesshope, A. Rushton, A. Cruz and J. Stewart   81

Parallel Memory Management in a SIMD Computer
M. Auguin and F. Boeri   97

Performance Analysis of a Data-Driven Multiple Vector Processing System
N.P. Topham   111

II. Algorithms and Mappings onto Systolic Arrays

Matching Parallel Algorithms with Architectures: A Case Study
M. Cosnard, Y. Robert and M. Tchuente   127

A Linear Systolic Array for Romberg Integration
D.J. Evans   145

On the Synthesis of Systolic Structures
H.N. Djidjev   157

The Solution of Ordinary Differential Equations by Systolic Array
   Extrapolation Tables
D.J. Evans   175

The Utilisation of Bit Level Systolic Arrays in Word Level Systems
J.V. McCanny   191

MIMD Machines and Sparse Linear Equations
F.J. Peters   201

III. Connections and Communications between Processors

A Systolic Scheme for Fast Parallel Communication in VLSI
   Mesh-Connected Parallel Computers
M.V.A. Hâncu and K.C. Smith   211

Hypercube Argument Flow Multiprocessor Architecture with
   Arbitrary Number of Links
R. Lauwereins and J.A. Peperstraete   223

IV. Architectures for Special Applications

Experiments on a Data Flow Machine
M. Iwashita and T. Temma   235

A VLSI-Oriented Architecture for Parallel Processing Image Generation
W. Strasser   247

Parallel Processing of Video Images
G.L. Reijns, U.E. Kraus, G. Kirana and W.C. Hildering   259

Author Index   271

HIGHLY PARALLEL COMPUTERS
G.L. Reijns, M.H. Barton (editors)
Elsevier Science Publishers B.V. (North-Holland)
©IFIP, 1987

RATIONALE AND CONCEPTS FOR THE SUPRENUM SUPERCOMPUTER ARCHITECTURE

P.M. Behr, W.K. Giloi, H. Mühlenbein

Gesellschaft für Mathematik und Datenverarbeitung (GMD)
Birlinghoven and Berlin
W. Germany

Supercomputer architectures can be based on either of
two major principles, SIMD vector machines or MIMD
multiprocessor systems. In the report both solutions
are briefly characterized and compared in terms of
performance, cost-effectiveness, and software problems
involved. The discussion outlines the rationale for
the decision to develop a MIMD multiprocessor supercomputer rather than a SIMD vector machine. The hardware architecture and the software issues of the
system, called SUPRENUM-1 are discussed.

OPERATIONAL PRINCIPLES FOR SUPERCOMPUTERS

In this paper the term "supercomputer" refers to very high performance machines
for numerical applications; though our considerations to some extent hold true
as well for non-numerical supercomputers. Supercomputers obtain their performance from two contributing factors. Firstly, they operate at the highest possible speed technology can provide. Secondly, additional performance is gained
through parallel processing.

An algorithm may be generally defined as a partial order of operations, the
partial order being determined by the data dependencies between the operations.
We call the parallelism of an algorithm explicit if the data dependencies are
well-defined by the nature of the data types to be processed and, consequently,
are known a priori. We call the parallelism implicit if it is not a priori
known but must be determined through data dependence analysis.

What makes the dataflow principle so attractive is its property to enable the
machine to perform the data dependence analysis at run time and, thus, to
provide a convenient way of exploiting implicit parallelism. Since implicit
parallelism includes explicit parallelism, dataflow is a most general operational principle for parallel processing. Therefore, the expectation has often
been voiced that the dataflow machine may become the major parallel processing
architecture of the future. However, the forte of the data flow solution to
provide parallel processing in a "self-synchronizing" manner comes at the price
of considerable overhead and, therefore, is also its major disadvantage in
parallel processing applications where the parallelism is primarily the one
inherent in the data structure objects.

Unlike implicit parallelism, explicit parallelism can be exploited with minimal
control overhead, using either the SIMD or the MIMD mode of operation. Figure 1
presents a taxonomy relating the nature of parallelism (explicit or implicit)
to the appropriate control structures, processor structures, and communication
structures (Giloi, 1986).

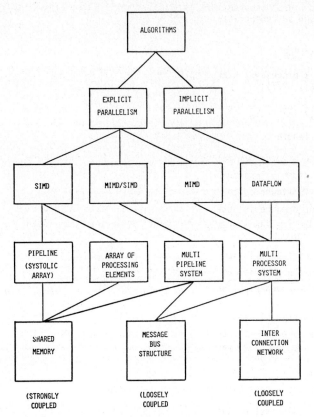

Figure 1
Taxonomy of parallel computer architectures

PERFORMANCE CONSIDERATIONS

In the following it is considered how the a priori known parallelism inherent
in data structure objects, i.e., in regularly ordered sets of data elements,
is exploited by the two types of machines, SIMD and MIMD, respectively.

The SIMD machine is assumed to be a vector machine operating with a number
of pipeline processors. The MIMD machine is assumed to consist of a large number

of "processing nodes" (conventional processor with private memory) which communicate through an appropriate interconnection structure.

SIMD Vector Machine

A pipeline of k processing stages operating within a clock interval T_p performs
(Ramamoorthy/Li, 1977):

$$P = \frac{k}{1 + (k-1)/L} \cdot \frac{1}{T_p} \quad \text{operations per second (OPS)}$$

on vectors of length L.

Note that for $L \to \infty$ the maximal performance, $P_{max} = k/T_p$, is reached. Conversely,
P may be considerably less than P_{max} if the vector length becomes very small.
A characteristic figure is the vector length $L_{\frac{1}{2}} = k-1$, for which only half of
the maximum performance is obtained. Since $1/T_p$ is the performance for k = 1,
$\frac{k}{1 + (k-1)/L}$ denotes the degree of parallel processing in the pipeline.
A higher degree of parallelism can be obtained only by multiplying the number
of pipelines in the machine. However, such an architecture is not SIMD anymore
but MIMD/SIMD, as each pipeline processor is controlled individually.

The performance gain of pipeline processing is lost if the vector length becomes short or - worse - if scalar operations are performed. In the latter case,
the execution time for a dyadic operation becomes:

$$T_{op} = 2\,T_m + T_s + k \cdot T_p$$

where: T_m = memory access time for an operand fetch

T_s = pipeline set up time (selection of operation, clearing of registers,
etc.)

$k \cdot T_p$ = pipeline flush time (i.e., time it takes an operand to travel
through (and be processed by) the pipeline.

This is much larger than the time per operation for the processing of long
vectors, which is $T_{op} \approx T_p$. This effect is known as the "scalar gap" of pipeline
processing. To minimize the scalar gap effect, the following measures can be
taken.

- keep T_m as small as possible (this is a matter of memory bandwidth)
- keep T_s as small as possible (this is a matter of pipeline processor design)
- keep the number of pipeline stages k low.

Consequently, pipeline processor design is a trade-off between high parallel
processing gain for long vectors (large k) and small scalar gap (small k).
A pipeline, in which each stage transforms a set of data values every T_p
seconds, requires that every T_p seconds as many operands as required by the
operation are fed into the pipeline. Likewise, if the pipeline produces a
result stream, there will be a new result value every T_p seconds. Since operand

and result values are stored in the main memory of the machine, the maximum
performance of the pipeline processor can be obtained only if the memory bandwidth is adequately high.

As a typical example we consider the inner product of 2 vectors: With each
step 2 operands must be fed into the pipeline, and 2 operations (multiplication and summation) are performed. Because of the reduction character of
the inner product, the entire operation produces only a single scalar result.
Thus, if the pipeline processor is to perform X MFLOPS, the memory it operates upon must be capable of delivering X million words per second.

With currently existing technology, the processing speed of the pipeline
stages is limited primarily by the packaging density which, in turn, is a
function of cooling. The technical limit for the processing bandwidth, in
any event, is much higher than the economical limit for the main memory bandwidth. This discrepancy can be overcome by executing strictly out of adequately
fast, small buffer memory. This seems only to shift the problem - since the
buffers must be filled or emptied at processing speed, a matching main memory
bandwidth is still required. However, a sufficiently high effective main memory bandwidth can now be obtained by memory interleaving, i.e., by filling
or emptying the buffers from several independent memory units in a time-skewed
fashion.

The price to pay for this simple solution is that the data must be read from
the interleaved memory in the same order in which they were stored. Consequently, the interleaving scheme works only if the machine does not perform
operations that change the order of vector elements.

THE CHOICE OF TECHNOLOGY

For the sake of discussion, two main technologies called "microcomputer technology" (MCT) and "main frame technology" (MFT) shall be characterized.

Microcomputer Technology:

- TTL or MOS, highly integrated low-power logic and memory (some 10^4 to 10^5 transistors per chip);

- predominant use of standard ("off-the-shelf") components, therefore lower design cost;

- low cost of packaging and cooling (forced air only);

- lower operating speed.

Main Frame Technology:

- ECL, less highly integrated high-power logic (some 10^3 transistors per chip); ECL or CMOS memory;

- predominant use of custom gate array logic, therefore higher design cost;

- higher cost of packaging and cooling;

- higher operating speed.

Of course, the cost-effectiveness of a computer depends not only on the technology but also on the architecture. Two examples shall illustrate that fact.

(A) A microcomputer with floating-point coprocessor has about the same cost per FLOPS as the MFT based vector machine. Hence, the conclusion can be drawn that the higher cost-effectiveness of MCT compensates for the lower efficiency of the conventional architecture.

(B) Comparing MCT vector machines with MFT vector machines, the former exhibit a much higher cost-effectiveness. The reason why nevertheless MFT is the dominating supercomputer technology is the much higher absolute performance MFT may provide.

This discussion can be summarized by stating that a supercomputer development based on MCT is less costly and risky. However, if one wants to reach the same performance as with MFT, a higher degree of parallel processing is required to make up for the lower operating speed of MCT. Whether the MCT solution is more cost-effective than its MFT counterpart is a question that can be answered affirmatively only if the vector machine architecture is chosen. In the case of a MIMD machine one will be quite satisfied if the cost-effectiveness of a MFT-based vector machine can be met. In this case the MIMD machine is the better choice, for it is more flexible and does not exhibit the "scalar gap".

The relationship between the two technologies, MCT and MFT, and the two architectural forms, SIMD and MIMD, can be summarized as follows:

MIMD multiprocessor systems with a large number of nodes (as needed to achieve supercomputer performance) can be realized only in MCT.

SIMD vector machines may be realized in both, MCT and MFT.

To conclude this section, we shall take a look at the absolute performance obtainable in either technology by contrasting the two cases, SIMD vector machine and MIMD multiprocessor system, respectively.

SIMD Vector Machine, MFT

As paradigm for maximal performance obtainable in ECL technology (MFT), we take the vector machines of Cray Research Inc. (CRAY-1, CRAY-X MP, CRAY-2). The following table presents the major parameters of these machines.

Model	Clock time T_p	Max. number of pipelines	Max. performance	Year
CRAY-1	12.5 nanoseconds	1	160 MFLOPS	1977
CRAY-X MP	9.5 nanoseconds	2	400 MFLOPS	1983
CRAY-2	approx. 5 nanoseconds	4	1000 MFLOPS	1986

MIMD Multiprocessor Machine, MCT

The maximal performance of an MIMD multiprocessor system with N nodes, obtained under most favorable conditions, is

$$P_{max} = q \cdot N \cdot P_n$$

if P_n is the performance of a node and q is an overhead factor, $q < 1$.
The conditions under which P_{max} can be reached are:

1. The algorithms executed by the machine must have a sufficiently high inherent parallelism in order to allow for the linear performance increase.

2. There is no communication bottleneck in the system.

If these conditions are violated, the performance actually obtained may be much smaller than P_{max}.

SIMD vector machines impose the constraint that the same operation is applied to all the elements of a vector. MIMD machines do not have that restriction and, thus, are more flexible. Because of the higher performance of a pipeline processor compared to an equally expensive conventional processor, however, SIMD vector machines provide more MFLOPS per cost unit than a comparable MIMD multiprocessor system.

Hence, the decision between the two architectural forms involves a trade-off between the higher cost-effectiveness of SIMD and the higher flexibility of MIMD. However, the latter exists only if it is not unduly constraint by the system's communication structure. To illustrate this point by an example, a communication structure which allows each node to communicate only with its nearest neighbors would constrain the use of the system to "nearest neighbor problems". This would unduly restrict the application spectrum of a MIMD machine and thus handicap its competitiveness with respect to the SIMD architecture. Consequently, the communication structure of a general purpose MIMD machine should provide total internode connectivity.

Highly integrated (256 Kbit) dynamic MOS memory allows a stream of up to 16 million words per second to be read into a pipeline processor. Static CMOS memory has become available with an access time of down to 15 nanoseconds. The paradigm of a highly integrated floating-point pipeline processor is the Weitek WTL 2264/2265 chip set (Weitek, 1986), which features the following performance:

    Floating-point operation (ADD, SUBTRACT, MULTIPLY), IEEE single precision:

    20.0 MFLOPS

    Floating-point operation (ADD, SUBTRACT, MULTIPLY), IEEE double precision:

    12.5 MFLOPS

If one wants a higher performance, one can cascade several such pipeline processor elements into a "macropipeline".

MIMD/SIMD Multiprocessor System, MCT

A single node that is based upon the use of the Motorola MC68020 microprocessor in connection with the Weitek floating-point pipeline processor and non-interleaved, static-column dynamic memory is able to perform 8 MFLOPS. Cascading multiplication and addition, e.g., to perform the dot product, results in 16 MFLOPS per node. A supercomputer with 256 nodes therefore has a peak performance of 4 MFLOPS, provided the nodes can communicate with each other in a bottleneck-free manner. These are the SUPRENUM specifications.

COMMUNICATION STRUCTURES IN PARALLEL COMPUTERS

SIMD Vector Machines

SIMD vector machines process operand data streams flowing from a storage to the pipeline processor, thereby producing result data streams flowing back to the storage. Thus their performance is determined either by the memory bandwidth or the processor bandwidth limitation, whichever comes first, and no further communication bottleneck exists. The same holds true for multipipeline machines in which the tasks running on the different processors are only "loosely coupled" (i.e., in which there is little data dependency between the tasks).

MIMD Multiprocessor Systems

To overcome the memory bandwidth limitation problem, each processor of a MIMD multiprocessor system must have its private memory. Such a processor-memory combination usually is called a "node". This approach puts the emphasis on the problem of providing an adequate <u>interconnection structure</u> (IS) to handle the inter node communication.

An adequate IS should satisfy the following conditions:

(1) It must provide total connectivity to maintain the potential flexibility of a MIMD machine.

(2) It must exhibit a sufficiently high bandwidth to avoid communication bottlenecks.

(3) It must be technically and economically feasible.

(4) It must be highly reliable.

The Problem With Interconnection Networks

Interconnection networks (IN) that are capable of connecting a number of source nodes with a number of destination nodes are considered by many as the solution to the interconnection problem in large scale SIMD multiprocessor systems. Many papers have been published dealing with such structures, their complexity, and their interconnection properties. Hardly any of these many papers is addressing the topic of the technical feasibility and the interconnection bandwidth obtainable in view of such mundane parameters as pin limitation, packaging problems, driving power limitation, cost, etc.

INs come in two major categories: single-stage (permutation) and multi-stage networks. In single-stage networks, a data packet may have to travel through the network several times in order to reach a given destination from a given source. In contrast, in a multi-stage network the data can flow directly from the source to the destination. Another distinction is that between circuit switching, where a physical connection is provided from source to destination, and packet switching, where a logical connection is provided for a packet traveling through the network. Furthermore, control may be centralized or decentralized.

If one takes a closer look, the seemingly large variety of INs proposed can be identified as variants of one of the 4 basic classes listed in the following table (Ermel, 1985).

Class	Network Type	Complexity
A	CROSSBAR SWITCH	$0 \ (n^2)$
B	BENES NETWORK	$0 \ (n \cdot \log n + n/2)$
C	N-CUBE, BASELINE, BANYARD, OMEGA, FLIP, DELTA	$0 \ ((n/2) \log n)$
D	DATA MANIPULATOR, INVERSE DATA MANIPULATOR	$0 \ (n + n \log n)$

Networks with (N·log N)-komplexity are not suitable for circuit switching, since they exhibit at any time a large incidence of mutual blockages of data paths. This leaves the crossbar switch, which provides total point-to-point connectivity, as the only viable solution for a circuit switching network. Packet switching networks, on the other hand, can readily deal with blockages, since the nodes have the capability of storing and keeping a packet for the duration of a blockage.

The switching elements of a circuit switching crossbar network are extremely simple (simple bus connection by tri-state logic). In addition, some hardware is needed to arbitrate the access to the crossbar busses. The switching elements of packet switching networks, on the other hand, must be intelligent communication processors that are orders of magnitude more complex than the simple switching elements of a circuit switching network. By the same token, they are also much slower, as they have to execute a complex microprogram to handle a packet. Therefore, if one compares only the switching complexity of different networks, one may be comparing apples with oranges.

A more detailed feasibility study conducted by Ermel (1986) has shown that the size of a crossbar network should not exceed that of a 32 x 32 switching matrix in order to be packagable in a reasonable manner; and 64 x 64 would absolutely be the technical limit. This means that the direct interconnection of, say, 256 or more nodes through a crossbar switching network is technically not feasible. Packet switching networks for the interconnection of an equally large number of nodes, even if still feasible in terms of pin limitation and packaging constraints, would be too slow for supercomputers.

The way out of this dilemma is a two-stage approach by forming clusters of nodes and connecting these clusters either via a crossbar network or an equally fast packet switching network. The interconnection of the nodes of a cluster may be performed through either a very high-speed cluster bus or, again, a crossbar network.

SOFTWARE PROBLEMS

Historically the parallel processing user has been a rather knowledgeable scientist or engineer who is willing to assume the burden of creating application programs using rudimentary environments. Detailed architectural and operating system knowledge as well as the intricate ability to manually map parallel algorithmus onto a virtual parallel architecture are some of the hurdles such users had to overcome.

Programming of Single-Pipeline Vector Machines

The programming of single pipeline vector machines usually is carried out in FORTRAN. A number of vectorizing compilers have been developed which map the inner loops of conventional, sequential FORTRAN programs onto the vector operations of the machine. The conditions under which such a mapping is possible and the techniques involved have become a well-understood topic.

Programming of Multi-Pipeline Vector Machines

Presently, multi-pipeline vector machines are programmed in a multitasking manner. Typically, a task is a part of a program that can be run in parallel with some other parts of the program. The work to be done is partitioned into at least as many tasks (processes) as there are pipelines. The system then maintains a task queue, to which an unoccupied pipeline can go in order to find a task to execute. This "task attraction" scheme works only in strongly coupled systems, i.e. systems with shared logical memory.

The primary tools for multitasking can be classified into three categories. They are: task creation, critical sections monitoring, and task synchronization. The most advanced tools can be found in the Denelco HEP system, whereas for example the Cray computers offer only low-level constructs such as LOCK and EVENT variables. The following little example demonstrates some of the problems:

```
SERIAL PROGRAM:      DO 1  I=1, NPIPES
                   1 CALL COMPUTES (I)
PARALLEL PROGRAM:    DO 1  I=1, NPIPES
                   1 CALL TASKSTART (ID, COMPUTES, I)
```

The two programs do not produce the same results. The reason is that FORTRAN calls are made by reference and the main task with the I-loop and the other tasks are running asynchronously.

Despite this and other classical "multitasking" problems the simple "task partioning" approach works on the presently existing vector machines with a small number of pipelines. The application programmer is assumed to be a knowledgeable system programmer capable of using the low-level multitasking tools.

This approach will not be acceptable when the number of pipelines becomes larger. The above mentioned low-level multitasking tools are fare too error prone for problems of higher complexity.

Experiences with MIMD Multi Processor Systems

The experiences with multitasking programming so far gained were made by system programmers and can be summarized as follows:

(1) The behaviour of even short parallel programs may be astonishingly complex.
(2) Tracking down a bug in a parallel program can be exceedingly difficult. This results from the combination of logical complexity, nonrepeatable behaviour, and the lack of existing tools.

No really satisfactory solutions to these difficulties are at the horizon. At best, only partial solutions can be expected. The following postulates can be given:

(1) Whenever possible, rewrite at least the "skeleton" of the parallel program from scratch.
(2) Given the great difficulty of finding bugs, much greater emphasis must be placed on writing code which is correct from the beginning.
(3) Use high-level synchronization policies wherever possible and hide (encapsulate) them as much as possible.

Programming of MIMD Multi Processor Systems

The problem of programming a MIMD multiprocessor system with a very large number
of nodes has been attacked only lately. Realistically, we see four different
ways how applications software may be written during the next 5 - 10 years.
Each of them currently has some severe drawbacks that limit their usefulness.
McGraw/Axelrod (1984) discuss the following four approaches:

(1) Extend existing languages, like FORTRAN, with new operations that
    allow users to express concurrency and synchronization.

(2) Extend existing compilers to identify concurrent operations wherever
    it can and insert the necessary synchronization (automatic paralleliza-
    tion).

(3) Add a new "language layer" on top of an existing language that describes
    the multitasking and the desired concurrency, while allowing the basic
    applications program to remain "relatively" unaltered (metalanguage
    approach).

(4) Integrate new languages and appropriate compilers which incorporate
    the concepts of concurrency and synchronization (e.g., a very high
    object-oriented and process-oriented procedural language or a func-
    tional language).

These four ways do not represent totally orthogonal approaches, and therefore
there can be no hard lines drawn between them. All of them involve some amount
of language and compiler alteration.

It is not the place here to identify the motivations behind persuing a specific
way and the critical "unsolved" issues that limit its acceptance at the present
time.

SUPRENUM-1: A MIMD SUPERCOMPUTER

Rationale for SUPRENUM-1

SUPRENUM-1 is a MIMD supercomputer development project funded by the Ministry
of Research and Technology (BMFT) of the German Federal Government. To carry
out the project a task force has been formed consisting of several research
institutions and companies. Specifically the Gesellschaft für Mathematik und
Datenverarbeitung (GMD) is involved in the following tasks:

• development of a first prototype hardware and system software (in close
  cooperation with the participating industry)

• development of specific program development environments

• development of application software, e.g., multigrad partial differential
  equation solvers (Trottenberg, 1984).

The rationale for the decision to build a MIMD multiprocessor system rather
than a super fast SIMD vector machine is multifold:

(1) The market for SIMD vector machines is highly competitive, whereas
    the market for MIMD supercomputers is just beginning to evolve.

(2) The higher flexibility of MIMD machines allows for a broader applica-
    tion spectrum.

(3) The "scalar gap" problem of SIMD vector machines does not exist in
    MIMD multiprocessor systems.

(4) It is expected that the MCT-based multiprocessor system will eventually become more cost-effective than the MFT-based vector machine of comparable performance.

(5) Given the appropriate hardware solution, the development cost of the MCT-based multiprocessor system is lower than would be the cost of developing an MFT-based vector machine.

(6) The MIMD multiprocessor system development will produce technological spin-offs that will benefit a whole spectrum of products (such a general spin-off effect could not be expected from the more specialized pipeline machine development).

The SUPRENUM-1 research and development project is product-oriented. This means that, in contrast to pure research, additional market-oriented requirements must be satisfied such as:

- the desired absolute performance must be obtained at competitive cost-effectiveness;

- the programming development environment provided must find user acceptance;

- the machine must be manufacturable, testable, and maintainable;

- there exists a time window during which the research and development project must lead to a production model.

In order to meet the time window requirement, the architectural design of SUPRENUM-1 will be based upon already proven yet highly innovative concepts and solutions. In this sense, the SUPRENUM-1 development is influenced in many ways by the solutions and experiences gained by the preceding UPPER-project (Behr/Giloi, 1984).

UPPER is the prototype of a high-performance, distributed multiprocessor system developed at the GMD Research Center for Innovative Computer System and Technology at the Technical University of Berlin (GMD-TUB FIRST). The project was funded by the BMFT under grant no. 413-5839-ITR8402 5.

The design of the UPPER system was based upon the following concepts:

- The task to be performed by the system is decomposed into a number of cooperating processes. Inter process cooperation is based on a simple client-server model, for the programming of which the user is offered an appropriate set of high-level clauses as extension of a programming language if his choice (PASCAL, MODULA 2, ...). Program decomposition into a set of cooperating processes is supported by a specific program development library.

- Synchronization of cooperating processes is based on the dataflow schema, i.e., is of the "no wait" variety (wait states occur only if necessitated by true data dependencies).

- Inter process communication is based upon the use of specifically declared communication objects and carried out by built-in mechanisms. Hence, the programmer has a high-level, abstract view of inter process communication.

- Communication objects, at the hardware level, are capability-addressed. Thus the system has complete control of the use of such objects and, consequently, system security and integrity is ensured by the hardware. The programmer, when using a communication object, specifies implicitly its intended use. This enables the system to grant the sharing processes appropriate access rights. By having a fast memory management hardware, which exercises access right control simultaneously to the address translation needed for the segmented virtual memory, the capability addressing of the communication objects causes no additional overhead.

- The nodes of the system communicate through a medium with practically
  unlimited transmission bandwidth, provided by the UPPERBUS, a fault-
  tolerant, bit-serial slotted ring bus with a data transfer rate of 560
  megabits per second. Since the slotted ring protocol is a collision-free,
  low-overhead protocol, the guaranteed net data rate of the UPPERBUS is
  50 megabytes per second.

SUPRENUM-1 HARDWARE ARCHITECTURE

In order to obtain a manageable, bottleneck-free interconnection structure,
SUPRENUM-1 has a hierarchical hardware structure consisting of nodes, clusters,
and hyperclusters.

As indicated in Figure 2, the basic processing node of SUPRENUM-1 is a single
board computer consisting of the following major components:

- powerful 32-bit ('front end') microprocessor, to function as program
  execution machine as well as scalar processor, in connection with 8 M-byte
  of high-speed dynamic memory;

- powerful floating-point vector processor (4 MFLOPS, IEEE standard single
  and double precision), performing a variety of complex numerical operations
  under microprogram control;

- microprogram controlled dedicated communication unit, to support the object-
  oriented communication mechanisms of the machine by an appropriate, fast
  memory management as well as by a copy processor which allows the objects
  of application-specific data types to be copied at high-speed from node to
  node.

Each node has a local operating system whose task is to boot-up the node on power-
on, manage and schedule the processes in the node, exchange communication objects
with other nodes, manage the local resources (e.g., disks), and perform comprehen-
sive self-testing and fault diagnosis routines.

Figure 3 depicts a block diagram of the cluster. The cluster contains up to 16
nodes plus a disk controller for local disks, the cluster monitor, and the communication unit for inter cluster communication. A cluster is accommodated in one
19" rack. The processors of the cluster communicate via an ultra-fast, proprietary,
message switching parallel bus, which allows several communication partners to
exchange messages simultaneously. The overall communication bandwidth of the
cluster bus is 256 megabits per second, a value that can hardly ever been ex-
hausted.

Smaller systems may consist of one hypercluster ring, comprising up to 4 clusters
(64 nodes) which are interconnected by one slotted ring bus (modified UPPERBUS)
with a transmission bandwidth of 560 M-bit per second.

Larger systems are structured in the form of a matrix of clusters whose rows
and columns, respectively, are hypercluster rings. That is, each cluster belongs to two hyperclusters, row and column. The hypercluster bus is not fault-
tolerant itself; rather, fault tolerance is achieved by alternate routing in
the matrix. The hypercluster bus controller provides a gateway between the row
and column each cluster belongs to, and it is intelligent enough to handle the
alternate routing task arising in the case of bus transmission faults. The bus
controller takes care of the protocol hierarchy that regulates the exchange of
packets or larger logical entities, formed by a number of packets, via the
slotted ring bus. It consists of: receive/transmit unit (RTU), transfer control
unit (TCU), and block transfer unit (BTU) (Zuber, 1985). The RTU is realized
by propriatory ECL gate array chips to achieve electrical stability and compact

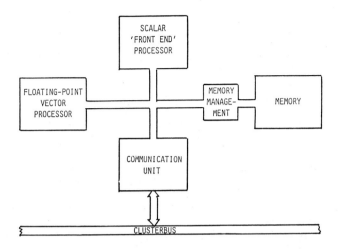

Figure 2
Structure of a node

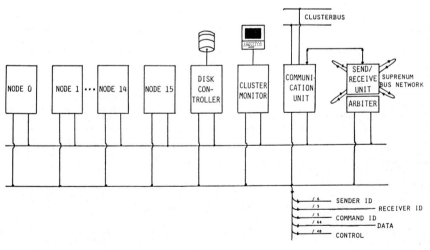

Figure 3
Structure of a cluster

packaging. Figure 4 illustrates the matrix structure of a SUPRENUM-1 configuration with 1024 nodes.

The SUPRENUM-1 system includes a separate operating system machine, whose tasks is to manage the global system resources such as global disk storage, take care of the workload distribution and system initialization, and perform the recovery procedures required in the case of fault detection. The operating system machine, however, is not involved in the actual program execution. Program execution is strictly handled by the collective of local node operating systems. In addition to the operating system machine, SUPRENUM-1 contains a dedicated diagnosis and maintenance machine. Moreover, additional 'peripheral computers' can be added such as: one or more program development machines and special graphics processors for graphical representation of results. Note that these additional machines can be arbitrarily inserted into any of the rings of the orthogonal network of ring busses and that it is specifically the (ultra high bandwidth) ring bus structure that allows for the wide-range configurability of the system.

SUPRENUM-1 SOFTWARE ARCHITECTURE

The SUPRENUM Software Environment

The SUPRENUM software system forms a hierarchy consisting of:

'firmware' (PROMed software) and software for node monitoring, process management, and inter process communication

operating system machine software providing the language interface as well as the central database management

appropriate parallel processing languages

program constructor

application constructor.

Every layer provides services to the upper layers. The language layer will be based upon the services of an abstract SUPRENUM machine.

The abstract SUPRENUM machine specifies the run-time environment the (distributed) 'global operating system' (collective of node operating systems) will support. Its basic features can be characterized as follows:

• The logical entity of computation is the process.
• The logical entity of communication is the communication object.
• Only communication objects can be shared by several processes; all other objects are local to the process who owns it.
• A structure is provided for aggregating processes with communication objects. This structure is called a task.
• The task provides the scope of protection.
• Multiple users may be given partitioned access to the machine.

The following basic features of the abstract SUPRENUM machine will be reflected in the programming languages

• dynamic creation of explicit processes;
• asynchronous inter process communication (IPC);
• messages received at a single process entry point.

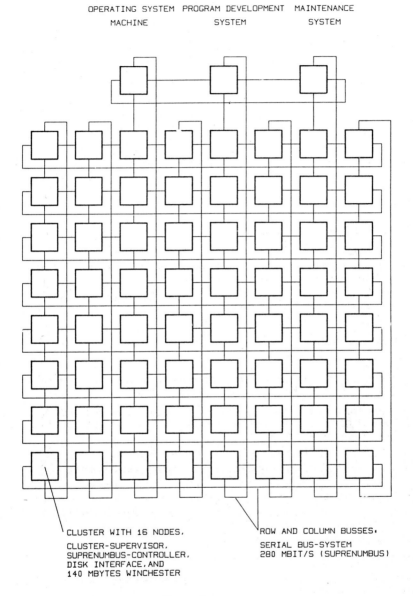

OPERATING SYSTEM PROGRAM DEVELOPMENT MAINTENANCE
MACHINE   SYSTEM   SYSTEM

CLUSTER WITH 16 NODES.
CLUSTER-SUPERVISOR.
SUPRENUMBUS-CONTROLLER.
DISK INTERFACE.AND
140 MBYTES WINCHESTER

ROW AND COLUMN BUSSES.
SERIAL BUS-SYSTEM
280 MBIT/S (SUPRENUMBUS)

Figure 4
SUPRENUM System With 64 Clusters (1024 Nodes)

Asynchronous communication through messages received at multiple entry points
have been explored by Behr/Giloi (1984) and Muehlenbein/Warhaut (1985). These
papers also deal with such pertinent issues as the granularity of program decomposition into processes (Muehlenbein/Warhaut) and the support of the programmer provided by a program development library (Behr/Giloi, 1984). The approach is
reflected in appropriate **extensions of PASCAL (Haenisch, 1984) and MODULA 2**
(Warhaut, 1986). In the SUPRENUM system, the languages extended for program
decomposition into cooperating processes with data-driven synchronization will
be FORTRAN and MODULA 2.

The SUPRENUM Program Constructor

The program constructor consists of language-specific syntactic editors and
interpreters. The constructor is based on the programming system generator
PSG developed by Bahlke/Snelting (1985). The constructor can deal with incom-
pletely specified program templates, called <u>fragments</u>, and comprises a 'hybrid'
editor, which accepts textual input and/or prompted input from an abstract syntax tree.

Program fragments called <u>program templates</u> will be implemented for specific
types of generic interprocess communication. One example is a program template
for a ring process structure, where every process sends messages only to its
left and right neighbor. Another example is the 2D-mesh, where each process can
send messages to its four neighbors, etc.

Other components of the programming environments are run-time debuggers of
different flavors. For example, language interpreters may be used for debugging
small modules, simulators may be used for debugging larger programs, and a
performance monitor may be used for performance-related debugging on the physical SUPRENUM machine.

The SUPRENUM Application Constructor

The SUPRENUM Application Constructor will allow users who do not want to do
low-level programming to implement applications by using existing application
software packages.

The development of the SUPRENUM Application Constructor is a very research-
oriented topic. The constructor will have to contain specialized application
languages for restricted application domains, as well as a knowledge base for
guiding the user in the task of generating applications by some heuristics.

First examples will be a very high level language for specifying the resolution of partial differential equation solving and an expert system for creating
the appropriate multigrid programs.

REFERENCES

Bahlke/Snelting (1985)   Bahlke R., Snelting G.:"The PSG Programming System
                         Generator", ACM SIGPLAN Notices 20,7 (July 1985)

Behr/Giloi (1984)   Behr P.M., Giloi W.K.:"Obtaining a Secure, Fault-
                         Tolerant, Distributed System With Maximized Performance",
                         in G. Reijns (ed.): Hardware Supported Implementation of
                         Concurrent Languages in Distributed Systems, North Holland,
                         Amsterdam 1984

Ermel (1985)   Ermel W.:"Untersuchungen zur technischen Realisierbarkeit
                         von Verbindungsnetzen für Multicomputer-Architekturen",
                         Ph.D., Technical University of Berlin, 1985

Ermel (1986)   Ermel W.:"Vorschlag zum Aufbau eines 32x32 Crossbar
                         Networks", GMD FIRST Internal Report 1986

Filman/Friedman (1984)   Filman R.E., Friedman D.P., Coordinated Computing,
                         McGraw-Hill, New York 1984

Giloi (1986)   Giloi W.K.:"Principles of Computer Architecture" in
                         R. Gueth (ed.): Computer Systems for Process Control,
                         Plenum Press, New York - London, 1986

Haenisch (1984)   Haenisch R.:"PARALLEL PROCESSING PASCAL Manual",
                         GMD FIRST 1984

McGraw/Axelrod (1984)   McGraw J., Axelrod T.S.:"Exploiting Multiprocessors:
                         Issues and Options", Lawrence Livermoore Preprint
                         UCRL-91734, 1984

Muehlenbein/Warhaut   Muehlenbein H., Warhaut S.:"Concurrent Multigrid in an
         (1985)   Object-Oriented Environment", in Degroot D. (ed.):
                         Proc. 1985 ICPP

Ramamoorthy/Li (1977)   Ramamoorthy C.V., Li H.F.:"Pipeline Architecture",
                         ACM Computing Surveys 9,1 (March 1977), 61-102

Trottenberg (1984)   Trottenberg U. (ed.):"Rechnerarchitekturen für numerische
                         Simulation auf der Basis superschneller Lösungsverfahren",
                         GMD Studien Nr. 88, Sept. 1984

Warhaut (1986)   Warhaut S.:"Concurrent MODULA 2 Specification",
                         GMD Report 1986

Weitek (1985)   Weitek Corp.:"WTL 1264/WTL 1265 Preliminary Data",
                         Sunnyvale, CA., 1985

Zuber (1984)   Zuber G.:"UPPERBUS - A Bit-Serial Computer Interconnec-
                         tion Bus With 280/560 Mbps", GMD FIRST Tech. Report 12,
                         1984

HIGHLY PARALLEL COMPUTERS
G.L. Reijns, M.H. Barton (editors)
Elsevier Science Publishers B.V. (North-Holland)
©*IFIP, 1987*

A HIGHLY PARALLEL ARCHITECTURE BASED
ON A DISTRIBUTED SHARED MEMORY

Bode, A., Fritsch, G., Händler, W., Henning, W., Volkert, J.

Institut für Mathematische Maschinen
und Datenverarbeitung (Informatik III)
Universität Erlangen-Nürnberg
Martensstr. 3, D-8520 Erlangen, F.R. Germany

For a large number of scientific computations (e.g. multigrid
algorithms) an enormous amount of data has to be handled and
processed. Therefore in the context of a parallel computing
system the organization and access to primary memory and the
close coupling of secondary memories is crucial to the overall
system performance. For applications with local character we propose the concept of a distributed shared memory as the basis for
a hierarchical NN (nearest neighbour) multiprocessor system. The
systems architecture, applications and first results on the EGPA
and DIRMU multiprocessors are presented.

1. INTRODUCTION

The analysis of scientific computations, especially the class of numerical simulations of physical phenomena shows the need for very powerful supercomputers
concerning computational performance as well as memory capacity ([1] , [2] ,
[3]). In order to obtain from computer experiments both mathematical converg-
ency and physically significant results, the approximative discretization steps of
the variables involved in the real phenomenon must be sufficiently fine. Thus in
simulation calculations large amounts of data are generated and processed. Furthermore these simulations will be applied to more and more complex real systems.

On the other hand the performance of computers can be increased both by technological advance and by parallel architecture. Physical laws limit the performance
improvement to be obtained by the first factor. On the other hand, parallel
systems, especially multiprocessor organizations can be combined to large
system size.

To obtain important speedups relative   to monoprocessor systems a suitable
mapping of the problem structure onto the multiprocessor structure must be found
concerning the organization of the elements of storage, transformation and transportation as well as the overall control and programming strategy.

In the following we discuss a proposal for a high performance multiprocessor
system whose structure was derived from the ample class of scientific user problems with gridlike data structure. For instance many phenomena in physics,
chemistry, engineering sciences can be described by systems of partial differential equations. The numerical treatment starts with some discretization which leads
to a system of linear equations.

2. CONCEPT OF A MULTIPROCESSOR WITH DISTRIBUTED SHARED MEMORY

2.1 PROBLEM STRUCTURE AND MULTIPROCESSOR ARCHITECTURE

In order to compute large problems efficiently on multiprocessor systems the problem structure must be mapped suitably onto the multiprocessor structure. For this purpose, the problem has to be partitioned appropriately into subtasks. On the other hand the multiprocessor system should have suitable architectural and performance features. In the following we discuss the requirements as to the interconnection system, the computation speed of the node processors, the organization of primary memory, the processor-memory, memory-peripheral bandwidth etc. for multigrid algorithms as one sub-class of the extensive user problem class in question. Presently, multigrid methods are widely used and implemented with various numerical simulation problems.

The analysis of multigrid algorithms [4], [1] gives the following requirements for a computer suited to the processing of this class of applications:
- 10^9 or more grid points per time step in 2D or 3D problems
- between 5 and 30 variables per grid point depending on type of algorithm and applications
- 300 to 10^5 time steps to be calculated
- 100 to 4000 arithmetical operations per grid point and time step.

All of the variables and operations are on data of the floating point type with 32 or 64 bit accuracy.

The algorithms used in multigrid applications may be divided into four classes [4]:
- interpolation: coarse-to-fine transfer between 2 grids: generation of values for the finer grid from values of the coarser grid
- restriction: fine-to-coarse transfer between 2 grids: generation of values for the coarser grid from values of the finer grid
- relaxation: smoothing process only on one type of grid
- direct solver executed on the coarsest grid.

Interpolation, restriction and relaxation are algorithms of local and homogeneous type. They are operating on restricted neighbourhoods concerning grid point values and for the major part of the grid they perform identical operations.

From this specifications of the tasks to be performed we derive the following architectural features of a multiprocessor system.

1. The enormous amount of data to be used makes it impossible to hold resident all the values needed in the main memory of the system. The main memory (or memories) must be organized as a window of secondary storage with larger capacity. On the other hand, fast access to the data is crucial for performance. This is only obtainable by closely coupling the secondary to the primary memory i.e. a high bandwidth to the peripheral memories must be realized by fast disc devices (10 MBytes per second), parallel use and parallel access by parallel channels.

   Separate and parallel channels to secondary storage can only be used if the primary memory is subdivided into independently accessible modules. This leads to the concept of a distributed primary memory (which will nevertheless be a shared one for other reasons). With 64 disc units and associated channels a secondary storage of at least 32 G Bytes and a transfer rate of 640 M Bytes per second should be obtainable.

2. Since multigrid algorithms have a regular data structure (grid structure), a regular computer structure should be a good solution for this problem. We propose a rectangular nearest neighbour (NN-) array of processor-memory modules (PMMs) with toroidal closing, where each processor has direct access to his associated module of the distributed shared memory and to the associated modules of his four nearest neighbours (to be explained under 4.) With a 256 PMM system and 4 MBytes for each associated memory module total main memory capacity would be 1 G byte.

The mapping of data onto the multiprocessor structure cannot be a 1 to 1 mapping (number of grid points is too big). Rather, a 2D or 3D subarea of the entire data structure consisting of several hundreds or thousands of grid points should be mapped onto an individual PMM.

3. Interpolation and restriction work on grids with changing granularity. To maintain the direct access to neighbouring points in a NN-structure with coarser grids, a hierarchy of NN-arrays interconnected in a pyramidal structure should be used. This pyramidal structure can also support the implementation of control and I/O functions. The pyramid should at least contain two physical levels. It is possible to represent the uppermost levels by a virtual system, physically realized by a very high speed bus concept.

4. Multigrid algorithms mostly consist of local operations within and between grids. This implies that the access time to local data must be short. Within a 2D or 3D subarea of the data mapped onto one PMM this access time corresponds to one primary memory access (we assume that data are already loaded from secondary memory). Most interesting are the possibilities of access to data which are on the borders of such areas that might need data from subareas mapped onto neighbour-PMMs. With the concept of a distributed shared memory, where each processor has access to his own associated module and the associated modules of his four nearest neighbours, it can be shown that every data access to a 2D or 3D border value requires the time of a simple main memory access. Of course, as the individual memory module may be accessed by different processors, it must be multiported. The time penalty for the multiport is significantly smaller than for any type of I/O - or message-oriented information transfer. Once again, as access to "bordering" data occurs rather frequently, it seems to be most important for the overall system performance to execute it in the order of a memory access time.

5. Multigrid methods use subalgorithms with homogeneous operations. Intelligent microprogrammed coprocessors with multiple ALUs and autonomous address calculation units can be used to implement a "multigrid macroinstruction set". Such a macroinstruction set benefits from the effects of vertical migration (mostly in the sense of the reduction of main memory accesses for machine instruction fetches) and of data structure architectures (addresses calculation of complex data structures in hardware/firmware instead of machine code). With fairly conventional technology (highly integrated floating point chips as AMD 29325, WEITEK 1164/5 or Analog Devices ADSP 3220) between 5 and 20 MFLOPS per PMM may be obtained or 1 to 4 GFLOPs for the overall system.

6. To cope with the evaluation of algorithms and the changing number of grid points for different applications the system performance should be variable in all dimensions. The proposed structure with the concept of a distributed shared memory is fully extensible in this sense, since it consists strictly of a variable number of elementary pyramids with constant local interconnections complexity (processor and memory fan-in / fan-out independent from the number of PMMs in the whole system).

A. Bode et al.

Figure 1 shows the topology of the proposed system, figure 2 the details of the NN connection of PMMs and the mapping of the application (2D case) onto the PMM array.

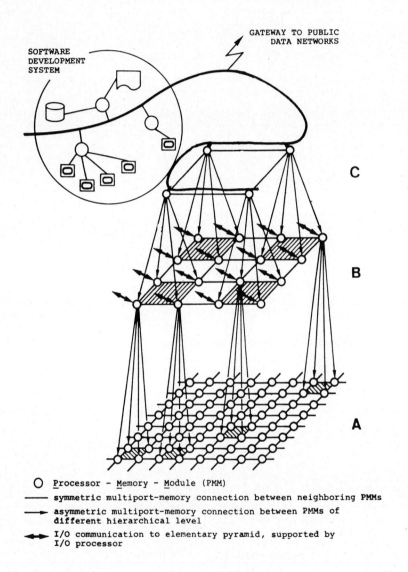

GATEWAY TO PUBLIC DATA NETWORKS

SOFTWARE DEVELOPMENT SYSTEM

C

B

A

O <u>P</u>rocessor - <u>M</u>emory - <u>M</u>odule (PMM)

⸺ symmetric multiport-memory connection between neighboring PMMs

⟶ asymmetric multiport-memory connection between PMMs of different hierarchical level

⟷ I/O communication to elementary pyramid, supported by I/O processor

Figure 1: Topology of a multiprocessor structure for gridlike application based on the concept of distributed shared memory.

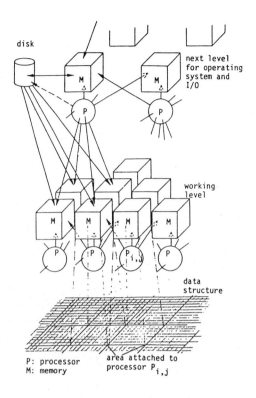

Figure 2: Mapping of a 2D gridstructure onto the system structure (partial view)

2.2 Erlangen multiprocessor systems

The proposed system structure is derived from previous multiprocessor systems developed at the IMMD of the University of Erlangen-Nürnberg. The EGPA-pilot system (Erlangen General Purpose Array supported by the German Ministry for Research and Technology, 1978 - 1983) is a 5 processor system (elementary pyramid) consisting of 5 microprogrammable 32 Bit process control computers AEG 80-60 with a distributed shared memory. With this system important speed-ups against the monoprocessor case for a large number of applications could be obtained. System details and results have been described elsewhere ([5], [6], [7], [8], [9], [10]).

The DIRMU system (DIstributed Reconfigurable MUltiprocessor kit supported by the German Science Foundation, SIEMENS AG and the German Ministry for Research and Technology) provides the basic building blocks for multiprocessor systems with different plugable topologies. A 25 processor system is running since summer 1985. The individual processor consists of 8086 and 8087, and local primary memory, the interprocessor communication is achieved through an additional distributed shared memory. System details have been described elsewhere ([11], [12], [13], [14]).

For DIRMU, a microprogrammable coprocessor ([15] has been designed and
tested with a theoretical internal performance of 8 MFLOPS and 16 MIPS, The
coprocessor structure is shown in figure 3. With the current 8086/8087 DIRMU
the maximum internal speed can not be obtained since the system is bus- and
memory bound. Nevertheless the coprocessor allows for studies in future 32-Bit
processor-oriented systems based on distributed shared memory.

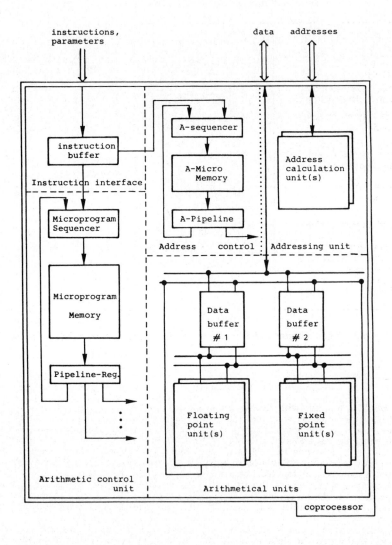

Figure 3: Structure of microprogrammable coprocessor for the multigrid oriented
multiprocessor architecture

3. IMPLEMENTATION RESULTS on **EGPA** SYSTEMS

In order to demonstrate the capacity of an EGPA system, some algorithms have
been implemented on the pilot system (4 worker processors at the lowest level)
and recently on a 21-processor pyramid (16 worker processors at the lowest
level) built with DIRMU-node processors (processor-memory-module, PMM). As
programming languages were used ALGOL 68 (subset) and MODULA 2. In
comparison with monoprocessor program runs, speedup values were calculated
from the computation times (Table 1).

Algorithm / problem	problem size	number of processors	speedup
Electrical power nets	< 650 nodes	4	3.6
Matrix inversion by column substitution	dense matrix with dimension 200	4	3.9
Matrix inversion by Gauß Seidel	dense matrix with dimension 200	4	nearly 4.0
Steady Stokes equation solved by multigrid using V-cycles	16K cells with 3 variables each in the finest grid	8	7.92
Sparse matrix inversion	dimension 1200 with about 4 % non-zeros	16	9.7
Matrix multiplication	dense matrix with dimension 800	16	15.4
Poisson equations with Dirichlet conditions solved by full multigrid using V-cycles	64 K points in the finest grid	16	15.3

Table 1: Speedups measured for different applications implemented on EGPA
multiprocessors

One should note that with EGPA systems only the worker PMMs contribute to the
overall performance so that the maximal speedup is equal to the number of
worker PMMs (at the lowest level). There is some loss of computational performance because the PMMs of the higher levels are used for operating system
functions. For instance the PMMs at the second level control the access to the
disks (with efficiency calculations, usually I/O-processors are not considered).
The processor on the top (for instance at the third level) represents a comfort-
able interface which allows the user to communicate with the system as with a
monoprocessor. Moreover, at the higher levels part of the user program can be
executed. This possibility was used for the implementation of multigrid methods.

All the algorithms given in Table 1 were parallelized by data partitioning. Thereby,
the user partitions the data in positions, e.g. sub-matrices. The data portions
are associated with the PMMs of the nearest-neighbour array in a natural way
(Fig. 2). The aim is to achieve load balancing on the processor array. Each pro-

cessor works on its data portion being controlled by usual monoprocessor programs to which only some communication parts have to be added . Actually the programming technique for these multiprocessor systems is essentially the same as for a monoprocessor. Because of the inherent data locality of the studied user problems, it was sufficient that all processors of the array have access to the memories of their neighbouring PMMs. In particular, this was shown with multigrid problems.

In several cases data locality can be only accomplished by modifying considerably the algorithms. For instance this has to be done for matrix multiplication. We used the well-known CANNON-algorithm . This algorithm was changed to the effect that sub-matrices instead of single elements were shifted over the processor array and were simultaneously treated during this operation [16] . Another consequence of data locality is local synchronization, that is, a processor merely waits for data generated by its direct neighbours. These neighbour-PMMs signal the readiness of the data by setting a certain state of a SPINLOCK variable (often represented as a time stamp). Only with direct methods for solving linear equation systems there is some need for global synchronization. This can be achieved easily by using the tree in the EGPA structure. We explain this for the Gauss elimination. Each processor calculates, per step, a pivot within its data portion and communicates this proposal to its master at the next higher level of the EGPA system. Finally the processor on the top selects a pivot from the proposals and broadcasts it to all processors. Then the next step of the algorithm starts (for more details see [16]).

The speedup values measured for most studied problems were approximately equal to the number of PMMs at the lowest level (worker processors), provided that the problem size was sufficiently large. Sparse matrices are an exception because of the irregularity of the data structure and because of the sequential portion of the program which was higher in comparison to the other problems. The measured efficiency of more than 50 % (see Table 1) can be considered as satisfying with regard to this problem class.

Summarizing the results, we can conclude that multiprocessor systems with EGPA architecture are well suited for user problems with a gridlike data structure. This was shown by the speedup values. Furthermore theoretical results on this issue are published in [17, 18] .

4. OUTLOOK

Further research work is aimed to other problem classes. We believe that multiprocessor systems with EGPA architecture can be used successfully for a broad spectrum of applications which do not necessarily have a gridlike data structure. For instance, we intend to study algorithms which make more use of the hierarchical feature of EGPA systems (e.g. methods of artificial intelligence). Presently, we are going to analyse the problem structure of VLSI simulation algorithms (logic, circuit and device level).

Moreover, applications will be analyzed which are characterized by large data amounts and a high computation demand. We think that large EGPA systems are well suited to treat such applications, provided that they are sufficiently equipped both with many I/O-channels (at the second level) and with a powerful floating-point co-processor in each PMM as described above (see also [19] .

The discussion, so far, has referred to single user systems. However, it is conceivable to use EGPA systems in a space sharing mode (see [20], i.e. partitioning the worker processor array (and correspondingly the higher level arrays) into several continuous parts each one performing a user task independently of the others. Such a system with space sharing operating mode could be used in a computing center.

5. REFERENCES

[1] Bode, A.; Fritsch, G.; Henning, W.; Volkert, J.: High performance multiprocessor systems for numerical simulation. Proc. SCS 85 / First International Conference on Supercomputing Systems, St. Petersburg, Florida, 1985

[2] Hockney, R.W.; Eastwood, J.W.: Computer Simulation Using Particles. McGraw-Hill (1981)

[3] Rodrigue, G.; Giroux, E.D.; Pratt, M.: Large-scale Scientific Computation. Computer 13, 11, 65-80 (1980)

[4] Stüben, K.; Trottenberg, U.: Multigrid methods: Fundamental algorithms, model problem analysis and applications. In: Multigrid Methods. Proceedings of the Conf. held at Köln-Porz, Nov. 23-27, 1981 (W. Hackbusch; U. Trottenberg, eds). Lecture Notes in Mathematics. Springer Verlag Berlin, 960, 1-176 (1982)

[5] Händler, W.; Hofmann, F.; Schneider, H.J.: A General Purpose Array with a Broad Spectrum of Applications. In: Händler, W.: Computer Architecture, Informatik Fachberichte, Springer Verlag Berlin Heidelberg New York 4, 311-35 (1976)

[6] Fritsch, G.; Kleinöder, W.; Linster, C.U.; Volkert, J.: EMSY85 - The Erlangen Multiprocessor System for a Broad Spectrum of Applications. Proc. 1983 Int. Conf. on Parallel Processing, 325-330 and in: Supercomputers: Design and Applications (K. Hwang, ed.), IEEE Comp. Soc. (1984)

[7] Händler, W.; Bode, A.; Fritsch, G.; Henning, W.; Volkert, J.: A tightly coupled and hierarchical multiprocessor architecture. Computer Physics Communications 37 (1985) 87-93, North-Holland, Amsterdam

[8] Hofmann, F.; Händler, W.; Volkert, J.; Henning, W.; Fritsch, G.: Multiprocessor-Architekturkonzept für Mehrgitterverfahren. In: U. Trottenberg, Wypior (eds): Rechnerarchitekturen für die numerische Simulation auf der Basis superschneller Lösungsverfahren I: GMD Studien Nr. 88, 65-76 (1984)

[9] Fromm, H.J.; Hercksen, U.; Herzog, U.; John, K.-H.; Klar, R.; Kleinöder, W.: Experiences with Performance Measurements and Modelling of a Processor Array. IEEE-TC, C-32, 1, 15-31 (1983)

[10] Händler, W.; Herzog, U.; Hofmann, F.; Schneider, H.J.: Multiprozessoren für breite Anwendungsgebiete: Erlangen General Purpose Array. GI/NTG-Fachtagung "Architektur und Betrieb von Rechensystemen", Informatik-Fachberichte, Springer Verlag Berlin Heidelberg New York, 78, 195-208 (1984)

[11] Händler, W.; Rohrer, H.; Thoughts on a Computer Construction Kit. Elektronische Rechenanlagen 22, 1, 3-13 (1980)

[12] Händler, W.; Schreiber, H.; Sigmund, V.: Computation Structures Reflected in General Purpose and Special Purpose Multiprocessor Systems. Proc. Int. Conf. on Parallel Processing (1979)

[13] Händler, W.; Maehle, E.; Wirl, K.: DIRMU Multiprocessor Configurations, Proc. 1985 Int. Conf. Parallel Processing, 652-656

[14]   Händler, W.; Maehle, E.; Wirl, K.: The DIRMU Testbed for High Per-
        formance Multiprocessor Configurations. Proc. SCS '85, First Interna-
        tional Conference on Supercomputing Systems, St. Petersburg,
        Florida 1985

[15]   Bode, A.: Ein Mehrgitter-Gleitkomma-Zusatz für den Knotenprozessor
        eines Multiprozessors. In: U. Trottenberg, Wypior (eds).: Rechnerar-
        chitekturen für die numerische Simulation auf der Basis superschneller
        Lösungsverfahren I: GMD Studien Nr. 88, 153-60 (1984)

[16]   Henning, W.; Volkert, J.: Programming EGPA systems. Proc. IEEE
        Computer Society Press 1985. 5th Int. Conf. Distributed Computing
        Systems, 552-559

[17]   Mierendorff, H.: Transportleistung und Größe paralleler Systeme bei
        speziellen Mehrgitteralgorithmen. GMD-Studien Nr. 88, GMD,
        D-5205 St. Augustin/FRG, 41-54 (1984)

[18]   Kolp, O.: Parallele Rechnerarchitekturen für Mehrgitteralgorithmen.
        Workshop "Rechnersimulation", GMD, D-5205 St. Augustin/FRG (1984)

[19]   Bode, A.; Fritsch, G.; Händler, W.; Henning, W.; Hofmann, F.;
        Volkert, J.: Multigrid oriented computer architecture. 1985 Int. Conf.
        on Parallel Processing, 89 - 95

[20]   Händler, W.: "Thesen und Anmerkungen zur künftigen Rechnerent-
        wicklung". In: Gert Regenspurg (ed): GMD Rechnerstruktur-Work-
        shop, München 1980, S. 17 - 47

HIGHLY PARALLEL COMPUTERS
G.L. Reijns, M.H. Barton (editors)
Elsevier Science Publishers B.V. (North-Holland)
IFIP, 1987

PARALLEL PROGRAMS FOR NUMERICAL AND SIGNAL PROCESSING ON THE MULTIPROCESSOR SYSTEM DIRMU 25

Erik Maehle and Klaus Wirl

Department of Computer Science (IMMD)
University of Erlangen-Nuremberg
D-8520 Erlangen
Federal Republic of Germany

For the execution on a multiprocessor system a problem has to be decomposed into concurrent processes that run in parallel on several processors. In this paper problem decomposition is discussed for two sample problems from numerical mathematics (Laplace PDE) and signal processing (speech preprocessing). The resulting parallel programs are described and their implementation on the multiprocessor system DIRMU 25 - a 25-processor system that is operational in Erlangen - is discussed.

INTRODUCTION

MIMD multiprocessors with a large number of processors are an attractive architecture for high-performance computing systems for numerical and signal processing applications [1]. While commercial high-speed systems are still mostly based on vector processors, some practical experience already exists with experimental MIMD machines like C.mmp [1], Cm* [2], Cosmic Cube [3] or Butterfly [4] having various interconnection structures (crossbar switch, hierarchical bus system, n-cube, Banyan network). Another interesting approach is the Inmos transputer [5], a VLSI component for the construction of large MIMD machines. Programs for MIMD machines consist of a set of concurrent processes which operate simultaneously and cooperatively to solve a given problem (parallel programs).

In this paper we will discuss the design of parallel programs for two simple (but typical) problems from numerical mathematics and signal processing as well as their implementation on the multiprocesor system DIRMU 25 [6]. First the application problems and sequential algorithms for their solution will be presented. Next we will derive the corresponding parallel programs. So far the discussion will be machine-independent. Then the mapping of the parallel processes on DIRMU 25 will be discussed. Note that DIRMU 25 has neither a fixed number of processors nor a fixed interconnection structure. Being a multiprocessor kit the machine structure can be matched to the program structure as closely as possible. Of course synchronization and communication between processes play an important role. Finally speedup measurements for the resulting implementations are presented which show that high speedups can really be achieved on DIRMU 25.

SAMPLE APPLICATIONS AND SEQUENTIAL PROGRAMS

The numerical problem, we will take as an example, is to solve the Laplace partial differential equation (PDE)

$$\partial^2 u/\partial x^2 + \partial^2 u/\partial y^2 = 0 \qquad (1)$$

with given boundary conditions (Dirichlet's problem). Though more efficient
solutions exist for this problem, for reasons of simplicity we will only consider
the classic Gauss-Seidel method here. Other PDE-solvers on DIRMU are for example
described in [6] and [7].

The problem is solved on an n x m grid U with the boundary values given. The
values in the interior of U are computed iteratively according to the following
formula

$$U[i,j]:=(U[i-1,j]+U[i,j+1]+U[i+1,j]+U[i,j-1])/4, \quad 1<i<n, 1<j<m \qquad (2).$$

For the Gauss-Seidel method new grid points are computed row by row starting in
the upmost left corner (U[2,2]). Computed values U[i,j] are replaced immediately,
i.e. the western and northern values (U[i-1,j] and U[i,j-1]) are values from the
current iteration while the eastern and southern values (U[i+1,j] and U[i,j+1])
are old values from the previous iteration. After all inner points of U have been
replaced, the next iteration is started. The computation stops after convergence
has been reached, i.e. for all grid points the difference from the previous
iteration to the current one is smaller than a given epsilon.

Depending on epsilon, the number of grid points and the given initial conditions a
large amount of computation may be required (Table 1). Though the Gauss-Seidel
method is known to converge rather slowly its computations are very similar to the
computational-intensive parts of more modern and faster methods (e.g. multigrid
methods). So parts of the following discussion on parallel Gauss-Seidel programs
apply to these methods as well. Being of large practical importance there is a
great interest in fast parallel PDE-solvers [7].

Grid Size (inner pts)	Iterations	DIRMU (8086, 5MHz)	CADMUS (68000, 10MHz)
50x50	701	696.98	256.22
100x100	1133	4500.33	1679.04
150x150	1322	11842.28	--

Table 1
Execution Times [sec] for the Sequential Gauss-Seidel Program on Monoprocessor
Systems (Fixed-Point Arithmetic, Modula-2 Programming Language)

Our second sample application comes from speech processing. The sequential program
has originally been developed by the pattern recognition group at our university
for a PDP 11/34. It is part of a larger speaker-independent speech recognition
system for fluently spoken german speech [8].

After low-pass filtering the speech signal is sampled at a 10 kHz sampling rate
with a 12-bit A/D converter. The signal is divided into overlapping time frames of
20 msec. Due to overlapping the repetition rate is 12.8 msec. Here we will only
consider the first steps of this system which computes numeric features
(characteristic vectors) for the frames which are required for a classification
module. This module classifies the frames into phonetic classes which form the
input for the further modules of the entire speech recognition system.

In the sequential program four major steps are computed for each frame in the
following order:

(1) Preprocessing of the filtered speech signal (normalization, Hamming window)
(2) Computation of autocorrelation and linear prediction (LP) coefficients

(3) Calculation of smoothed frequency spectrum
(4) Computation of 17 numerical parameters (feature vector) for classification
(e.g. normalized energy, normalized autocorrelation coefficient at unit delay, first linear prediction coefficient, normalized amplitude, frequency and bandwidth of the absolute maximum in the spectrum)

Note that real-time processing means that all four steps must not take longer than 12.8 msec, the repetition time of the frames. Table 2 shows the execution times that have been measured on a PDP 11/34 for FORTRAN and on a DIRMU monoprocessor (8086/8087 microcomputer, 5 MHz clock) for PL/M with subroutines in assembler. Both machines are considerable slower than real time (a factor of 167 and 54 respectively). So a further speedup by parallel processing is highly desirable even if faster processors are used.

	PDP 11/34	8086/87
Normalization, Hamming window	60 msec	62 msec
Autocorrelation, LP-coefficients	240 msec	176 msec
Frequency spectrum	1680 msec	286 msec
Feature vector	160 msec	172 msec
	2140 msec	696 msec

Table 2
Execution Times of the Four Steps of the Speech Processing Program (Square Wave Input Signal)

PROBLEM DECOMPOSITION STRATEGIES

Two important decomposition strategies for MIMD multiprocessor programs are data partitioning and macropipelining [9]. Data partitioning is applicable if the same or similar operations have to be done on a large data set (e.g. a 2- or 3-dimensional array). In order to exploit parallelism the data set is partitioned into several parts. For each part a process is formed. These processes can be executed in parallel on different processors. To assure that the parallel program works correctly the processes must interact to synchronize and exchange data.

Macropipelining [10] is applicable if the computation can be divided into parts, called stages, such that the output of one stage is the input for another one. As the processes that form a stage remain fixed while data is flowing from one stage to the other this approach is also called macro-dataflow. To achieve parallelism the stages can be realized by different processors which must be able to communicate with the previous and the following stage. Sometimes macropipelining and data partitioning can be combined. This can for example result in a configuration with several processors working in parallel within one pipeline stage on a partitioned data set from the previous one.

PARALLEL PROGRAMS FOR THE PDE-PROBLEM

For the PDE-problem we have a large data set, grid U, where the computation from formula (2) must be done for each grid point. So the data partitioning approach seems to be appropriate. An obvious partitioning is to cut the grid into N horizontal strips of equal size (Fig. 1) and to provide one process for each strip (static decomposition). These processes can now work independently for the inner

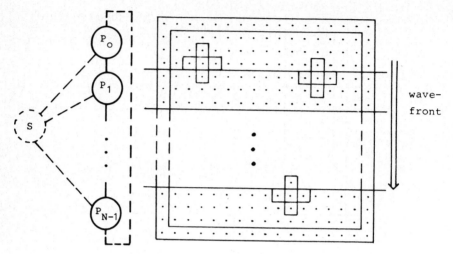

Figure 1
Partitioning of a Grid into Strips for the PDE-Problem

part of their strips. However, for the computation of their first row processes
1,2,...,N-1 need values computed by the last rows of processes 0,1,...,N-2
respectively. Similar, processes 0,1,..., N-2 need the values from the first rows
of processes 1,2,...,N-1 in order to compute their own last rows. Furthermore the
data transfer of the first and last rows must be synchronized.

As mentioned before, for the Gauss-Seidel method northern and western values come
from the current iteration, the eastern and southern values from the previous one.
For the parallel program this means that process k can start iteration i on its
strip only after iteration i has been completed by process k-1. The resulting
approach is very similar to the computational wavefront described by Kung et al.
for the wavefront array processor [11]. First process 0 executes iteration 1 for
all points of its strip with exception of the last row (exactly as in the
sequential program). For the computation of the last row the first row of process
1's strip (in this case the initial values) has to be transferred to process 0.
After process 0 has finished its strip, it passes its last row to process 1 and
starts with the second iteration. Having received the last row from process 0,
process 1 starts with its first iteration. Note that starting with the second
iteration processes 0 and 1 can work in parallel. After having finished its strip,
process 1 transfers its last row to process 2 which begins its first iteration,
while process 1 continues with the second one, etc. Finally, after N-1 iterations
all N processes can work in parallel on different iterations. Of course the total
number of iterations should be large in respect to N to make the influence of the
startup phase with only part of all processes working neglectible. Furthermore the
computation times for the processes should be the same. Otherwise the slowest
process will dominate the execution time for the whole iteration.

The iterations must be stopped if all strips have reached convergence. The easiest
way to implement this is to provide a central supervisor process S (Fig. 1). If
all N worker processes have reported convergence in their strips to it, this
supervisor stops the computations. In some multiprocessor systems central processes are not very desirable, so we will also present a distributed solution. The
main idea is to pass a convergence flag from one process to the other. There
exists one flag per iteration. Initially the flag is owned by process 0 and set to
TRUE. If a process k has reached convergence and the flag received has the value
TRUE, the value TRUE is passed to process (k+1) mod N. The resulting process

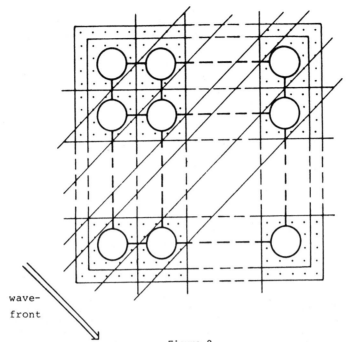

wave-
front

Figure 2
Partitioning of a Grid into Rectangular Fields for the PDE-Problem

intercommunication structure is a ring. If the value FALSE has been received or if
the strip has not yet converged, the value FALSE is passed. It is easy to see that
the whole grid has converged, when process 0 receives the flag set to TRUE from
process N-1. In this case process 0 sends a stop flag around the ring which causes
all computations to stop.

An alternative to the partitioning into strips is to partition the grid into
rectangular fields. Now each process in the interior of the grid has to communicate with four neighbours (Fig. 2) resulting in a mesh-like interprocess
communication structure. Again a wavefront approach can be used for the Gauss-
Sei el ethod with the wavefront travelling now from the upper left corner along
the diagonal to the lower right corner. For a distributed convergence test an
interconnection between the first processor and the last one in the wavefront can
be added. The advantage of this partitioning is that in general less grid points
have to be transferred to the neighbours than for strip partitioning, i.e. less
communication overhead. In addition the start-up time (wavefront travelling time)
is now proportional to the square root of N instead of N. A disadvantage is that
the parallel progam becomes more complex because communication and synchronizaton
with four neighbours must be programmed in contrast to two neighbours. Furthermore
a ring of processes has advantages for a fault-tolerant implementation [12] which
is however not the subject of this paper.

PARALLEL PROGRAMS FOR THE SPEECH PROCESSING PROBLEM

For the speech processing problem we have a continuous stream of data that is
transformed by various computation steps. In this case macropipelining seems to be
a promising strategy. However, in order to obtain a good processssor utilization it

E. Maehle and K. Wirl

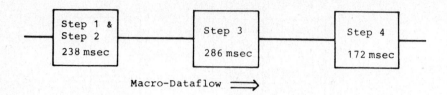

Macro-Dataflow $\Longrightarrow$

(a) 3-Stage Macropipeline

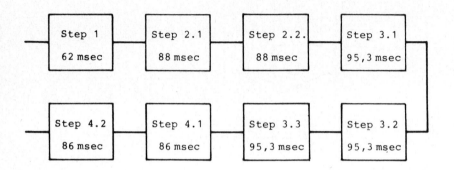

(b) 8-Stage Macropipeline

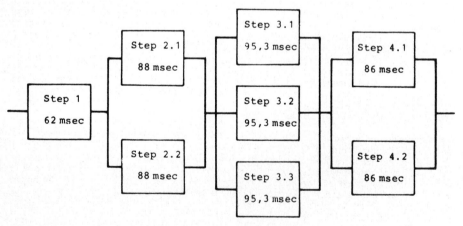

(c) 4-Stage Macropipleline with Concurrent Stages

Figure 3
Macropipelines for the Speech Processing Problem

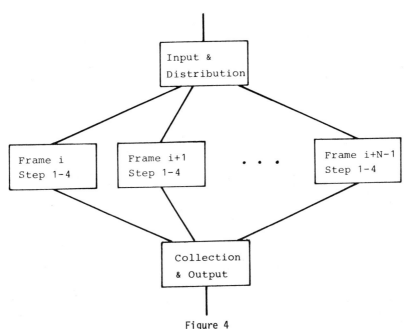

Figure 4
Data Partitioning by Concurrent Processing of Frames for the Speech Processing
Problem

is important that the pipeline is balanced, i.e. ideally all stages should have exactly the same computation time. If we look at Table 2, we see that a 4-stage pipeline is not at all balanced. The computation time is governed by stage 3 (frequency spectrum). In this case it is more suitable to combine steps 1 and 2 into one stage. The resulting 3-stage macropipeline with the execution times for the 8086/87 is shown in Fig. 3a. The speedup is 2.43 (81.1% efficiency) reducing the real-time factor to 22. Another problem is that the execution times of the steps can be data-dependent. If for a example a sine wave signal is used instead of a square wave signal as a test signal the total execution time increases to 709 msec. So also the efficiency of the pipeline will vary within a certain range depending on the actual load balancing.

In order to get a higher performance the number of processors can be further increased. One approach is to decompose the 4 steps into further steps that are again executed in parallel. A step can be decomposed either in a pipelined fashion into substeps which are executed one after another (Fig. 3b) or into a different set of substeps which can be executed concurrently on different parts of the input data. The execution times given assume that the corresponding steps are ideally decomposable which is certainly not realistic. The resulting theoretical speedup is 7.3 in both cases (91% efficiency) yielding a real-time factor of 7.4.

Also a data partitioning approach is possible for the speech processing problem. As all frames can be processed independently, we can provide N processes, one for each frame. The speech signal is sampled by one process and then distributed to the N processes which execute the complete algorithm for their frame. Finally an output process collects the feature vectors and passes them to the classifier (Fig. 4). If enough processes can work in parallel (e.g. more than 54 for the 8086/87) theoretically real-time processing can be achieved. The N procceses can again further be decomposed into macropipelines (e.g. those in Fig. 3) yielding a parallel/serial decomposition.

EXPERIMENTAL IMPLEMENTATION ON THE MULTIPROCESSOR DIRMU 25

The basic concept of DIRMU (DIstributed Reconfigurable MUltiprocessor) is to provide an universal microcomputer building block which allows system designers to configure a broad spectrum of task-oriented multiprocessor configurations. A DIRMU building block consists of a P-module and an M-module (Fig. 5). The P-module contains an 8086 microprocessor with 8087 arithmetic coprocessor, 320 KB of private RAM, 16 KB of PROM and some I/O interfaces (terminals, disks etc.). The M-module is a multiport memory of 64 KB. The processor can not only access the private memory in its P-module but also its own M-module and the M-modules of other building blocks if the corresponding P-ports and M-ports are connected by pluggable cables. Thus the memory in the M-modules can be shared by all processors connected to it. Usually program code and private data are stored in the P-module while common data is placed in the M-modules. In which configuration the DIRMU building blocks are interconnected depends on the application problem under consideration. As an example we will discuss now DIRMU configurations for the applications from the previous sections.

For the PDE-problem we have seen that a ring interconnection structure is required, if the grid is cut into strips and the distributed convergence test is used. A straightforward approach is to map the N processes from Fig. 1 onto N processors and to interconnect them as a ring such that each P-module has access to the M-modules of its two neighbours (Fig. 6a). If we store the grid points of each strip into the corresponding M-module the interprocess communication becomes very efficient: For computing the values of their first rows the affected processors can access the last rows of their neighbours immediately - simply by using the appropriate address for the shared M-module. The same is true for the computation of the last rows. So no real data transfer is required, only addresses are switched. Synchronization can be realized by Wait and Signal primitives for spin locks stored in the shared M-modules. We have implemented the resulting parallel program in Modula-2 on DIRMU 25 and have made speedup measurements on ring configurations with up to 25 processors (Fig. 7). As can be seen high efficiencies are observed (e.g. a speedup of 23.2 for 25 processors and a 150x150 grid meaning an efficiencies of 92.8%). This is mainly due to the high communication bandwidth to the neighbouring building blocks which keeps the communication and synchronization overhead very low. An interesting effect in Fig. 7 is that the speedup curve is not smooth but has some steps. For example the speedup of 20 for 22 processors is not increased for 23 and 24 processors. Only if we move to 25 processors it goes up again. The reasons for this behaviour is the rigid partitioning of the grid into strips with full rows which we have used in our program. In case of 22 to 24 processors some strips have 6 rows and some 7 rows. However, because of synchronization the computation time is always dominated by the processors working on 7 rows and does not increase if more processors are used. Only after all 25 processors are working the number of rows per strip is reduced to 6 for all strips which means a shorter total execution time and a jump in the speedup curve. We did not make experiments with mesh configuration for this PDE-problem yet. These configurations can also easily be configured with the DIRMU kit (Fig 6b). It can be expected that the efficiency for a mesh configuration is even slightly better than that for the ring.

For the speech processing problem various possible configurations exist as discussed before. So far we have only practical experience with the 3-stage macropipeline of Fig. 3a which was impemented on 3 DIRMU building blocks in PL/M. The predicted speedup of 2.4 was really measured [13] showing again that the synchronization and communication overhead in DIRMU is very small. The other macropipelines from Fig. 3 can also easily be realized with DIRMU (which remains to be done). However, the configuration in Fig. 4 can only be implemented for N<=7 because a DIRMU building block has no more than seven P-ports, which can be connected to the distributing building block, and seven M-ports for the connection to the collecting one. If more building blocks shall be used, we can either built upup to 7 macropipelines or provide intermediate distribution and collection

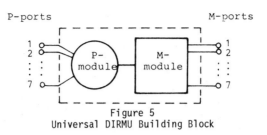

Figure 5
Universal DIRMU Building Block

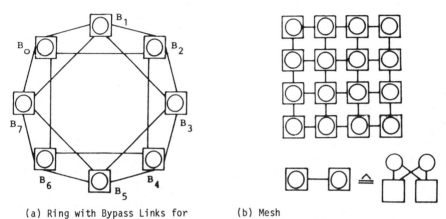

(a) Ring with Bypass Links for   (b) Mesh
    Fault-Tolerance Reasons

Figure 6
Fault-Tolerant Ring and Mesh Configuration from DIRMU Building Blocks

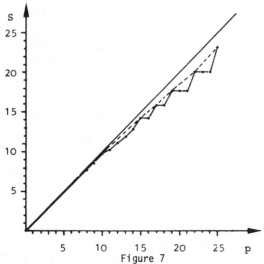

Figure 7
Speedup S Measured on a p-Processor DIRMU Ring Configuration for the parallel
Gauss-Seidel Program

building blocks increasing the "fan-in/fan-out". Of course these additional
building blocks do not contribute to the actual work and thus decrease the
efficiency for this kind of configurations.

CONCLUDING REMARKS

In this paper we have discussed various problem decompositions taking a parallel
program from numerical mathematics and one from signal processing as an example.
For both problems a high degree of parallelism can be exploited on multiprocessors. First experiments with implementations on DIRMU 25 have shown that
high efficiencies can really be observed in practice. An important advantage of
the DIRMU approach in contrast to true special-purpose processors is that the
individual building blocks are general-purpose and can easily be programmed in
conventional programming languages. Only the interconnection structure is tailored
to the process intercommunication structure for a particular class of applications. So also rather complex parallel algorithms can be implemented on the DIRMU
multiprocessor. Furthermore this concept is independent of the speed of the
building blocks used. So, as more powerful microprocessors and faster memory chips
are becoming available very high-performance configurations with a large number of
processors and an attractive cost/performance ratio can be built.

ACKNOWLEDGEMENT

The authors want to thank Prof. Dr. W. Handler for his continuous support of this
work as well as D. Japel, P. Regel, W. Schubert and M. Wiendl for their con-
tributions to the speech processing problem.
The project DIRMU has been supported by the DFG (Deutsche Forschungsgemeinschaft),
BMFT (Deutsches Bundesministerium fuer Forschung und Technologie) and Siemens,
Munich.

REFERENCES

[1] Patton, P.C., Multiprocessors: Architecture and Applications, IEEE Computer 6
     (1985) 29-40.

[2] Jones, A.K., Swarz, P., Experience Using Multiprocessor System - A Status
     Report, ACM Computing Surveys 2 (1980) 121-165.

[3] Seitz, C.L., The Cosmic Cube, Communications of the ACM 1 (1985) 22-33.

[4] Cowther, W., Goodhue, J., Starr, E., Thomas, R., Williken, W., Blackadar, T.,
     Performance Measurements on a 128-Node Butterfly Parallel Processor, Proc.
     1985 Int. Conf. on Parallel Processing (St. Charles 1985) 531-540.

[5] Whitby-Stevens, C., The Transputer, 12th Annual Int. Conf. on Computer
     Architecture (1985) 292-300.

[6] Handler, W., Maehle, E., Wirl, K., DIRMU Multiprocessor Configurations, Proc.
     1985 Int. Conf. on Parallel Processing (St. Charles 1985) 652-656.

[7] Bode, A., Fritsch, G., Handler, W., Henning, W., Hofmann, F., Volkert, J.:
     Multigrid Oriented Computer Architecture, Proc. 1985 Int. Conf. on Parallel
     Processing (St. Charles 1985) 89-95.

[8] Regel, P., A Module for Acoustic-Phonetic Transcription of Fluently Spoken
     German Speech, IEEE Trans. on Acoustics, Speech and Signal Processing 3
     (1982) 440-450.

[9] Hwang, K., Briggs, F.A., Computer Architecture and Parallel Processing (McGraw Hill New York, 1984).

[10] Handler, W., The Concept of Macropipelining with High Availability, Elektronische Rechenanlagen 6 (1973) 269-274.

[11] Kung, S.-Y., Arun, K.S., Gal-Ezer, D.V., Bhaskar Rao, Wavefront Array Processor: Language, Architecture and Applications, IEEE Trans. on Computers 11 (1982) 1054-1066.

[12] Maehle, E., Fault-Tolerant DIRMU Multiprocessor Configurations, Computer Architecture Technical Committee Newsletter, IEEE Computer Society (June 1985) 51-56.

[13] Schubert, W., Wiendl, M., Parallel-Serien-Zerlegung eines Progamms zur Sprachsignalverarbeitung fuer DIRMU Multiprozessorkonfigurationen, Studienarbeit am IMMD III (University of Erlangen-Nuremberg, 1984).

HIGHLY PARALLEL COMPUTERS
G.L. Reijns, M.H. Barton (editors)
Elsevier Science Publishers B.V. (North-Holland)
©IFIP, 1987

A PARALLEL REDUCTION ARCHITECTURE

T. D. Burnett *

University College London
Torrington Place
London WC1E 7JE
U.K.

A parallel machine architecture is presented aimed at digital
signal processing applications. The ability of the reduction
language F.P. to express parallelism within algorithms is used
as the basis for this parallel processor. Efficiency of
operation of each individual processing element is stressed
and a novel garbage collection technique which imposes
negligible time penalty makes a major contribution to this
efficiency. This paper reports simulation results which
indicate that the architecture is well suited to high
performance signal processing.

INTRODUCTION

Most digital signal processors in use at present are based on the sequential
von Neumann model for computation. This paper discusses one approach to a
parallel digital signal processing architecture. Many parallel machine
architectures have been proposed in the past and a large proportion have met
practical difficulties in real applications because the design has not been
guided by a reasonable programming model. The design presented here is a
product of the 'language first' approach to computer architecture, being
designed to execute a single functional language. Functional languages would
not normally be considered as a basis for signal processing applications due
to their inefficiency, but that used here, F.P. is particularly simple and
avoids the major sources of inefficiency found in lambda calculus based
functional languages. F.P. was proposed in 1977 by Backus [3] as an algebra of
programs because the syntax of the language was developed as a rigorously
defined algebra. Consequently programs written in F.P. are suitable for direct
mathematical manipulation to provide correctness proofs and efficiency
transforms. The combination of speed potential through parallelism and
mathematical tractability suggested that F.P. could be a highly suitable
language for signal processing applications, which, like the language, tend to
be simple and well defined mathematically.

The following sections explain the structure and operation of the parallel
processing system. A few features are described in detail, in particular the
garbage collection algorithm is described as it contributes greatly to the
efficiency of the system. Results obtained from a simulation of the processor
are presented for several algorithms and it is found that the processing rate
compares very favourably with established designs. For completeness a brief
introduction to the F.P. algebra is given in appendix A.

* This research is jointly funded by the Science and Engineering
Research Council and Racal Research Limited.

SYSTEM CONCEPTS

The machine architecture is tailored to the features of the F.P. language.
The mechanism used for computation in this language is function evaluation and
the form of the architecture reflects this basic requirement. Functions
within F.P. are either primitive or user defined. Primitive functions can be
directly evaluated by the hardware, whereas user defined functions are
evaluated from their definitions. A complete program is one function, usually
defined in terms of many simpler functions. The order in which these
subsidiary functions are to be evaluated is only partially specified in the
definition and it is this partial ordering which provides the potential for
parallelism.

The machine organisation is built around the distributed evaluation of
functions by processing elements. The processing elements are arranged in an
array and are connected via an orthogonal bus network (see figure 1).
Evaluation begins when a function is sent by the host to the processing
element which contains the root node of the source data. If the function is
primitive it is evaluated directly and the result is passed back to the host.
If the function is user defined its definition is looked up in local memory.
The definition will consist of further user defined functions, primitive
functions and some operations to combine the functions (see Appendix A). All
functions in the definition are, in due course, applied to their source
objects to produce the required result. If the source object is resident in a
remote processing element the function is passed to that processing element to
be evaluated. When all the component functions have returned results, the
combined result is returned to the host and computation ceases.

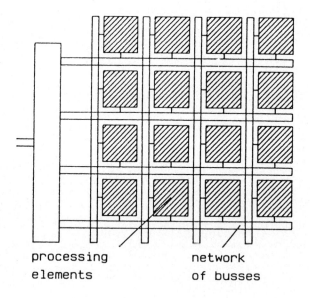

processing   network
elements   of busses

Figure 1.
System Configuration

OPERATION OF THE PROCESSING ELEMENT

To explain the process of evaluating user-defined functions the structure of
the processing element   should be explained (see figure 2).   The processing
element consists of a network interface, two separate blocks of memory, an
arithmetic processor, a central controller, and five special purpose
registers.   The network interface controls access to the two busses connected
to the processing element, all packets are dispatched and received through
this interface. The function definition memory is initialised with a
description of each user defined function.   Each processing element in the
array contains the complete set of function definitions in local memory.   The
data structure memory initially contains some part of a single data structure
which is distributed throughout the array of processing elements. Each of the
registers in the processing element has a unique function.   The source and
destination pointer registers point to the source and destination data
structures for the function being processed.   These registers have to be used
to access the data memory. The stack pointer is used to manipulate a stack
area in the data memory. The allocation registers are used to allocate memory
for new data structures and to reclaim the memory when the structures are no
longer required, this process of garbage collection is explained in more
detail in a later section.

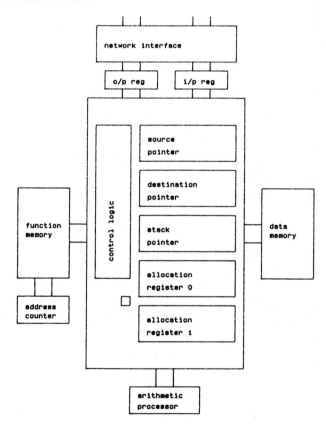

Figure 2.
Processing Element Architecture

When the processing element receives a function across the network which is user defined it has to obtain the definition of the function from memory. The internal function name is equal to the address at which the function definition starts. The function definition memory address generator is loaded with this address and the definition is sequentially read out. The function definition is represented internally as a list of instructions. The instructions that the processing element executes are a compiled form of the F.P. language. Each instruction corresponds to a primitive function, a user defined function or a combining form. The combining forms are frequently compiled into more than one word. For example, the F.P. source code below (read from right to left):

$$[1, \quad 2, \quad 3]$$

is compiled into the executable form:

CHECK,ENDCON,S_1,CONTCON,S_2,CONTCON,S_3,3,INITCON

The processing element responds to each of the symbols differently. INITCON allocates the memory for the construction, saves the source data structure pointer on the stack, fills the data structure with blank values and pushes the address of the first element to be filled in on the stack. CONTCON reinstates the source data structure pointer register and increments the address to be written by the next function. ENDCON cleans up the stack. CHECK suspends evaluation until all the elements of the data structure have been changed from their blank values. The other combining forms are similarly compiled into a sequence of instructions for the processing element.

Functions when read out from the function definition memory are handled in two ways. If the function is primitive it is directly evaluated using the data pointed to by the source data structure pointer and it puts the result in the location pointed to by the destination data structure pointer. If the result is a data structure then sufficient space is allocated in the data memory and a pointer to it is put in the destination data structure pointer register. When a function which operates on remote data is encountered the name of the function along with the source and destination addresses are passed to the remote processing element in a data packet. The packet has four fields as shown below. The combining form field contains any relevant combining form controlling the execution of the function, the function field contains the name of the function, the source data structure pointer field contains the address of the source data or an atom and the destination data structure pointer field contains the address that the function should return its result to.

| Combining form | Function | Source | Destination |

It is the process of remote function invocation which spreads the load across the system. Keeping the processing load spread evenly across the array is a fundamental requirement for any parallel processor. Functions are evaluated remotely when their source data is remotely located so it is imperative that the source data is distributed across the processors before evaluation starts. Placing the components of the source data structure must be done with care to obtain optimum load spreading, and this task must be done by the programmer as part of the programming function.

Communication between processors is achieved by sending packets across the network of busses. The network is simple but simulations show that bus conflicts are very infrequent. Any processing element can take control of the busses connected to it but control is only awarded to one processing element on each bus during any one bus cycle.

REPRESENTATION OF DATA

The only data that needs to be represented in the system are F.P. objects (see appendix A). The following allowed objects must be consistently represented.

        (a)   The undefined object.
        (b)   Atoms.
        (c)   Lists of objects.

Several restrictions have been imposed on the data to be used in the system. In the F.P. specification an atom can be an integer, a floating point number, a character, a string or a logical value true or false. It is clearly impracticable and undesirable to support all these data types in a machine aimed at signal processing applications, and so only integers and logical values are represented. Logical values are in fact represented by integers, zero corresponding to false and any non-zero integer corresponding to true. The manner in which the undefined object is handled by the simulation is also a departure from the F.P. specification. All functions within F.P. are strict, that is, if the argument to the function is undefined then the output of the function is undefined. Also if an element of a list is the undefined object then the whole list is undefined. Consequently if the undefined object is generated at any time during the evaluation of a function then the function will evaluate to the undefined object. The simulation does not have a representation of the undefined object, instead if a function ever produces the undefined object an error is reported and evaluation terminates. The effect of this procedure is exactly the same as if the evaluation had continued with the undefined object being passed from function to function, but reporting the error and where the error occurred is an informative debugging aid.

The data structures to be represented are atoms, lists of atoms and lists of lists. Each word in the data memory is divided into two fields, the data field which is thirty two bits wide in the simulation, and a pointer field which is one bit wide. Atoms are represented as values in the data field with the pointer field set to zero. Lists are represented as a continuous block of memory words starting with a one word header which contains the length of the list in the data field with the pointer field set to zero. If an element of a list is itself a list the pointer field is set to one and the data field contains a pointer to the start address of the second list. The list

$$< 11, < 21, 23>>$$

would be represented in memory as:

	Pointer field	Data field
start:	0	2
	0	11
	1	pointer = start + 3
	0	2
	0	21
	0	23

This representation is consistent with F.P. in that elements of lists are numbered from 1 to n so a straight forward translation to start address plus index obtains the correct word in memory and also the length count is both the number of words in the current list and also the correct length count as returned by the 'length' function in F.P.

COMMUNICATION STRATEGY

Data is passed from one processing element to another in the form of packets.
Only single items of data (i.e. either atoms or pointers to data structures)
need to be moved across the network, no block moves are necessary, so all
communication is performed by individual packets. The form of the packet is
shown below.

| Combining form | Function | Source | Destination |

Packets are routed to the processing element specified in the source address.
This routing is consistent with the policy of routing a function to the data
it is applied to.

Communication in F.P. occurs between functions. Arguments are passed to
functions and results are returned from functions and this is the only mode of
communication permitted. When a function is applied to a data structure a
packet of the form shown above is sent across the network to the processing
element containing its source data. The function is evaluated to produce a
result, the result is either an atom or a data structure. If the result is an
atom it is sent directly back to the processing element that sent the function
packet, if the result is a data structure a pointer to the data structure is
sent back across the network. This process of returning a result is
accomplished with a packet of the form below.

| 0 | 'point' | destination address | pointer or atom |

When the above packet arrives at the original processing element the function
'point' is executed and places the result into local memory at the destination
address. The simpler approach of allowing the result to over write the
contents of the destination data structure pointer register fails if any other
function is in the process of evaluating on the processing element. A
consequence of returning the result to memory is that before the following
function can evaluate it has to perform one level of indirection through its
memory. To keep the control algorithm consistent for all functions this
indirection is always performed, even if the previous function executed
locally.

GARBAGE COLLECTION

Evaluating a function in F.P. typically involves evaluating subsidiary
functions each of which takes an input argument and returns a result. The
results and arguments will usually be data structures and as these data
structures become redundant the memory they occupy must be liberated for
future use. The process by which memory is re-allocated is called garbage
collection and is a crucial issue in the design of reduction machines. For
this particular design it was important to keep the time spent garbage
collecting down to a minimum. The technique described below imposes negligible
overhead with little extra hardware.

In each processing element the data memory space is divided into two blocks.
For each user defined function one block of memory is used for data structures
which need only be preserved while the function is being evaluated and the
other block is used for data structures which form the output data structure.
After the user-defined function has been evaluated the memory used by its
temporary data structures is reclaimed. Memory is only reclaimed at the end of
the evaluation of a user defined function. Whether or not the output from a
particular function is to be saved is decided at compile time using a strategy
described later. Each function has a 'scratch' block and a 'save' block in
which to deposit results but the mapping between the logical scratch and save

blocks and the physical memory blocks is dynamically swapped as functions evaluate. For any one function the mapping is constant but when the function invokes a subsidiary function the mapping may or may not change. If the function is marked as 'save' at compile time the mapping is not changed and the subsidiary function uses the same scratch and save blocks as the calling function. If on the other hand the function has been marked as 'scratch' at compile time the mapping between logical and physical memory blocks is swapped so that the physical block that the calling function used as a scratch area is used by the subsidiary function as a save area and the physical block used by the calling function as a save area is used by the subsidiary function as a scratch area. For example, the following line defines f0 in terms of f1 and f2.

def f0 = f1 s ... f2

The three dots stand for any group of functions and combining forms. The symbol s before f1 is a marker inserted at compile time which indicates that the output of f1 is to be saved. So the output from f2 will be placed in the part of memory designated as scratch space for f0 and the output from f1 will be placed in the part of memory used to store results from f0.

Typically f1 and f2 will also be user defined and will consist of many functions. Let f1 be defined as below:

def f1 = f4 ... f3 s

The output of f4 is not required after f1 has completed but the output from f3 is. The algorithm would deposit the results from f3 in the block of memory nominated as the save area for f1 and the results from f4 in the block of memory nominated as a scratch area for f1. As f1 was marked as save before being invoked from f0, the save and scratch status of the two blocks of memory would not have been swapped. So the results from f3 would be put in the same block of memory as the results to be saved from f0 and consequently no memory will be reclaimed when f0 has been evaluated completely and the results from f1 and f3 will remain intact in memory. However, the scratch block will be reclaimed when f0 has been evaluated and the memory used by f2 and f4 will be re-allocated.

The hardware required to implement the garbage collection algorithm described in this section is simple. Two pointer registers in the controller are needed to point to the next free byte in each of the two physical blocks of data memory and a single flip-flop is needed to swap the mapping between the register used to allocate scratch space and that used to allocate save space. Some time overhead is also incurred as the register that points to the scratch area needs to be saved on the stack before the function is evaluated and needs to be restored at the end of the function. Although this overhead is undesirable it is a very small proportion of the overall time it takes to evaluate each function.

A COMPILATION TECHNIQUE FOR GARBAGE COLLECTION

At present the F.P. source code is compiled manually into the executable code, and so the save mark is placed by inspection which is a very straight forward process. This section outlines a suitable algorithm for automatically placing the save mark.

Initially each function in the system is tested to determine whether the input data structure is referenced in the output data structure as this is crucial to the rest of the compilation algorithm.

The next stage is to place the save mark in each function definition. The
result returned by the last component function in the definition must always
be saved in order to retain any output from the defined function. So the
savemark starts just to the right of the last component function and is moved
further to the right when this proves necessary. Whether it is necessary to
move the savemark to the right depends on both the combining forms and the
component functions within the definition. Each combining form is handled in
a different manner, so a brief description of the algorithm for each combining
form will be given.

Composition: The savemark will start to the left of the composition
              symbol, whether it is propagated to the right of
              the composition symbol and next function depends
              whether that function references its input in its
              output (a property which will have been determined
              in the first stage of the algorithm).

Construction: The whole algorithm must be recursively applied to
              each element of the construction. So the savemark
              starts to the right of each element in the
              construction. The whole algorithm is recursively
              applied to each of the elements in the
              construction.

Condition: The condition combining form has three elements, a
              predicate element and two other elements which are
              controlled by the predicate. The predicate element
              never produces an output to be retained. To
              determine where the savemark should be placed in
              the other two elements the whole algorithm is
              recursively applied to each element.

The three other combining forms are special cases of the three that have just
been covered so the algorithms will not be described in detail. This
compilation algorithm is extremely simple and places the savemark in the
optimal position within the function definition.

SIMULATION RESULTS

A simulation of the architecture described in the preceding sections has been
developed. Several different signal processing algorithms have been run on
the simulation and the performance studied under different conditions.
Two measures of performance were required from the simulation. The most
important. characteristic, was the relationship between the number of
processors in a particular configuration of the machine and the throughput for
that configuration. The second result needed was the penalty incurred by
executing F.P. on a single processing element in comparison with conventional
machine code executing on a von Neumann machine. The factors expected to
influence the throughput against number of processors were the communication
strategy, network conflicts and load spreading. The principle overheads to
adversely affect the throughput of any individual processor were expected to
be garbage collection and the properties of F.P. which dictate the repeated
construction of intermediate data structures.

Three different representative signal processing algorithms were chosen,
convolution, the fast fourier transform and an adaptive filter. The
programs are shown in fig 3, for an introduction to the syntax of F.P. see
appendix A.

A few points about these programs should be made at this stage. The first
property to note is the brevity, conventional programs to express the same
algorithms are considerably longer in terms of lines of code. None of these
functions specifies a length to its argument and so they perform their
functions on arbitrary length samples of vectors. All the functions are
recursively defined and operate on a tree of data. This departs from the
programming style advocated by Williams [5] which is based around 'closed
form' functions using the 'apply_to_all' combining form. Closed form
solutions are often more compact but the 'apply_to_all' combining form implies
central control of a function being applied to each element of a data
structure which is inherently slower then recursively dividing the
responsibility for control.

```
def FFT -  endcon ->Stage; Stage o [FFT o 1. FFT o 2, 3]

def endcon - atom o 1 o 1

def Stage - endcon -> Butt;  [Stage o [1 o 1.  1 o 2,  1 o 3],
                              Stage o [2 o 1,  2 o 2,  2 o 3]]

def Butt - [Cadd. Csub] o [1, Cmul o [2, 3]]

def Cmul - [- o [* o [1 o 1,  1 o 2], * o [2 o 1,2 o 2]],
            + o [* o [1 o 1,  2 o 2], * o [2 o 1,1 o 2]]]

def Cadd - [+ o [1 o 2,  1 o 1], + o [2 o 2,  2 o 1]]

def Csub - [- o [1 o 2,  1 o 1], - o [2 o 2,  2 o 1]]

        (a)   A fast Fourier transform program


def AdFir - atom o 1 o 2 -> TapStage;
            + o [AdFir o [1,  1 o 2], AdFir o [1,  2 o 2]]

def TapStage - * o [2 o 2, + o [1 o 2, * o [2 o 2,  1]]]

        (b)   An adaptive filter program


def Conv - atom o 1 -> *; + o [Conv o 1, Conv o 2]

        (c)   A convolution program

            Figure 3.
    Examples of F.P. programs
```

The results of the simulation are shown in histogram form in fig 4. It can be
seen that the throughput is an almost linear function of the number of
processors in the system for all the algorithms. This was a most surprising
result as it showed that the problems of communication and load sharing were
playing a small part in the overall performance of the system.

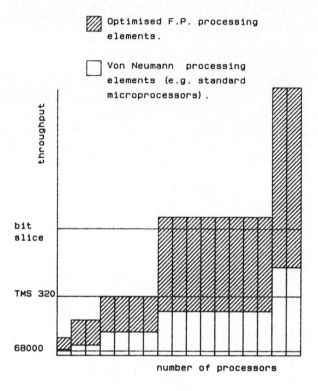

Figure 4a.
Speed improvement against
number of processors for
a 256 point F.F.T.

The crucial issue is how the performance of this system compares against that
of a conventional system. There are several features of F.P. which directly
militate against efficiency. The repeated construction of intermediate data
structures is the prime source of wasted cycles and is a consequence of the
restriction that each function can only take one argument. Consequently if a
sequential processing element is assumed several processing elements will be
necessary to provide performance equivalent to a conventional computer.
Relatively little parallelism has to be introduced into the processing element
to obtain a dramatic improvement in throughput. The shaded set of histograms

in figure 4   shows the performance obtained when certain instructions are
performed in parallel. In practice the actual performance will probably fall
between these two extremes. Making any firm predictions of the processing
speed of a hardware realisation of the architecture discussed in this report
is not possible at this stage but it is quite feasible that for equivalent
size and power the architecture will produce a significant improvement in
performance of at least a factor of two over the equivalent size von Neumann
machine. The performance of the different machines was compared on a cycle
for cycle basis, assuming that simple arithmetic functions can be evaluated in
one cycle but allowing multiple cycles for combining forms.

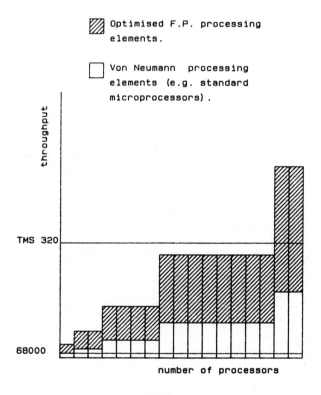

Figure 4b.
Speed improvement against
number of processors   for
a 256 tap adaptive filter.

It can be seen that a sixteen processor system has between three and four
times the performance of a TMS 320 signal processing microprocessor. The
processing rate of the TMS 320 for the F.F.T. example was taken as being 2.5
MOPS, so a sixteen processor system has a performance of about 10 MOPS. It is
interesting to compare these figures with other von Neumann computers. Timed
over a 4096 point F.F.T. the Cray 1 computer achieved 52 MFLOPS whilst the FPS
AP-120B, which is an array processor designed for the F.F.T., averaged 8
MFLOPS [9]. Although these comparisons have to be treated with caution they
illustrate the potential of the parallel processor described here.

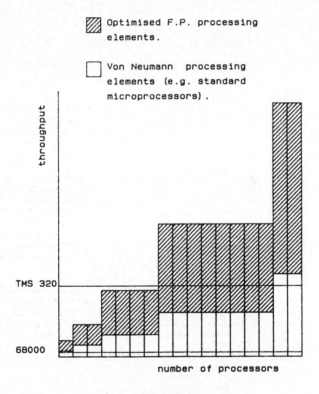

Figure 4c.

Speed improvement against
number of processors for
a 1024 point convolution.

CRITICAL APPRAISAL OF THE ARCHITECTURE

A simple reduction machine has been described which has been specifically designed to execute the reduction language F.P. Throughout the design stress has been placed on simplicity and efficiency, one of the principle objectives being to make each individual processing element of comparable efficiency with a von Neumann processor. Particular factors which contribute to the efficiency of the processing element are garbage collection with very low overhead and the use of parallelism within the processing element itself. Multiple processors can then be used to produce a speed improvement over the equivalent von Neumann processor. It is believed that reduction languages will only gain wide acceptance if they can be executed with efficiency exceeding that of von Neumann languages [4]. The ability to phrase parallelism naturally in reduction languages could mean that for applications requiring the greatest speed, reduction languages become the fastest solution. At that stage the other advantages of reduction languages could come to the fore, it is most unlikely that an inherently slow programming system will be accepted due to other benefits like easier mathematical manipulation.

RELATED RESEARCH

Two other designs for machines based on F.P. have appeared in the literature. Mago [6] suggested a tree structure of processors with storage elements at the leaves of the tree. An alternative architecture presented by Villemin [7] is based on clusters of processors around one input / output processor. The architecture presented here has been influenced by these and many other parallel processors [1][2], but it offers a different solution which stresses efficiency of operation. The garbage collection technique reported here contributes greatly to the speed of operation.

ACKNOWLEDGEMENTS

The author wishes to thank the Science and Engineering Research Council and Racal Research Limited for their financial support and Owen Davies and Simon Peyton Jones for many useful discussions.

CONCLUSION

The simulation of the F.P. machine described in this report shows that it is feasible to use F.P. style functional languages for digital signal processing applications. A sixteen processor system performs at an effective rate of about 10 million operations a second over a range of applications which compares well with signal processing architectures based on the von Neumann model. The combination of the speed advantage and the rigorously defined programming system could produce a very effective digital signal processing system.

REFERENCES

1. Keller R.M., Lindstrom G., Patil S. 'A loosely coupled   applicative
    multiprocessor system'. National Computer Conference 1979.

2. Darlington J., Reeve M. 'ALICE- A multi-processor reduction machine for
    the parallel evaluation of applicative languages'. Proc ACM Conf. on
    Functional Programming and Computer Architecture (1981).

3. Backus J. 'Can programming be liberated from the von Neumann style'.
    A.C.M. Turing Award Lecture C.A.C.M. Vol. 21, No. 8, August 1978.

4. Boyer R.S and More J.S. 'The correctness problem in computer science'.
    Academic press 1981.

5. Williams J.H. 'Notes on the F.P. style of functional programming'. in
    'Functional programming and its applications'. Darlington, Henderson and
    Turner (Eds) Cambridge 1982.

6. Mago G.A. 'A network of microprocessors to execute reduction languages'.
    International Journal of Computer and Information Sciences. Part 1
    in Vol 8., No5, 1979, and part 2 in Vol 8., No6, 1979.

7. Villemin F.Y. 'SEFRE- A general purpose multiprocessor reduction
    machine'. I.E.E.E. conference on parallel processing. 1982.

8. Backus J 'The Algebra of functional programs: function level reasoning,
    linear equations and extended definitions'. Lecture Notes on Computer
    Science No 10, pp 1-43 1981.

9. Hockney R.W. and Jesshope C.R. 'Parallel Computers', Adam Hilger 1981.

APPENDIX A. THE F.P. ALGEBRA

F.P. is best viewed as a machine executable algebra as opposed to a
programming language because one of the principle advantages of reduction
languages like F.P. is that programs can be mathematically manipulated
directly as 'source code'. Some of the syntax and ideas are unfamiliar but
there are strong arguments in favour of F.P. which are particularly eloquently
stated by J. Backus who proposed the language in [3][8]. To make this paper
self contained a brief outline of the language will be given. As the example
algorithms shown in the text do not use all the facilities of the language
only the relevant features will be discussed.

F.P. is a simple functional programming language. The fundamental operation
in F.P. is function application which can be compared with the basic von
Neumann operation of instruction execution. So the basic mechanism by which
computation is performed is the application of a function to an object to
obtain an object.

An object is either:

> (a) The undefined object, represented by '?'.
> (b) An atom, i.e. a single datum like 4, 3.142, TRUE, etc.
> (c) A list of objects. e.g. <0.1 , 0.2>.

So applying the function 'add' to a suitable data structure such as:

add:<0.1,0.2>

would return the result, or reduce to, 0.3. The colon denotes function application.

The F.P. language definition includes about twenty functions such as add. These functions can be classified into three groups: arithmetic and logic functions; data structure manipulating functions and predicate functions. Each function takes just one argument and returns one result, however each argument can be a data structure of arbitrary complexity. The function 'add' above takes one argument which is a data structure consisting of exactly two atoms. If the data structure passed to any function is not of the correct form then the function returns the undefined object ('?') as its result. An important property of F.P. functions is that they all return the undefined object if their input contains the undefined object, so that if at any time during the evaluation of a function the undefined object is generated the result of the function will be the undefined object.

More complex functions can be built up from primitive functions by combining the functions using 'combining forms'. The language definition includes eight combining forms but only the five used in this paper will be described.

Composition: Two functions can be combined using the
                 'composition' combining form to produce a single
                 function. The resulting function is the same as
                 applying each of the component functions in turn.
                 So given two functions f1 and f2 the composition
                 of the two is written f1 o f2, and is identical to
                 the two functions being applied in order from
                 right to left, f2 applied first and f1 applied to
                 the result of f2. Composition is one of the few
                 combining forms which specifies the order of
                 evaluation of its function arguments.

Construction: The construction combining form is used to build
                 data structures from the results of a group of
                 functions. Construction is denoted by [f1,f2]
                 where the results from the two functions will form
                 a two element data structure as below.

                 If f1:a reduces to b
                 and f2:a reduces to c, then
                 [f1,f2]:a reduces to <b,c>.

                 The functions f1 and f2 can be evaluated in any
                 order.

Condition: An if-then-else facility is provided by the
                 condition combining form. Given three functions
                 f1, f2 and f3 the line:

                 f1 -> f2; f3 : a

                 applies f1 to a, if the result is the Boolean
                 value 'true' then f2 is applied to a otherwise f3
                 is applied to a.

Apply to all: The 'apply_to_all' combining form applies a
                function to each element of a data structure in
                turn. For example the expression

                    & f: <x0, x1, ..,xn >

                where the '&' stands for apply to all, reduces to

                    <f:x0, f:x1, f:x2, ..,f:xn>

Tree Insert: The 'tree_insert' combining form allows one dyadic
                function to be applied recursively to a data
                structure. The structure is recursively split
                until the function can be applied to pairs of
                elements. For example

                    | + : < 1, 2, 3, 4 >

                where '|' stands for 'tree_insert', reduces to

                    + : < + : < 1, 2 >, + : < 3, 4 > >

                which in turn reduces to the atom 10. This
                combining form is a useful way of expressing
                parallelism in summations and similar operations.

The functions used in the examples are confined to arithmetic functions and
selector functions. Selector functions return a specified element of the data
structure they are applied to. The name of the function is the number which
represents the position of the required element.

Example: 2 : < 0.1, 0.2 > reduces to 0.2
            2 : < 0.1, < 0.2, 0.1 > > reduces to < 0.2, 0.1 >

The '2' to the left of the colon is the name of the function which selects the
second part of any data structure.

The convolution program used in the text is a useful example to illustrate how
these functions and combining forms can be used to perform a practical
algorithm. The convolution function has the form:

    def conv = atom o 1 o 1 -> *; + o [conv o 1, conv o 2]

and is designed to act on a data structure which is a binary tree. Take the
example of the convolution of a four element vector.

                        s0 s1 s2 s3

With four samples from another vector.

                        h0 h1 h2 h3

The first sample of the convolution vector y would be given by.

    y0 = s0 * h3 + s1 * h2 + s2 * h1 + s3 * h0

The function conv evaluates to y0 when applied to the appropriate data structure. The data structure conv requires is a tree with pairs of elements grouped together at the leaves. In the case of the above vectors the required data structure is:

< < < s0, h0 > < s1, h-1 > > < < s2, h-2 > < s3, h-3 > > >

The function conv recursively applies itself to each half of the data structure. So after the first application the computation could be represented by:

+ : < conv : < < s0, h0 > < s1, h-1 > >, conv : < < s2, h-2 > < s3, h-3 > > >

after three more applications of conv the computation has progressed to the point where no more applications of conv are needed and all the functions in the expression are primitive.

+ : < + : < * : < s0, h0 >, * : < s1, h-1 > >,
        + : < * : < s2, h-2 >, * : < s3, h-3 > > >

These functions evaluate to produce the one atom, y0, which is returned to the host. There is a high degree of parallelism in this expression which can be exploited.

The other algorithms used in this paper evaluate in a similar manner to conv; each acts on a tree of data and recursively applies itself to part of that tree. This structure maps well onto the architecture and covers many signal processing applications, but it should be stressed that there are many different ways of coding these functions in F.P. and it is possible to formally transform between one form of the F.P. code which maps well onto the architecture to another which can be directly related to the definition of the convolution summation.

HIGHLY PARALLEL COMPUTERS
G.L. Reijns, M.H. Barton (editors)
Elsevier Science Publishers B.V. (North-Holland)
©IFIP, 1987

A Pipelined Code Mapping Scheme for Tridiagonal Linear Equation Systems

GUANG R. GAO

Laboratory for Computer Science
Massachusetts Institute of Technology
Cambridge, MA 02139
May 1986

Massive parallelism in numerical computation can be exploited effectively utilizing data flow principles in future generation computers. The key is to organize the data flow machine program graph such that array operations can be fully pipelined. In this paper, a pipelined code mapping scheme for tridiagonal linear systems of equations is developed which introduces fine-grain parallelism in a way that may be effectively exploited by static data flow computers. A comparision with other parallel solution schemes is outlined.

1. Introduction

A major driving force in the development of high-performance parallel computers has been scientific computation. The kernels of such computations consists of many array operations, processed in a regular and repetitive pattern. The massive parallelism in vector computation can be exploited effectively utilizing data flow principles in future generation computers [12]. The key is to organize the data flow machine program graph such that

---

1. The research described in this paper was supported by the Department of Energy and the National Science Foundation.

array operations can be fully pipelined. The applicative nature of the data flow graph model allows flexible scheduling of the execution of enabled instructions in the pipeline data flow programs. Accordingly, program transformation can be performed on the basis of both the global and local data flow analysis to generate efficient pipelined data flow machine code. A pipelined code mapping scheme for transforming array operations in high-level language programs into pipelined data flow machine programs is described in [13].

Tridiagonal systems of linear equations form a very important class of linear algebraic equations. For example, the heart of finite difference solutions of partial differential equations may consist of tridiagonal systems of equations. A tridiagonal system of linear equations can be solved on a conventional computer using the classical *Gaussian elimination algorithm*. However, such solution method is sequential in nature and hence unsuitable for parallel computers without drastic alteration.

In the past decade, new techniques have appeared for solving tridiagonal systems of equations with parallel computers [14, 18]. The best known parallel algorithm is based on the cyclic reduction technique, first proposed by Golub and Hockey and applied by Buzbee et al, for solving tridiagonal system of equations efficiently [3]. One approach is using such parallel technique to solve the recurrences established by the LU-decomposition method of Gaussian elimination algorithm. One such algorithm, known as recursive doubling suggested by Stone and originally designed for Illiac IV, was later modified for other vector computers [19]. Another approach has resulted from considering the needs of parallel processing in the first place and trying to design fundamentally new algorithms which are inherently more parallel. The *odd-even cyclic reduction* algorithm is base on such a principle [3]. A major difficulty with the algorithms based on cyclic reduction technique is the overhead of data rearrangement between computation steps and the considerable variations of degree of parallelism between computation steps.

In this paper, a new method for solving tridiagonal systems of equations is proposed which introduces parallelism in a way that may be effectively exploited by data flow computers. The algorithm is based on the maximally pipelined solution of linear recurrences presented in a companion paper [9]. It performs a program transformation of the recurrences generated in the Gaussian elimination method to produce machine code which can be executed in a maximally pipelined fashion. The new method eliminates the substantial data rearrangement overhead incurred by many existing parallel algorithms and it sustains a relatively constant parallelism during various phases of program execution. Based on this scheme, the code structure of a maximally pipelined tridiagonal equation solver is outlined for a static data flow supercomputer. The principle outlined in the paper may be extended to other data flow computers.

2. Background and Related Work

In this section we state briefly the problem of tridiagonal system of linear equations and review the directed methods for solving them — such as the Gaussian elimination algorithm, in particular the linear recurrences established by the LU-decomposition technique. We also survey the related work of parallel tridiagonal solution methods, such as the well-known cyclic reduction technique.

2.1 Statement of The Problem

We consider the solution to the following tridiagonal set of linear equations:

$$
\begin{pmatrix}
b_1 & c_1 & 0 & - & - & - & 0 \\
a_2 & b_2 & c_2 & & & & \\
0 & a_3 & b_3 & & & & \\
& & & \ddots & & & 0 \\
& & & & a_{n-1} & b_{n-1} & c_{n-1} \\
0 & - & - & - & 0 & a_n & b_n
\end{pmatrix}
\begin{pmatrix}
x_1 \\
x_2 \\
\cdot \\
\cdot \\
\cdot \\
x_n
\end{pmatrix}
=
\begin{pmatrix}
k_1 \\
k_2 \\
\cdot \\
\cdot \\
\cdot \\
k_n
\end{pmatrix}
\tag{2.1}
$$

or expressed in matrix-vector notation

$$\Lambda x = k \tag{2.2}$$

In this paper, our major concern will be the case where the coefficient matrix A is positive definite or at least pivoting is not required.

2.2 LU-Decompusition

There are a number of serial methods for solving the tridiagonal system as expressed in (2.1). The maximally pipelined solution method to be developed in this paper is based on the well-known *LU-decomposition* technique [6]. The Stone's recursive doubling algorithm to be discussed later is also based upon such technique. In this method, we find two matrices, L and U, such that

(1) LU = A;
(2) L is a lower bidiagonal matrix;
(3) U is an upper bidiagonal matrix with 1s on its principal diagonal.

When A is non-simpler, its LU decomposition is unique. In fact, it is shown that

$$U = \begin{pmatrix} 1 & u_1 & 0 & - & - & - & 0 \\ 0 & 1 & u_2 & & & & \\ & & 1 & & & & \\ & & & \ddots & & & 0 \\ & & & & & & u_{n-1} \\ 0 & - & - & - & - & 0 & 1 \end{pmatrix}$$

and

$$L = \begin{pmatrix} c_1^{-1} & 0 & - & - & - & - & 0 \\ a_2 & c_2^{-1} & & & & & \\ 0 & a_3 & c_3^{-1} & & & & \\ & & & \ddots & & & 0 \\ 0 & - & - & 0 & & a_n & c_n^{-1} \end{pmatrix}$$

where

$$u_1 = c_1/b_1$$
$$u_i = c_i/(b_i - a_i u_{i-1}) \qquad i = 2,3...n-1 \qquad (2.3)$$
$$e_i = u_i/c_i$$

After computing L and U, it is relatively straightforward to solve the system of equations by a two-step process. First, letting $Y = Ux$, we have

$$Ly = K \qquad (2.5)$$
$$Ux = y \qquad (2.6)$$

and together, we have $Ax = LUx = Ly = k$.

The equation $Ly = k$ can easily be solved for y as follow.

$$y_1 = k_1/b_1$$
$$y_i = (k_i - a_i y_{i-1})/(b_i - a_i u_{i-1}) \qquad i = 2,3...n \qquad (2.7)$$

Note that in the solution process, as indicated by (2.7), there is no need to compute e_i explicitly unless the matrix L is needed in other places. Next, we solve $Ux = y$ for x by noting that

$$x_n = y_n$$
$$x_i = y_i - u_i x_{i+1} \qquad i = n-1, n-2...1 \qquad (2.8)$$

The two steps of (2.7) and (2.8) are often called *forward-elimination* and *backward-substitution*. The recurrences (2.3), (2.7) and (2.8) constitute a complete solution for $Ax = k$. and a sequential algorithm to perform such a solution is the so-called *Gaussian elimination algorithm*.

2.3 Cyclic Reduction Technique

In this paper, we make no attempt to survey all parallel algorithms for tridiagonal linear equation solvers, but review only two well-known methods which are based on the cyclic reduction. This discussion will motivate the pipelined solution presented in this paper.

2.3.1 Recursive Doubling Algorithm

The recursive doubling algorithm proposed by Stone [19] began with the observation that the formula required by I U factorization, such as (2.7) and (2.8), are first-order linear recurrences (FLR). The equation (2.3) appears not to be a linear recurrence. However, if we introduce a new variable q_i such that $u_i = -q_i/q_{i+1}$, then (2.3) can be transformed into the following second-order linear recurrence (SLR):

$$a_i q_{i-1} + b_i q_i + c_i q_{i+1} = 0 \qquad i = 2,3,...,n-1 \qquad (2.9)$$

where $q_1 = 1$, $q_2 = -b_1/c_1$.

Stone pointed out that (2.9) can be transformed into a first-order linear recurrence except that the sequence is now a set of vectors instead of scalar values. The recursive doubling algorithm uses standard cyclic reduction method for handling linear recurrences to solve them.

It is helpful to review the cyclic reduction technique for solving linear recurrences before we outline its disadvantages. For instance, we consider the evaluation of the sequence of x_i from the following first-order linear recurrence relation.

$$x_i = a_i x_{i-1} + b_i \qquad \text{for } i = 2...n \qquad (2.11)$$

where $x_1, a_1,...,a_n$ and $b_1,...,b_n$ are known values. The basic idea of standard cyclic reduction technique is to back up the recurrence in (2.11) such that a new recurrence can be obtained which relates every other term, every fourth term, every eighth term, etc.

For example, from (2.11) we have

$$x_i = a_i a_{i-1} x_{i-2} + a_i b_{i-1} + b_i$$
$$= a_i^{(1)} x_{i-2} + b_i^{(1)} \tag{2.12}$$

where $a_i^{(1)} = a_i a_{i-1}$, $b_i^{(1)} = a_i b_{i-1} + b_i$. The superscript (1) denotes the fact that this is a first level backup. Such a backup process can be repeated (in a cyclic fashion) and we obtain a set of equations as follow.

$$x_i = a_i^{(l)} x_{i-2^l} + b_i^{(l)} \tag{2.13}$$

where

$$a_i^{(l)} = a_i^{(l-1)} a_{i-2^l}^{(l-1)} \tag{2.14}$$
$$b_i^{(l)} = a_i^{(l-1)} b_{i-2^l}^{(l-1)} + b_i^{(l-1)} \tag{2.15}$$

with $l = 0,1...\log_2 n$, $i = 2,3...n$. An important observation is that if any of a_i, b_i or x_i is outside the defined range, its value can be taken as zero. Therefore, when $l = \log_2 n$, all x_i are solved by

$$x_n = b_n^{(\log_2 n)}$$

We can have the following observation:

(1) high parallelism exists at certain phases (steps) of the algorithm, i.e., at a fix level l, (2.14) and (2.15) can be evaluated for all i in parallel;
(2) the parallelism grows roughly linearly with the size of the vectors — i.e. n in this case;
(3) the useful parallelism decreases as the computation progressing through different phases.

The amount of parallelism varies between phases of computation. This will increase the difficulty of fully utilize the parallelism of the machine.

2.3.2 Odd-even Reduction Algorithm

The *odd-even cyclic reduction algorithm* is perhaps the most successful cyclic reduction algorithm applied to solve tridiagonal systems [3]. It starts directly from the system of equations defined by (2.1), i.e.,

$$a_i x_{i-1} + b_i x_i + c_i x_{i+1} = k_i \qquad i = 1,2...n^1$$

The algorithm first eliminates the odd numbered variables in the even numbered equations by performing elementary row operations. In each level, we cut down the total number of equations by 1/2, hence, in $\log_2 n$ levels, the middle element $x_{n/2}$ can be computed directly from the coefficients. The remaining unknowns can be found by a refilling procedure. This algorithm also involves the recursive calculation of coefficients for equations at each level. One important advantage of the odd-even reduction over the recursive doubling algorithm is that it reduces the number of operations considerably at each level, and the total number of operations is on the order of $O(n)$.

One major difficulty with odd-even reduction is the data rearrangement of variable and coefficient vectors between phases of computation. For example, on the Cyber 205 one cannot apply vector operations directly to every other elements of the vector. Thus extra operations must be employed to reformat those elements into a new vector [17]. On the Cray it is possible to access elements of a vector at a fixed increment, but this may result in a performance degradation [15]. Because of the overhead of data rearrangement, the cyclic reduction algorithm may run slower than a serial algorithm for sufficiently small n [18].

Another problem is the degree of variation of parallelism between different phases of computation. Because the parallelism decreases very rapidly, this problem becomes more serious than that for the recursive doubling algorithm. A parallel version of odd-even reduction algorithm has been proposed to keep a high parallelism throughout the computation. However, it increases the number of operations significantly to $O(n\log n)$ [14].

---

1. In the remaining discussion of this section, we assume n is a power of 2, but this is not an essential assumption.

3. A Pipepined Solution for Linear Recurrences

3.1 Overview of the Pipelined Solution Scheme

In cyclic reduction scheme, the goal is to increase the speed through fully exploiting the parallelism in the original problem. High concurrency is obtained by replicating the operations as much as necessary to compute all elements in the result vector in parallel. In contrast, we propose a new solution method which can explore and organize the parallelism in a way that best matches a suitable computer architecture, i.e. the static data flow architecture. It is based on a maximally pipelined code mapping scheme developed in our previous work [4,7].

Two forms of parallelism exist in a data flow machine level program, as shown in Figure 1, which consists of seven actors divided into four stages. In Figure 1 (a), actors 1 and 2 are enabled by the presence of tokens on their input arcs, and thus can be executed in parallel.[1] This is called *spatial* parallelism. Spatial parallelism also exists between actors 3 and 4, and between actors 5 and 6. The second form of parallelism is *pipelining*. In static data flow architecture, this means arranging the machine code such that successive computations can follow each other through one copy of the code. If we present a sequence of values to the inputs of the data flow graph, these values can flow through the program in a *maximally pipelined* fashion — i.e. input/output values are consumed/produced at maximum rate allowed by the machine architecture. In the configuration of Figure 1 (b), two set of tokens are pipelined through the graph, and the actors in stage 1 and 3 are enabled and can be executed concurrently. Thus, the two forms of parallelism are fully exploited in the graph.

The power of pipelined computation in a data flow computer can be derived from machine-level programs that form a large pipeline in which many actors in various stages are executed concurrently. Each actors in the pipe are activated in a totally data-driven

---

1. A solid disk on an arc represents the presence of a token.

Fig. 1. Pipelining of Data Flow Programs

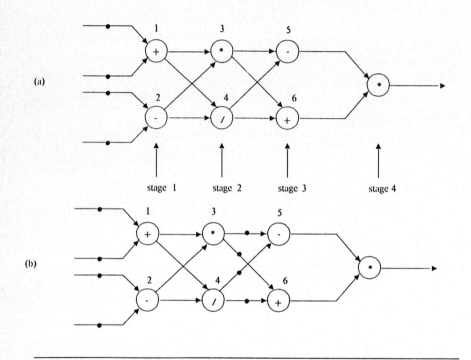

manner, and no explicit sequential control is needed. With data values continuously flow through the pipe, a sustained parallelism can be efficiently supported by the data flow architecture.

3.2 Maximally Pipelined Mapping of Linear Recurrences

An attractive way to implement recurrence on data flow computers is to introduce feedback paths in the data flow graph. This, however, presents particular problems when maximum pipelining of the program is desired. A direct translation of the first order recurrence is shown in Fig. 2. The value x_i depends on the value of x_{i-1}, therefore, a *feedback path*, such as the one marked in the graph, is generated. The key is to understand the role of the merge operator (denoted by M in Fig. 2): (1) under the *merge control* input values (<FT...T>), the initial output value of the loop is taken from the second input of the merge, i.e., x_1. (2) the upper output of M is routed under the *feedback control* values, i.e. <T...TF>, therefore all but the last element of the array will be fed back; and (3) the lower output of the merge is forwarded as the output of the loop unconditionally. Due to the existence of cycles, the data flow graph produced by such a scheme, in general, cannot be fully pipelined. More specifically, the feedback link between the output of cell 3 and the input of cell 1 prevents the whole graph from being fully pipelined.

The problem of the above example and its solution have been studied by the author

---

Fig. 2. The Pipelined Mapping of a FLR

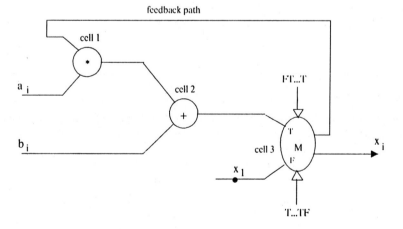

in [4, 7]. The problem is essentially a mismatch between the *dependence delay*— the dependence inherent in the recurrence (i.e., x_i depends on x_{i-1}, therefore a two-stage feedback delay is required) and the *computational delay*—the actual length of the loop in the data flow graph generated by the direct translation scheme (3 stages in this example). In [9], the author described a solution for such a problem on a static data flow computer, based on the concept of *companion functions* [4,16]. It is essentially a way to remove the dependence of x_i on x_{i-1}, thus, easing the feedback constraints in order to match the computational delay of the data flow graph. For the above example, we have:

$$x_1 = b_1$$
$$x_2 = a_2 b_1 + b_2$$
$$x_i = a_i a_{i-1} x_{i-2} + a_i b_{i-1} + b_i \quad \text{where } i \geq 3 \qquad (3.1)$$

This transformation is interesting to us because x_i now depends on x_{i-2} instead of x_{i-1}. Therefore, we can map our example, now expressed as in (3.1), into a data flow graph as shown in Fig. 3. Note that we have introduced two additional pipelines a_i and b_i as

---

Fig. 3. Maximually Pipelined Mapping of FLR

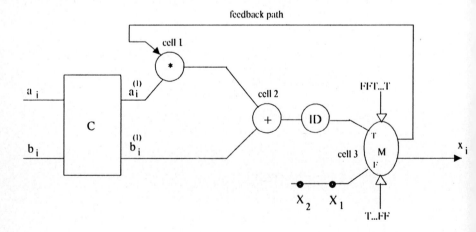

denoted by the dotted lined box C, where

$$a_i^{(1)} = a_i a_{i-1}$$
$$b_i^{(1)} = a_i b_{i-1} + b_i \qquad\qquad \text{where } i \geq 3.$$

This added pipeline is named the *companion pipeline* in [4], and its structure is shown in Fig. 4. To understand how the scheme works we first examine the loop in Fig. 3. The role of the merge operator is as before except that two initial values are presented to the second input of the merge, i.e. $x_1 = b_1$, $x_2 = a_2 b_1 + b_2$. The ID cell plays the role of a FIFO of size 1, and is inserted to tune the computational delay in the feedback path to match exactly the dependence delay. The two boxes in Fig. 4 are also FIFOs, and they can introduce proper skew needed in the pipelining of array operations [7]. The rest of the

---

Fig. 4. The Companion Pipeline fo Example (3.1)

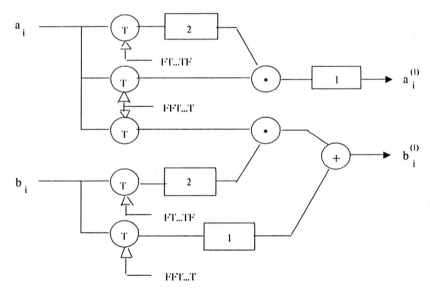

72   *G.R. Gao*

graph is self-explanatory and the reader should be convinced that the graph is maximally pipelined.

The transformation shown in the above example is equivalent to dividing the first-order linear recurrence into two equivalent classes of computation. In fact, since x_i now depends on x_{i-2}, we may split the sequence of results into two subsequences:

$$X' = \langle x_1, x_3, x_5 \ldots x_{2i-1} \ldots \rangle$$
$$X'' = \langle x_2, x_4, x_6 \ldots x_{2i} \ldots \rangle.$$

Either sequence can be computed independently by sharing the same loop, and the companion pipeline provides the appropriate input coefficients.

The advantage of this scheme is obvious. First, it does not require data rearrangement during the computation. In fact, it even eliminates the requirement that the input vectors be completely filled before the computation starts. If the input coefficient vectors themselves are generated by some preceding code block in a pipelined fashion, the producer-consumer type of interface technique (as described in [7]) can be applied to save considerable storage space for the intermediate values. Moreover, we observe that the degree of parallelism remains constant (5 floating point arithmetic operations and several other operations) in the computation.[1] The high throughput is achieved by the maximally pipelined execution of each actor in the data flow program, hence, the storage usage by the machine code is very efficient. Finally, there are no essential limitation on the length of the vectors which can be computed.

4. A Maximally Pipelined Solution Method

Starting from LU-decomposition, we can observe that the major equations, such as (2.7) and (2.8), are first-order linear recurrences. Therefore, the pipelined method as described in the last section can be applied directly. Now consider (2.9) which can be transformed into the following second-order linear recurrence:

---

1. Here the variation of the parallelism during the start and finish time of the computation is not considered

$$q_i = \alpha_i q_{i-1} + \beta_i q_{i-2} \qquad i = 3,4...n \qquad (4.1)$$

where $q_1 = 1, q_2 = -b_1/c_1$ and

$$\alpha_i = -b_{i-1}/c_{i-1}$$
$$\beta_i = -a_{i-1}/c_{i-1}$$

Performing one level backup we obtain

$$q_i = \alpha_i^{(1)} q_{i-2} + \beta_i^{(1)} q_{i-3} \qquad i = 4,5...n \qquad (4.2)$$

where $q_1 = 1, q_2 = -b_1/c_1, q_3 = b_2 b_1/c_1 c_2 - a_2/c_2$, and

$$\alpha_i^{(1)} = \alpha_i \alpha_{i-1} + \beta_i$$
$$\beta_i^{(1)} = \alpha_i \beta_{i-1} \qquad i = 4,5...n$$

Fig. 5 shows a maximally pipelined data flow machine level program for mapping (4.2). The loop in the middle of Fig. 5 can easily be understood by noting its similarity with the loops in Fig. 3. The code in the dotted lined box is the companion pipeline generating values for $\alpha_i^{(1)}$ and $\beta_i^{(1)}$. The node labeled N performs a negation of its input. The boolean value sequences C0 - C5 can be found in Fig. 7. The boxes denote the FIFO buffers which are introduced for balancing the graph [5,7] to achieve maximum pipelining, and the number written inside the box is the number of stages in that buffer. It is easy to check that Fig. 5 correctly computes (2.9) and it is maximally pipelined.

We rewrite the first-order linear recurrence in (2.7) as

$$y_i = g_i y_{i-1} + h_i \qquad i = 2,3...n \qquad (4.3)$$

where $y_1 = k_1/b_1$, $g_i = -a_i/(b_i - a_i u_{i-1})$, $h_i = k_i/(b_i - a_i u_{i-1})$. Performing one level backup we obtain

$$y_i = g_i^{(1)} y_{i-2} + h_i^{(1)} \qquad i = 3,4...n \qquad (4.4)$$

where $y_1 = k_1/b_1$, $y_2 = (-a_2 k_1 + b_1 k_2)/(b_2 - a_2 u_1) b_1$.

Fig. 5. Pipelined Tridiagonal Linear Equation Solver -- Part 1

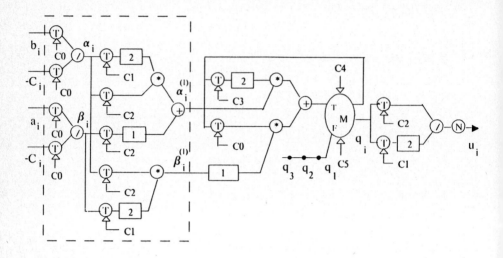

and

$$g_i^{(1)} = g_i g_{i-1}$$
$$h_i^{(1)} = g_i h_{i-1} + h_i.$$

Fig. 6 shows a maximally pipelined mapping of (4.4). The dotted lined box is the companion pipeline and the boolean sequences C1,C2,C7,C8 can be found in Fig. 7.

Finally, (2.8) can be conveniently treated as a first-order linear recurrence by introducing new variables $\bar{x}_i, \bar{y}_i, \bar{u}_i$ such that $\bar{x}_i = x_{n-i+1}, \bar{y}_i = y_{n-i+1}, \bar{u}_i = u_{n-i+1}$. Hence, (2.8) can be rewritten as

$$\bar{x}_i = r_i \bar{x}_{i-1} + s_i \qquad\qquad i = 2,3...n \qquad\qquad (4.5)$$

where $\bar{x}_i = \bar{y}_i, r_i = -\bar{u}_i$ and $s_i = \bar{y}_i$ We can note that (4.5) is a standard first-order linear recurrence, hence we can solve it by one level backup:

Fig. 6. Pipelined Tridiagonal Linear Equation Solver -- Part 2

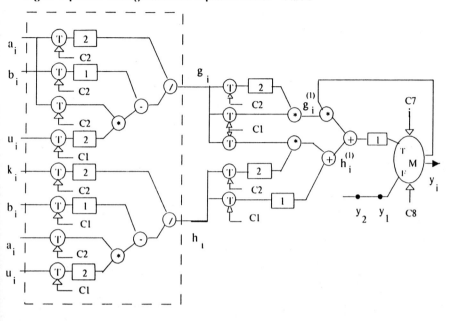

$$\bar{x}_i = r_i^{(1)}\bar{x}_{i-2} + s_i^{(1)} \qquad\qquad i = 3,4...n \qquad\qquad (4.6)$$

where $\bar{x}_1 = \bar{y}_1, \bar{x}_2 = \bar{u}_2\bar{y}_1 + \bar{y}_2$ and

$$r_i^{(1)} = r_i r_{i-1}$$
$$s_i^{(1)} = r_i s_{i-1} + s_i$$

Fig. 7 shows a maximally pipelined mapping of (4.6).

Now we have constructed a complete pipelined machine code structure for a maximally pipelined tridiagonal solver as shown by Fig. 5 - Fig. 7. Fig. 5 and Fig. 6 can be combined into one maximally pipelined data flow graph by observing that the sequence of values of u_i produced by Fig. 5 can be directly fed into Fig. 6. The interface between the outputs of Fig. 5 and Fig. 6 and the inputs of Fig. 7 cannot be connected directly. The

Fig. 7. Pipelined Tridiagonal Linear Equation Solver -- Part 3

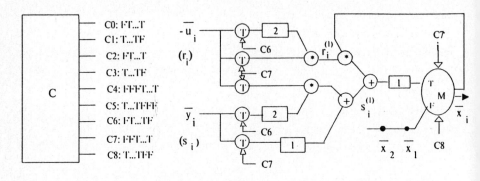

main reason is that the order in which the elements y_i and u_i are generated by Fig. 5 and Fig. 6 is opposite to the order in which they are used for the maximum pipelining of Fig. 7. Hence, we should first store the values of u_i, y_i into memory. Then, Fig. 7 will access the arrays in a reverse order. The code in Fig. 5 and Fig. 6 will sustain a constant parallelism such that there are 20 floating point operations and a number of other operations are concurrently in pipelined operation. When only the code of Fig. 7 is in execution, the parallelism will be reduced to a constant of 5. Although there is such a change of degree of parallelism between the forward elimination and backward substitution phases of the computation, the parallelism remain entirely stable during each phase, hence are easily to be handled by the processors. Furthermore, In Fig. 5 - Fig. 7, the pattern of runtime data routing is regular, thus eliminating the data rearrangement problem for cyclic reduction. Moreover, it essentially can work for tridiagonal systems regardless of their size, hence, has more flexibility and generality than the cyclic reduction scheme.

The reader may wonder if the 5 to 20 folds of parallelism available in the pipelined algorithm may not meet the appetite of a supercomputer. We argue that the major concern should be how the parallelism in the algorithm can be most effectively used by a suitable architecture. First, the new scheme maintains a relatively constant amount of parallelism and relatively simple data routing pattern. Thus, the resource management and allocation problems are more easy to handle, thereby providing better opportunity for parallel processing when the machine has extra power. Second, one is often faced with solving a set of m independent tridiagonal systems (say, m = 64), as frequently occurs in the solution of PDEs [14]. In this case, the new scheme can be best used by generating m independent pipelines for each system to obtain 20xm folds of parallelism (more than 1000 if m = 64 !). Finally, the new scheme is flexible enough to be extended to obtain more parallelism when such a requirement does occur [10].

5. Pipelining of Array Operations

In this section, we brief outline how the pipelined solution described above can be handled by a coherent code mapping scheme. The use of data flow languages such as Val [1] encourages an applicative style of programming which does not depend on the von Neumann style of machine program execution. The basic operations of the language, including operations on arrays, are simple functions that map operands to results. Data dependencies, even those involving arrays, should be apparent. Since our major concern is how to utilize the regularity of array operations in the source program, we concentrate on two array creation constructs -- the **forall** and **for-iter** [1] expressions. The **forall** construct allows the user to specify the construction of an array where similar independent computations can be performed on all elements of the array. The iteration construct, is used to specify construction of an array where certain forms of data dependencies exist between its elements. For example, the linear recurrences (2.7), (2.8) and (4.1) can be expressed by the Val iteration expressions, where all the vectors a,b,c,u,x,y,q are considered as arrays.

We have developed a pipelined code mapping scheme which concentrates on the analysis and handling of the two types of code blocks [11]. It is essentially a two-step process. The first step consists of the application of a set of basic mapping rules which can translate the code blocks into pipelined data flow graphs. In this step, the conceptual model of arrays in the source program -- i.e. the input and output arrays as seen by each code block -- remains   unchanged, but the array operations are translated into corresponding data flow actors in the result graph. The second step consists of the application of a set of optimization procedures which can remove the array actors from the result graphs of step 1 and replace them with ordinary graph actors. Thus, the links between code blocks become ordinary arcs of a data flow graph. The result graph for a pair of producer and consumer code blocks may be executed concurrently, both in a pipelined fashion, without involving array operations.

6. Sumary and Discussions

In developing new parallel algorithms, high importance attached not only to the speed of the greatest computation rate, but to the numerical stability problems as well. The stability aspect of the pipelined tridiagonal solver has been studied by the author in a second companion paper [11].

The entire code for the pipelined tridiagonal linear equation solver has been translated into the machine code of a proposed static data flow supercomputer, and preliminary simulation results indicate that the projected maximally pipelined throughput can be sustained for each of the three loops.

The pipelined solution scheme has several important advantages over other existing parallel algorithms. Although, the primary target machine used in this paper is a static data flow computer, we expect that the principle can also be applied to other data flow computers, such as the dynamic data flow machine [2], although a different perspective of pipelining may be required [8]. It is my belief that the basic ideas may also be useful for a conventional parallel machine architecture. A compiler which can perform the automatic program transformation to implement the pipelined solution scheme is an interesting challenge to the compiler construction for such computers.

7. Acknowledgements

The author is indebted to the constant encouragement and direction from Prof. Jack Dennis at MIT. Dr. Bill Ackerman and Kevin Theobald have read the draft and made interesting comments. Natalie Tarbet has provided valuable helps in the improvements of the English for this paper. Finally, the author is grateful to Gao Ping, for her typing of the entire manuscripts and preparation of the figures.

References

[1] Ackerman, W. B. and J. B. Dennis. "Val—A Value-Oriented Algorithmic Language Preliminary Reference Manual." Technical Report 218, Laboratory for Computer Science, MIT, Cambridge, MA, 13 June 1979.

[2] Arvind, Gostelow,K.P. and Plouffe,W, "An Asynchronous Programming Language and Computing Machine", TR-114a, Dept. of Information and Computer Science, Univ. of California, Irvine, Dec. 1978.

[3] Buzbee, B. L. Golub G. H. and Neilson C. W., "On Direct Methods for Solving Poison's Equations", SIAM Journal of Numerical Analysis, 7., 1970.

[4] Dennis, J. B. and Gao, G. R. "Maximum Pipelining of Array Operations on Static Data Flow Machine", Proceeding of the 1983 International Conference on Parallel Processing, Aug 23-26, 1983.

[5] Dennis, J. B., Gao G. R. and Todd, K., "Modeling the Weather with a Data Flow Supercomputer", IEEE Trans. on Computers, c-33, No. 7, July 1984.

[6] Forsythe, G. E. and Moler, C. B., "Computer Solution of Linear Algebraic Systems", Prentice-Hall, Englewood Cliffs, N. J., 1967.

[7] Gao, G. R. "An Implementation Scheme for Array Operations in Static Data Flow Computer" MS Thesis, Laboratory for Computer Science, MIT, Cambridge, MA, June 1982.

[8] Gao, G. R., "Maximally Pipelined Throughput and Its Token Storage Requirements for Dynamic Data Flow Processors", IBM Research Report, RC-10785, Computer Science, T.J. Watson Research Center, Oct. 1984.

[9] Gao, G. R. "Maximum Pipelining of Linear Recurrence on Static Data Flow Computers", Computation Structure Group Note 49, Lab. for Computer Science, Aug. 1985.

[10] Gao, G. R. "A Maximally Pipelined Tridiagonal Linear Equation Solver", Computers", To appear on the International Journal On Parallel and Distributed Computing, 1986

[11] Gao, G. R. "Stability Aspects of a Pipelined Tridiagonal Linear Equation Solver", Computation Structure Group Note 48, Lab. for Computer Science, Aug. 1985.

[12] Gao, G. R., "Massive Fine-Grain Parallelism in Array Computation — a Data Flow Solution", Proceedings of Future Directions of Computer Architecture and Software Workshop, Charleston, USA, May 5-7, 1986.

[13] Gao, G. R., "A Pipelined Code Mapping Scheme for Static Data Flow Computers", Ph.D dessertation in preparation, Dept. of Electrical Engineering and Computer Science, Cambridge, MA, 1986.

[14] Hockney, R. W. and Jesshope, C. R., "Parallel Computers", Adam Hilger Ltd., 1981

[15] Kershaw, D. "Solution of Single Tridiagonal Linear Systems and Vector Rization of the ICCG Algorithm on the Cray-1", in "Parallel Computations", Ed. by Rodrigue, G. et al., Academic Press, 1982.

[16] Kogge, P. M. "A parallel Algorithm for Efficient Solution of a General Class of Recurrence Equations." IEEE Trans. Comput., Vol. c-22, no. 8, Aug. 1973.

[17] Lambiotte, J. and Voigt, R., "The Solution of Tridiagonal Linear Systems on the CDC Star-100 Computer", ACM Trans. Math Software 1., 1975.

[18] Ortega, J. M. and Voigt, R. G., "Solution of Partial Differential Equations on Vector and Parallel Computers", NASA ICASE Report No. 85-1, 1985.

[19] Stone, H., "Parallel Tridiagonal Equation Solvers", ACM Trans. on Math. Software, Vol. 1, 1975.

HIGHLY PARALLEL COMPUTERS
G.L. Reijns, M.H. Barton (editors)
Elsevier Science Publishers B.V. (North-Holland)
©IFIP, 1987

THE STRUCTURE AND APPLICATION OF RPA - A HIGHLY
PARALLEL ADAPTIVE ARCHITECTURE

Chris Jesshope, Andrew Rushton, Adriano Cruz and Jimmy Stewart

Department of Electronics and Information Engineering
The University
Southampton SO9 5NH
England

ABSTRACT

The architecture and implementation of the
Reconfigurable Processor Array (RPA) is described.
It is being developed in the Department of Electronics and Information Engineering at Southampton
University and will provide low cost, high performance processing, on a wide range of applications.
The flexibility of the array is achieved under
software control, using a design ideally suitable
for implementation in VLSI.

INTRODUCTION

Parallelism is being increasingly used as a means of avoiding the diminishing returns obtained from circuit speeds on
computer performance. However, with this increasing use of
parallelism, the applications designer faces a new set of
programming problems. The discovery of parallelism in a
given algorithm is usually the least of these problems, both
in terms of programming and program efficiency.

Unless the parallelism within an algorithm is exploited
automatically, the programmer must be concerned with the
structure and topology of the target machine and with the
mapping of possibly non-conforming data structures onto that
machine. Moreover, there is a further constraint in the communication of operands between processing sites in the computer. These may be distant in a large fixed processor
array for example. This latter constraint is often a limit-
ing factor on the performance of a given algorithm.

The alternative of automatically generating parallelism is a
very immature field of study and to date, the inefficiencies
with which this process is achieved all but outweigh the
performance advantages to be gained from parallelism. The
possible exception to this is automatic vectorisation of

code for pipeline processors, although here the process can hardly be called automatic, for if vectorisation is to be achieved, the code must be written in such a way as to conform to one of the known templates to which it must be matched.

The generation of parallel code from functional based languages, although very desirable from a theoretical point of view, can lead to very inefficient computation. The popular counter argument to this is that hardware is cheap and we will just exploit further parallelism to make up for any inefficiencies. However most of the inefficiencies are concerned with communications, which are not cheap. It is also known that these inefficiences usually grow unfavourably with the degree of parallelism. This can be illustrated by example. Data flow machines require fast expensive matching stores[1] to match result tokens and further operations. This is a hardware solution to the problem of communications and yet data flow machines still become communications bandwidth limited where large numbers of processors are required. As an example of the degree of communications bandwidth limitation in a reduction architecture, consider the simulations of COBWEB [2], which relies on a regular fixed arrays of processors implementing a token pool. Karia has shown that the communication required to match tokens for reduction can dominate execution times by many orders of magnitude over the computational requirements.

In response to the lack of any known efficient method for the automatic generation of parallelism, INMOS with the Transputer and Occam has taken the pragmatic DIY approach, to the exploitation of parallelism. This approach relies on allowing a single code to be executed on different physical realisations of processors, without excessive restructuring. The converse problem can be conceptually equivalent and concerns the implementation of problems of differing sizes or structures onto a fixed processor structure. In occam these aims are achieved by the placed Par construct and the ability to execute many processes efficiently on a single transputer.

The architectural developments at Southampton University also follow this approach but in an SIMD like structure, rather than the MIMD structure of Occam. SIMD processor arrays are by no means new, being first proposed by Unger in 1958 [3]. Technological restrictions delayed the implementation of this architecture, with the first commercial processor array being ICL's DAP [4], which was started in 1974. The first DAP systems were delivered to customers in 1980 and consisted of a square array of 4096 simple processors implemented in MSI TTL technology.

The Reconfigurable Processor Array (RPA) is a VLSI processor array, which uses an extension of the SIMD model, which allows the structure of the architecture to adapt to the problem being implemented. This greatly simplifies the task of mapping, to obtain conformity with the array. The SIMD model is extended allowing processors to modify the broadcast instruction. In this way the processors may act in a different but locally preprogrammed manner. This extended local control provides both flexibility and efficiency in the most common data processing operations and communications. It will also be shown that it allows the fixed array structure to be viewed as variable in its size or shape, or indeed be viewed as an efficient implementation of another topology.

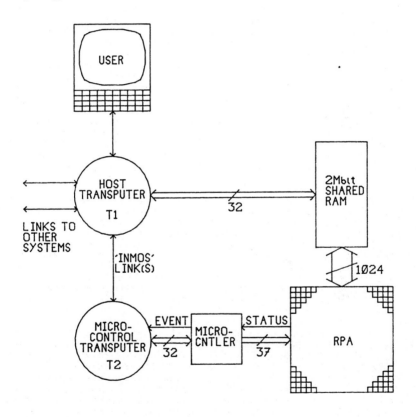

FIGURE 1   THE RPA SYSTEM ARCHITECTURE

THE RPA SYSTEM

The RPA system is organised as illustrated in figure 1. At the core of the system are two Transputers which provide the overall sequencing of program execution, and scalar data and address operations. Transputer T1 executes the host program and performs scalar data operations and data manipulation. It can be seen that as well as its own dedicated memory, it has the array data mapped into its 32 bit address space, thus providing fast backing store to the array. This is similar in design to the ICL 2900/DAP system. Transputer T2 provides a scalar address processor and buffer to the micro-controller. This transputer is responsible for issuing array orders via the microcode controller and in providing the more complex address calculations (the microcontroller can only increment an address). Feedback from the array, either as a single boolean variable or by the edge registers of the array is mapped into this transputers address space, together with all internal registers in the microcode con-troller chip.

The array instructions are interpreted as microprogram rou-tine calls by the microcontroller. Each routine can be a quite sophisticated function since the microcontroller has facilities for jump, loop and call operations within the microcode RAM. A 35 bit field in each microinstruction is sent to the RPA directly for execution. The microcode RAM is user programmable, giving the programmer the choice between programming the RPA directly in microcode or indirectly using existing general purpose routines.

THE RPA PROCESSOR ARRAY

The Reconfigurable Processor Array [5], like most other pro-cessor arrays, consists of a square array of processing ele-ments (PEs) working in lockstep under the control of a sin-gle master controller. For the prototype system an array size of 32x32 is proposed. The PEs operate bit serially, allowing flexibility in programming efficiency for all forms of data. These processing elements also provide selectable data connections to four orthogonally neighbouring PEs.

A feature of conventional processor arrays is that they present a large, fixed parallelism to the programmer. With very large data arrays this is not a problem, since the data array is fairly easily mapped onto the processor array either by splitting it into sub arrays or by mapping a locality onto a single PE. With small data arrays a conven-tional processor array can only be partially filled with data resulting in very inefficient use of resources. In the RPA however, the PEs are designed as bit slice processors which can be chained together to any length using the nearest neighbour interconnect. Local control of the direc-tion of communication allows any shape of processing unit to

be built. By using the interconnect as a carry path, bit
parallel (ripple carry) arithmetic can also be performed in
any connected chain of PEs. Thus the processing elements of
the RPA have been designed as bit slices of a more general
microprocessor, that can be configured from any connected
path of these bit slices.

The most useful paths for configuring multi-bit processors
are closed loops of processing elements and such configurations can support:

i)   all bitwise logical operations on two operands (two
      seperatly programmed operations can be performed in a
      single cycle);

ii)   single length cyclic and planar (arithmetic) shifts;

iii) double length cyclic and planar (arithmetic) shifts;

iv)   broadcast of one bit to all other bits within a proces-
      sor;

v)   ripple carry arithmetic with fast Manchester carry
      chain, performed in multiple 'byte' operations, with
      automatic handling of carry between sub-operations;

vi)   multiplication with full double length result, using
      multiple ripple carry adds (v), double length shifts
      (iii) and broadcast of bit data within 'bytes' (iv).

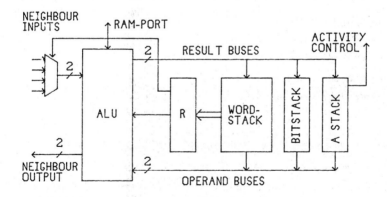

FIGURE 2 DETAILS OF THE RPA PROCESSING ELEMENT

The operations outlined above are performed with a processing element as shown in figure 2. It shows that a symmetrical 2 bit bus organisation has been adopted both internally
and via the neighbouring interconnects. The two operand
busses can be passed to a neighbour, where they are received
by the two result busses. Alternatively the ALU contains two
independent function generators, each of which can generate
any one of the 16 possible two variable logic functions.
Additional logic plus a carry register provides all four
permutations of addition and negation (A+B, A-B, -A+B, -A-B)
either bit serially using the carry register or as part of a
bit parallel processing unit.

There are two main storage structures in the PE. The
Bitstack is a bit wide stack with a stack depth of 8 bits,
and is used as a general bit store. The Wordstack is a much
more complicated structure, consisting of eight 8 bit shift
registers which can be connected together to form a word
wide stack. The word width is programmable in 8 bit steps
from 8 bits (giving a stack depth of 8 words) to 64 bits
(giving a stack depth of 1, i.e. a single 64 bit word). The
main use of the Wordstack is the storage of whole word
operands, though it can also be used as a large internal
store as an alternative to the Bitstack. Shift registers are
used so that the Wordstack fits into the general bit serial
organisation of the PE. They also preserve the bit ordering
of the words for arithmetic operations which are performed
least significant bit first.

The use of stacks simplifies the control of the array in two
ways. Firstly it simplifies the micro controller, since
there are no addresses to generate. Secondly the width of
the micro control bus entering the chip and distributed
around it is reduced. The cost of using stacks is the
increase in local control decoding within the PE.

Bit serial processors are not well suited to floating point
operations. The RPA therefore, has some additional features
to improve its performance on floating point operations.
There is a comparator circuit between the top two words of
the Wordstack, which makes it possible to perform magnitude
subtraction, always giving a positive result. Thus the sign
magnitude arithmetic that is used in floating point operations does not require a 2's complement to sign magnitude
conversion stage. There is also a decrementer circuit, which
is used in floating point addition to align the two mantis-
sas prior to adding them. This circuit provides local control of the Wordstack and shifts the appropriate mantissa by
the required amount. This is difficult to program with common broadcast control as found on conventional processor
arrays, since the shift distance varies with the data found
across the array.

A further form of local control, found in most other processor arrays, is the activity control, which usually consists
of a single bit register enabling the other storage elements
of a given PE when set. Activity control is the processor
array's equivalent to the IF..THEN statement in scalar processing. The RPA has activity control but uses a stack
identical to the Bitstack, which provides control of a large
number of environments by simply popping and pushing on context changes. Only the top bit of the activity stack is
used to control the PE.

The Reconfiguration register provides the local control
required to chain together PEs as bit slice processing
units. It contains three fields, one to label the PE as an
LSB, MSB or intermediate bit, the other two to contain the
direction of data movement in left and right shift operations. The register is loaded in parallel from the top 6
bits of the Bitstack, which could in turn have been loaded
from RAM.

An RPA chip is being designed to the design rules for the
Department's 3 micron n well CMOS process, which will contain a 4x4 sub array of PEs. Layout of the PE is about
three quarters complete. To minimise and equalise communication delays between PEs, the PEs are arranged on chip with
the same square topology as the conceptual array organisation. This optimisation of the data paths is at the expense
of control bus duplication for each row of PEs on the chip.
Layout should be complete by the mid 1986. The chip size is
larger than originally anticipated, about 8mm x 8mm, due to
the adoption of a very conservative design approach.

THE MICROCODE SEQUENCER ARCHITECTURE

The other major component of the array architecture is the
microcontroller chip, which is being implemented as a UK5000
CMOS gate array chip. The major component of this chip, the
microprogram sequencer, is shown in figure 3. This provides
the address of the microinstruction for the next machine
cycle. It receives two or more possible addresses, and based
on the current state of the machine decides which will be
the next active microinstruction. The architecture will be
best understood by describing the uses of its elements.

The chip contains one output bus, which normally supplies
the address inputs of the control memory and an input bus,
supplied from the current microword, which is used as an
alternative address during branch microoperations. The low
byte of the input bus can also supply immediate data in loop
operations. The third bus is used to input data and
instructions from transputer T2 via its memory interface.
Microprogram memory addresses are stored in a 16-bit register called the microprogram counter (MPC). This register
always holds the address of the current microinstruction
plus one.

The facility for subroutine calls at the microcode level is one of the more powerful features of the microengine, as sequences of microinstructions can be shared between microprograms, saving memory control words. A stack (MPC stack) has therefore been added to the architecture, making it possible to perform microroutine linking. This stack is 16 bits wide and four words deep.

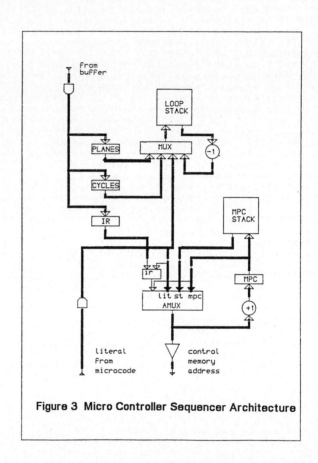

Figure 3 Micro Controller Sequencer Architecture

Due to the bit serial nature of the RPA PEs, most of the instructions executed by the array will consist of a series of simple operations repeated a number of times. Efficiency in this area has a direct impact on the system performance

and thus looping is another address operation that was given
hardware support. This was achieved using another stack,
the loop counter stack, which is 8 bits wide and four words
deep. This stack allows nested loops, which can also be
used with microsubroutines, as link information is held on a
separate stack. The top of the loop stack is always the
active loop counter and a decrementer and zero detector circuit are used to terminate 'For' loops. 'Repeat/Until' loops
are terminated by external condition signals. The stack
input can receive data from the output of the decrementer,
the literal field or one of two registers called Planes and
Cycles. These registers are used to store information about
the array configuration. Using these registers along with
the counter stack, it is possible to create a single microroutine that can be used to perform the same operation on
different formats of data or configuration. This avoids the
microcode explosion that would otherwise result from such a
flexible array structure.

Users will normally write programs to solve their problems,
using array instructions which perform operations such as
floating point addition, on user determined array sizes.
These will be preprogrammed and accessible from high level
languages. However if necessary, a user can download complete sections of code to microstore, to perform more complex applications oriented operations; matrix multiplication
would be one such example, for which a completely new
microroutine and instruction could be created. This is
achieved by decoding instructions entirely by microprogram
and implemented using a branch table in the bottom page of
microprogram memory. This supplies a vector to the appropriate routine. The instruction set can then be extended by
reserving one of the 256 orders as a primary vector to a
second page of orders, and decoding this page with a second
level of indirection.

ADAPTING THE RPA TO DIFFERING DATA STRUCTURES

Because the array structure can adapt to the data structures
of a given algorithm, mapping the user's problem onto the
array becomes a simple hardware assisted operation. As any
closed set of processing elements can form a general purpose, multi-bit processor, virtually any regular structure
can be mapped onto the array. It can be shown that although
local communication bandwidth is degraded by approximately
the square root of the number of processing elements in the
processor, as would be expected, the global communication
bandwidth remains constant for any configuration. Indeed the
communication bandwidth in less regular data structures or
in complex data movements can be much improved over a
software implementation, as would be required in the DAP for
example. In a software implementation, a great deal of
repetition may be required to obtain multiple-shift directions, by alternately masking and shifting. However, in the

RPA, this can be achieved by configuring the switch network to realise the various shift directions concurrently. Moreover the stack storage, which may be conditionally pushed or popped allows for irregular data storage, where stacks in different processing elements may be out of step.

Figure 4 Some modes of communication in the RPA

Key to Figs 4[a] to 4[d]

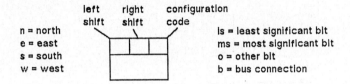

n = north
e = east
s = south
w = west

ls = least significant bit
ms = most significant bit
o = other bit
b = bus connection

A single RPA processing element

Figure 4 illustrates some regular configurations, which together give some idea of the power and flexibility of this adaptive array structure. As shown in the key above, three configuration fields are used in figures 4[a] to 4[d]. These are coded as shown and correspond to the configuration store state in an RPA PE.

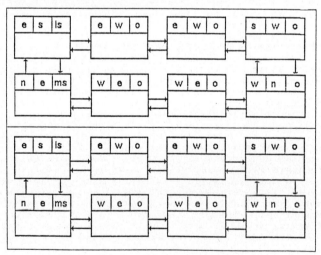

Figure 4[a]   Two eight bit processors

Figure 4[a] shows the configuration for two eight bit processors. Notice that these are closed loops and thus support the full range of 'byte' oriented operations.

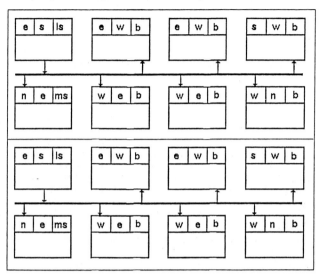

Figure 4[b] Multiple concurrent broadcast within 8 bit processors

To perform multiplication, it is possible to configure the processors of fig 4[a] to broadcast data from one bit to all other bits in a given processor and to do this in each processor simultaneously. This configuration (Fig4[b]) gives the facility of a parallel bus structure, in which multiple broadcasts can be performed concurrently.

Figure 4[c] shows how the array can be used to map a binary tree of single bit processors onto the RPA. This is achieved with a 50% utilisation of the processing elements. Some 25% of the processing elements are not used at all and another 25% are used in bus configuration and only pass inputs to outputs.

With larger processors it is possible to obtain a more efficient mapping. For example a 9 bit processor can be mapped onto the array with some 95% efficiency (fig 4[d]), provided processing is only required at the leaves. This structure uses 9 bit processors, 3 bit switch and communication processors at the lowest level and single bit switch and communications processors at all higher levels. Thus leaf to leaf communication is performed at full bandwidth, whereas communication higher in the tree is degraded by a factor of three.

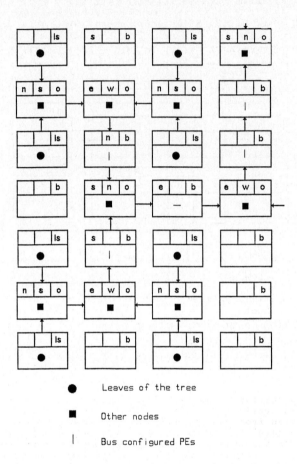

●   Leaves of the tree

■   Other nodes

| Bus configured PEs

Figure 4[c] A tree of one bit processing elements

This flexibility of the RPA in mapping such diverse structures would be a great disadvantage, were it not for the
power and flexibility of the microcontroller, which provides
for fully parameterised arithmetic coding, independent of
actual configuration. The only information the microcontroller needs concerning a given configuration is the number
of slices to be processed and the length of these slices to
determine propagation times for bus configuration propagation and for ripple carry propagation. Thus the processing
elements of figures 4[a] and 4[d] could well share common
arithmetic routines.

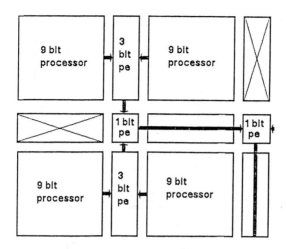

Figure   4[d] A Tree of nine bit processors

SOFTWARE DEVELOPMENT ON THE RPA

Both systems and applications studies are   underway   on   the
RPA   development   systems.   These systems comprise the occam
program development system from INMOS, and an RPA   microcode
development   system   and   simulator,   which has already been
implemented at Southampton on an ICL Perq. This puck   driven
system   provides   interactive   data configuration, microcode
editing and simulation, and graphical display of all   internal states and busses.

Microcode editing is performed without recourse to the   key-
board,   as   options for each field of the micro-control word
are selected from pop up menus. Similarly, running microcode
is   controlled   by the graphics cursor and puck, with single
step   and other modes of   execution.   The   graphics   display
which   is   present throughout all operations, can be updated
in real time; this is admittedly somewhat   slower   than   the
hardware (by a factor of about one million). Alternatively
a slight speedup can be obtained by updating the display   on
completion of a microcode fragment.

This microcode development system is being used to implement
the basic arithmetic operations for a wide variety of configurations. As indicated previously, the unbounded explosion
of microcode for an almost infinite set of configurations is
avoided by the design of the controller, which has registers
parameterising   the   configuration. These include Planes and
Cycles, which are used to store information about the number
of bit planes used to store a word and the number of cycles

required for the propagation of information, as found in
carry and bus communications. Using only these parameters
it is possible to create a single microroutine that can be
used to perform the same operation on different configurations of processing units, whatever their shape.

The implementation of high level languages, namely unbounded
array FORTRAN and C languages are being provided by a colla-
boration under the Alvey scheme, involving ICL, GEC and a
number of other Universities. The provision of these
languages for a virtual array architecture will enable many
array architectures to share the compiler development costs.
This project under the Alvey program will define a Compiler
Array Target Language (CATL) for a virtual array architecture of arbitrary size and implement compilers for it. The
RPA will benefit from this development, by implementing CATL
in microcode. It is obvious that the implementation of CATL
will be greatly simplified by the array's adaptability.

PERFORMANCE

The RPA as a transputer based workststion with a 32x32 array
card, will provide between 20 and 100 Mflops/sec on 32 bit
floating point numbers, assuming a clock rate of 10Mhz and a
carry ripple rate of 40Mhz. Because of the serial nature of
arithmetic implemented on the array, maximum performance
will be dependent on the precision of the data. For example
32 bit integer addition of 32 by 32 arrays will be performed
at a rate of 320 Mops/sec, whereas 8 bit integer addition
will be performed at almost four times this rate, which is
in excess of 1000 Million operations per second (1 Gop/sec).
Indeed boolean operations can be performed at a rate of 20
Gops/sec. We are currently investigating the performance
expected for a variety of applications and we expect to see
performance figures close to the theoretical maximum for a
given data type. These studies include the implementation of
the basic arithmetic functions and the exploitation of the
architecture for such diverse applications as signal processing and tools for VLSI design.

REFERENCES

[1]   Gurd J R, Kirkham C C, Watson, I, 1985 'The   Manchester
      Prototype Dataflow System', CACM Jan pp34-52.

[2]   Karia R, 1986 'Reduction on a   wafer'   in   Wafer   Scale
      Integration,   Adam Hilger Ltd (Eds C R Jesshope and W R
      Moore).

[3]   Unger S H, 1958, 'A Computer Oriented   Towards   Spatial
      Problems', Proc. IRE v.46 pp1744-50.

[4]   Hunt D J, Reddaway S F, Parkinson D,   1977,   'Efficient
      High-Speed Computing with the Distributed-Array Proces-
      sor' in, 'High Speed Computing and Algorithm   Organisa-
      tion' (Ed Kuck D J), Academic Press.

[5]   Rushton A J, Jesshope C R,   1986,   'The   Reconfigurable
      Processor   Array   -   An Architecture in Need of WSI' in
      Wafer Scale Integration,   Adam   Hilger   Ltd   (Eds   C   R
      Jesshope and W R Moore).

[6]   J R Grierson et all, 1983, ' The   UK5000   Successful
      collaborative   development   of   an integrated   design
      system for a 5000 gate CMOS array with   built-in   test,
      Proceedings of the 20th Design Automation Conference.

HIGHLY PARALLEL COMPUTERS
G.L. Reijns, M.H. Barton (editors)
Elsevier Science Publishers B.V. (North-Holland)
©*IFIP, 1987*

PARALLEL MEMORY MANAGEMENT IN A SIMD COMPUTER

M. Auguin F. Boeri

Laboratoire de Signaux et Systèmes
Université de Nice
UA N° 814 du CNRS
41 Bd Napoléon III
06041 Nice Cedex

In this paper we present a parallel memory organization for
a vector SIMD architecture. This memory is a compromise between conflictless access to vector objects and the overall
throughput. It is important that vector accesses with an odd
address skip be done without conflict as indeed the unity address skip is very often used. A Benes interconnection network allows data alignment with the processors, access conflict resolution and permutation on vectors of any length
for numerical processing.

1. INTRODUCTION

One of the most significant challenges in parallel SIMD computers is the parallel
memory organization. In order to obtain great performance, data in parallel memory have to be accessed at the highest throughput. Furthermore data must be routed to the processing elements such that they contain data processed together.
Classicaly SIMD computers perform vector processing (BARNES (1968), BATCHER (1974),
KUCK (1982)) so the parallel memory must hold data arrays processed by algorithms.
Generally, vector computing uses sub-arrays selected from arrays held in the parallel memory. For example, a two dimensional FFT may be performed by compounding
FFT on rows and FFT on columns. The parallel memory requires efficient accesses
to sub-array to supply processors with data.

The parallel memory consists of P memory modules. Associated with each of them,
an address generation is required to point out each datum. This computation
must be as fast as possible. Particularly, introduction of pipeline levels in
the system increases the overall start-up. Therefore we use a small number of levels
and in order to be efficient with short vectors, address generation must be obtained with combinational operators.

Two possible ways of parallel vector processing exist :

- Some high speed strongly pipelined operators are connected with the memory
  which is also pipelined. This is the CRAY-1S scheme.

- Several identical operators, a priori less complex, perform simultaneously
  the same operation on different vector elements. This is the BSP scheme.

In this latter case, processing elements are connected with the memory by an
interconnection network (figure 1). The interconnection network of ILLIAC IV
links processing element i with processing elements (i+1), (i-1), (i+8), (i-8)
modulo 64.

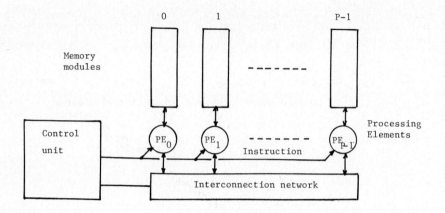

Figure 1 : SIMD Architecture Model

In the BSP, two full crossbar switching networks allow data exchanges. An inter-connection network is able to do data manipulations (FENG (1974)) which are dif-ficult to implement in a pipelined machine. This data manipulator realizes permu-tations on data during transfers between memory modules and processors. Since con-flicts may occur during vector accesses, it is important to reduce them. But the hardware must manage their occurrence to make it possible to program the machine. This point is well illustrated on the ILLIAC IV system (PERROT (1981)).

In this paper we present a parallel memory organization which takes into account these constraints.

2. SOME PARALLEL MEMORIES

First we define a N-vector V to be a N element set of the elements of a m dimen-sioned array A :

$$\{A (i_0, i_1, \ldots i_{m-1})_0 , A(i_0, i_1, \ldots, i_{m-1})_1, \ldots A(i_0, i_1, \ldots, i_{m-1})_{N-1}\}$$

Next we define a linear N-vector to be a N-vector formed by linear subscript ex-pression :

$$\{ A(i_0 + n_0 k, i_1 + n_1 k, \ldots, i_{m-1} + n_{m-1} k) \; / \; n_0, \ldots, n_{m-1} \in Z, k = 0, \ldots, N-1\}$$

where n_j is the skip associated with j^{th} dimension.

A number of memory systems have been discussed in the literature. In the associati-ve processor STARAN (BATCHER (1976)) the parallel memory only permits conflictless row/column linear vector accesses for two dimensioned arrays. A masking scheme selects row or column slices.

The hardware realization is very easy and efficient but sub-array access capabi-lities are limited.
Data in the ILLIAC IV parallel memory are stored using a skewing scheme (BARNES (1968)). Conflictless linear vector accesses are defined by the programmer. The implementation of the address generation is efficient but the interconnection

network induces numerous data exchanges. The BSP contains two switching networks
for assuming a maximum memòry throughput. Furthermore in order to reduce conflicts, the BSP has seventeen memory modules which is a prime number. Unfortunately computations modulo 17 are not straighforward (KUCK (1982), LAWRIE
and VORA (1982)).

As the BSP contains sixteen processing elements, some unused memory locations
are introduced by the storage scheme. This array mapping prevents from considering instructions like IDENTIFY of the Fortran 8 X that is weighty.
Finally, in the CRAY-1S arrays are mapped using a column major storage in order
to ensure the largest portability of Fortran programs. The address generation
system allows linear vector accesses with a hardware management of conflicts.
But it is a great pity that no mecanism is designed to deal with non linear
vectors.

A balance between the conflictless access capabilities of a parallel memory and
its hardware complexity must be defined with the object of obtaining low address generation response time. Conflicts have to be handled automatically by
the hardware for relieving the programmer and / or the compiler of this task.

In subsequent sections we will consider a power of two memory modules. This
choice restricts conflictless access capabilities to linear vectors. As mention-
ned below the vector is accessed without any conflict if and only if the distance
between two consecutive elements of a linear vector is odd. Is it advisable
to consider a complicate addressing system for taking into account even distances ? Our choice must be taken by considering that odd distances are more often encountered (unity is the only value used by the CYBER 205).

3. STORAGE OF ARRAYS

Firstly we define addresses of memory location in the parallel memory. This address is formed with two fields :

- The least significant bits give the memory module number.

- The most significant bits are the address in this module.

The element of the m dimensioned array $A(i_0, i_1,...,i_{m-1})$ is stored at the address :

$$a = base + i_0 r_0 + i_1 r_1 +...+ i_{m-1} r_{m-1}$$

Let us suppose A has d_j elements in the jth dimension, then typically

$$r_0 = 1, r_1 = d_0,..., r_{m-1} = d_{m-2} d_{m-3}...d_0$$

The value base is the address of the element A(0,0...0). An example of an array
A(0 : 4, 0 : 3) stored in four memory modules is given in figure 2.

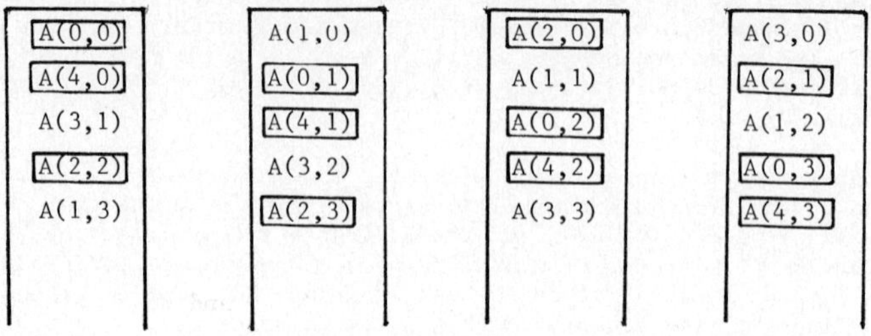

A(0,0)	A(1,0)	A(2,0)	A(3,0)
A(4,0)	A(0,1)	A(1,1)	A(2,1)
A(3,1)	A(4,1)	A(0,2)	A(1,2)
A(2,2)	A(3,2)	A(4,2)	A(0,3)
A(1,3)	A(2,3)	A(3,3)	A(4,3)

Figure 2 : Sub-array $A_1(0:4:2,0:3)$ built from
the array $A(0:4,0:3)$.

An advantage of this formulation is to work on sub-arrays of A without data transfers.
For example from the above array we can extract the sub-array $A1(0:4:2,0:3)$ by considering $r_o=2$ in the element address computation formula.

4. ACCESS TO LINEAR VECTOR ELEMENTS

A parallel memory composed of $P= 2^P$ memory modules can deliver at most P elements. Thus, to build a linear N-vector, (N div P) successive accesses followed by an access of (N modulo P) elements are necessary. Below we consider only the case of linear P-vectors.

The kth element of a linear vector is located at address :

$$a(k) = base + i_o r_o + .. + i_{m-1} r_{m-1} + k(n_o r_o + .. + n_{m-1} r_{m-1}) \qquad (1)$$

At memory module level, an address computation is needed in order to point out the element stored in that module. First at all, we have to define the number k of the element contained in the memory module x. Then we compute the element address inside the memory module.

The module x containing the kth element of the linear P-vector is defined by :

$$x = a(k) \text{ modulo } P$$

Then we get :

$$(k(n_o r_o + ... + n_{m-1} r_{m-1})) \text{modulo } P = (x-(base + i_o r_o + ... + i_{m-1} r_{m-1}) \text{ modulo } P)$$

O r :

$$(KR) \text{ modulo } P = (x-E) \text{ modulo } P \qquad (2)$$

where $R = n_o r_o + ... + n_{m-1} r_{m-1}$ and $E = base + i_o r_o + ... + i_{m-1} r_{m-1}$.

The element number k is obtained from (2) by :

$$k \text{ modulo } P = ((x - E)R^{-1}) \text{ modulo } P$$

The value R^{-1} is computed in the ring $\mathbb{Z}/P\ \mathbb{Z}$ with $P=2^P$

<u>Remark</u> : Existence of R^{-1}

We search $R^{-1} \in \mathbb{Z}/P \mathbb{Z}$ so that $RR^{-1} = 1$ modulo P

which gives $RR^{-1} = 1 + zP$, $z \in \mathbb{N}$

therefore $RR^{-1}-zP=1$

        From BEZOUT identity we have :

$\forall$ p, q $\in \mathbb{Z}$, p and q are relatively prime numbers if and only if $\exists$ u,v/up+ vq=1

Consequently, R^{-1} exists if and only if P and R are relatively prime. But $P=2^p$ is even so R must be odd.

        From equation (2) we get :

k modulo P = $((x-E)R^{-1})$ modulo P   (3)

The value of k is straighforwardly obtained with operations on p bits.
Linear vectors are accessed with conflicts if and only if R is even. The parallel memory system of the BSP is composed of 17 memory modules. Thus linear vectors are accessed with conflicts if and only if R is a multiplicative number of
17. Unfortunately the computation of k is laborious.

The value of k is known, then define the address $a_x(k)$ of   this k^{th} element
inside the xth memory module, i.e the most significant bits of the complete
address a(k) :

    $a_x(k) = a(k)$ DIV P

Hence, combining (1) -(3) above we get

    $a_x(k) = (E + ((x-E)R^{-1}$ modulo P) R) DIV P   (4)

It is easy to compute this address with a multiplication of R by k coded with
p bits and one addition with E. The integer division by P is obtained with the
most significant bits of the result of the addition.

Some calculations are common to all the address generation systems associated
with memory modules (values of E, R, R^{-1} modulo P). These values are computed
and brodcast _1 the control unit. Each address generation system number x performs k=$(x-E)R^{-1}$ modulo P and then computes the address $a_x(k)$ of the vector
element stored into the memory modulo x.

In order to execute vector operations, elements number k must be gathered in
the same processing element : it is the data alignment problem.
We choose to bind a processing element k with a vector element k. Thus we have
to perform the permutation illustrated in figure 3.

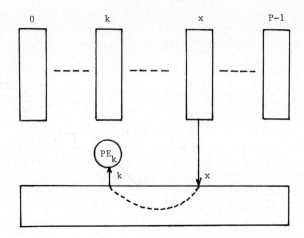

Figure 3 : Data alignment principle

For a read operation, the processing element k receives through the interconnection network the data from the memory module x . For a write operation, the processing element sends the data through the interconnection network towards the memory modulo x. We obtain for a read operation the permutation :

$$x \longrightarrow k = ((x-E)R^{-1}) \text{ modulo } P \qquad (5)$$

The network must realize this permutation efficiently.

A full crossbar interconnection network is able to perform these permutations, but the complexity varies as P^2, so we do not use it for large numbers of memory modules (greaterthan 16).

We consider the Benes network (figure 4) less complex than the previous one, with a complexity of $O(P \log_2 P)$ and which performs the P! permutations.

5. THE INTERCONNECTION NETWORK

The general control algorithm of the Benes network (OPFERMAN (1971)) is time consuming for setting up P connections.

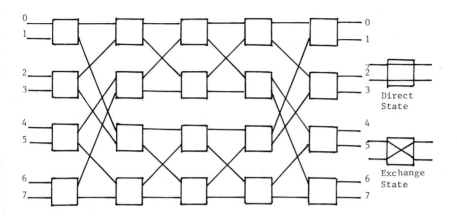

Figure 4 : Benes network with P=3.

Indeed $O(2^F)$ steps are needed to set up all the switching elements. For each vector access the system computes the states of all switching elements which produces a too large overhead. A more efficient control algorithm takes into account a subset of all the possible permutations grouped into five families (LENFANT (1978)). One of them called $\chi^P_{s,t}$ contains the following permutations :

$$x \to sx+t \text{ modulo } P = 2^P \quad ; s \text{ is an odd integer.}$$

The Benes network aligns vector elements by identifying s and t respectively with R^{-1} and $- ER^{-1}$ of (5). The control algorithm for the $\lambda^P_{s,t}$ family is mainly combinational which provides set up time of the network of the same magnitude order than the parallel memory access time. The (p-1) first switch stages of the Benes network are set up in the direct state by this control algorithm. Thus the p last stages are needed. Feng (1980) shows that these stages are topologicaly equivalent to the Omega network (LAWRIE (1975)) Figure 5 .

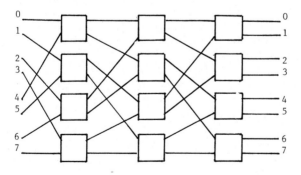

Figure 5 : Omega network

The symmetrical Benes network may be emulated by an Omega network by routing
two times data, the first time from the left side to the right side and vice-
versa after (TAHE (1979)).

Another family of permutations, used for access conflict management, is the family $\rho^P_{j,l,m,k}$. The binary representation of an input number x is divided into
four **fields** $(\hat{x}_4,\hat{x}_3,\hat{x}_2,\hat{x}_1)$ whose lengths are j,l,m,p-(j+l+m) respectively. Permutations of this family map $(\hat{x}_4,\hat{x}_3,\hat{x}_2,\hat{x}_1)$ onto $(\hat{x}_4,\hat{x}_1,\hat{x}_2,\hat{x}_3)\oplus$ k where $\oplus$ is the
exclusive or operator. The realization of these permutations requires the Benes
network.

We have introduced the Benes network which is able to align vector elements when
they are fetched or stored into the parallel memory with an odd distance between
vector elements. We consider in the following section the case R even.

6. MANAGEMENT OF CONFLICTS

An example of a P linear vector access with conflicts is given in figure 6.

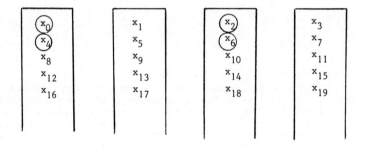

Figure 6 : Access of the vector x_0,x_2,x_4,x_6
into 4 memory modules.

The kth vector element is stored in the memory module x = (E+kR) modulo P. Let

$$R \text{ modulo } P = y \, 2^q \; ; \; y,q \in \mathbb{N} \; ; \; 0 < y < 2^P \; ; \; 0 \leqslant q \leqslant p, \; y \text{ odd.}$$

Firstly, we show that only 2^{p-q} memory modules contain the P elements. Then
we partition the set of the memory modules and the interconnection network into
2^q subsets of memory modules and 2^q subnetworks respectively.
The linear P-vector is split into 2^q linear subvectors of 2^{p-q} elements. Only
one subset of memory modules contains all the subvectors.

Let

$$(v^j_0 , v^j_1,\ldots v^j_{2^{p-q}-1}) \; ; \; j = 0,\ldots,2^q-1$$

be the set of the subvectors such that v^j_k is the element $v_{k+j2^{p-q}}$ of the linear
P-vector.

All the elements v_k^j ; $j = 0,\ldots,$ 2^q-1 are contained in the memory module

$$x = (E + k \, y \, 2^q) \pmod{P}$$

Indeed these elements are contained in memory module

$$x = (E + kj \, 2^{p-q} \, y \, 2^q) \pmod{P}$$

that is to say $x = (E + k \, y \, 2^q) \pmod{P}$

Therefore all the linear P-vector elements are mapped into a subset of 2^{p-q} memory modules.

We partition the set of memory modules (and the set of processing elements) such that the subset t includes the memory modules :

$$x = (t + k \, y \, 2^q) \pmod{P} \; ; \; k = 0,\ldots,2^{p-q} - 1$$

The 2^q subvectors are in the subset number E modulo P.

The Benes network with 2^p inputs can be partitionned into 2^q Benes subnetworks of 2^{p-q} inputs and 2^{p-q} outputs. This is obtained by setting up the q first stages and the q last stages of the Benes network in the direct state.

Inputs and outputs with number

$$x = (t + ky \, 2^q) \pmod{P} \; ; \; k = 0,\ldots,2^{p-q}-1$$

are connected with a Benes subnetwork.

Accordingly each subset of 2^{p-q} memory modules is connected with a subnetwork. After this partitionning, we get 2^q independent SIMD systems. In the following we describe conflicts management for fetching linear vector elements. For storing we proceed in a reverse way. We manage memory conflicts by dispatching a subvector towards memory module subsets in a first step, by aligning subvectors simultaneously inside each subset in a second step and at last by unscrambling the linear P-vector.

In each memory module subset t we renumber memory modules with the mapping :

$$t + k \, y \, 2^q \; \rightarrow \; ky$$

Thereby, subvector alignment consists in routing the kth element of the subector j, mapped in memory module $x = ky$ of the subset t, to the processing element k of the same subset. That is to say :

$$x \; \rightarrow \; (xy^{-1}) \text{ modulo } 2^{p-q}$$

This bijection is a permutation $\lambda_{y^{-1},0}^{p-q}$

After this first phase we get 2^q linear subvectors aligned into 2^q subsets of 2^{p-q} processing elements.
The element v_k^j is contained in the processing element k of the subset j, i.e. the processing element $j + k \, 2^q$.
Now the element v_k^j is the element $v_{k+j \, 2^q}$ of the linear P-vector.

Thus we have to perform the permutation

$$(\hat{x}_2, \hat{x}_1) \quad \rightarrow \quad (\hat{x}_1, \hat{x}_2)$$

where $\hat{x}_2$ and $\hat{x}_1$ are the q most significant bits and the p-q least significant bits of the processing element binary representation number respectively. This permutation is a

$$\beta \, ^P_{0,0,p-q,0} \quad \equiv \quad \beta \, ^P_{0,p-q,0,0}$$

The overall conflict management algorithm is :

begin

    for j:= 0 **to** 2^{q-1} **do**

    fetch subvector j from memory module subset E modulo P ;

    perform a permutation $\lambda^P_{1,j-E}$ in order to send suvector j to the subset j

    end
    for all the subsets **do**

    the permutation $\lambda \, ^{p-q}_{y-1,0}$ in order to align elements inside

    each subset

    end

    perform the permutation $\beta^P_{0,0,p-q,0}$ to unscramble the linear P-vector elements.

end

Notice that this algorithm is valid when q=0 i e when the access is conflictless. Indeed permutations $\lambda^P_{1,-E}$ and $\lambda^P_{y-1,0}$ may be combined in one permutation $\lambda^P_{y-1,-Ey-1}$.

Furthermore the permutation $\beta^P_{0,0,p,0}$ is the identity bijection. As y=R modulo P and q=0 we get the alignment permutation of the conflictless case previously presented. In order to optimize the overall implementation, the conflictless case must be separately processed since one passing through the Omega interconnection network is required.

An interconnection network in a SIMD architecture allows to access non linear P-vectors. Next, we present an illustration of this capability with the bit reversal permutation.

7. BIT REVERSAL REALIZATION

This permutation is often used in the FFT algorithm which is basic in numerous fields. Its purpose is to associate the ith element, with binary representation $(i_{n-1}, i_{n-2},...i_0)$ of the source N-vector (N=2^n) with the element $(i_0, i_1,...., i_{n-2}, i_{n-1})$ of the outcome vector. We can consider source or outcome vectors as linear vectors but not both simultaneously.

The bit reversal permutation ρ^P performed by the Benes network allows the optimal realization of ρ^n (n >p). Optimal means that only N/P conflictless accesses to the source vector and N/P conflictless access to the outcome vector are sufficient.

Let us define $\tilde{i}$ as the bit reversal operation on the integer i.

The bit reversal control algorithm is divided into two cases :

First case : $n < 2 \ p$

Let $a_s(0)$ and $a_r(0)$ be the base addresses of the source and outcome vectors respectively.

The algorithm is :

begin
    For i:= 0 to 2^{n-p} do

    . the memory module x supplies the element $(i \oplus (x \text{ modulo } 2^{n-p}), x) + a_s(0)$;

    . Perform the composition

$$\rho^p \circ \beta^p_{0,n-p,0,\tilde{i}} \quad ;$$

    . The memory y which receives an element stores it at address

$$((y \text{ modulo } 2^{n-p}) \oplus \tilde{i}) + a_r(0)$$

    End
End

Proof :

Let us consider the jth element of the source vector. The binary representation of this number is divided into 3 fields (a_3, a_2, a_1) where (a_3, a_2, a_1) have lengths n-p, 2p-n, n-p bits respectively. Recall that the bit reversal permutation maps the element (a_3, a_2, a_1) onto the element $(\tilde{a}_1, \tilde{a}_2, \tilde{a}_3)$.

The memory module x such that

$$x = (a_2, a_1) \text{ supplies the element } (a_3, a_2, a_1)$$

when
$$a_3 = i \oplus (x \text{ modulo } 2^{n-p}), \text{ i.e}$$
$$a_3 = a_1 \oplus i$$

The permutation ρ^p sends this element to the processing element.

$$(\widetilde{a_2, a_1}) = (\tilde{a}_1, \tilde{a}_2)$$

Then $\beta^p_{0,n-p,0,\tilde{i}}$ sends it to the processing element $y = (\tilde{a}_2, \tilde{a}_1 \oplus \tilde{i})$

Since $a_3 = a_1 \oplus i$, we have $\tilde{a}_3 = \tilde{a}_1 \oplus \tilde{i}$ and $y = (\tilde{a}_2, \tilde{a}_3)$.
This element is stored at the address

$$a_r(0) + (y \text{ modulo } 2^{n-p}) \oplus \tilde{i}$$

that is to say $a_r(0) + \tilde{a}_3 \oplus \tilde{i}$. As $i = a_3 \oplus a_1$ this address is equal to $\tilde{a}_1 + a_r(0)$.

Consequently the element (a_3, a_2, a_1) source vector is sent to the memory module $(\tilde{a}_2, \tilde{a}_3)$ with the index $(\tilde{a}_1, \tilde{a}_2, \tilde{a}_3)$.

Second case : $n \geqslant 2p$

Let (i_2, i_1) the binary representation of i such that lengths of i_2 and i_1 are p and $n-2p$ bits respectively

In this case the algorithm is :

<u>Begin</u>

   <u>For</u> i := 0 <u>to</u> $2^{n-p}-1$ <u>do</u>

   The memory module x supplies the element $(i_2 \oplus x, i_1, x)$;

   Perform the composition

$$\rho^p \ o \ \beta^p_{0,0,0,\ i_2} \ ;$$

The memory module y which receives an element stores it at the address

$$(y \oplus \tilde{i}_2, \tilde{i}_1)$$

    <u>End</u>

<u>End</u>

Proof :

Let (a_3, a_2, a_1) be the binary representation of the element index such that lengths of a_3, a_1 are p, n-2p, p bits respectively.

The bit reversal permutation maps this element onto the element $(\tilde{a}_1, \tilde{a}_2, \tilde{a}_3)$ of the outcome vector.

The memory module $x = a_1$ supplies this element when $i = (a_3 \oplus a_1, a_2)$. The $\beta^p_{0,0,0, i_2}$ permutation sends it to the processing element $(a_1 \oplus a_3 \oplus a_1) = a_3$.

The ρ^{υ} permutation sends it towards the processing element $y = \tilde{a}_3$. In the associated memory module the received element is stored at address :

$$(y \oplus \tilde{a}_1 \oplus \tilde{a}_3, \tilde{a}_2) = (\tilde{a}_1, \tilde{a}_2)$$

So, the element with address $(\tilde{a}_1, \tilde{a}_2)$ in the memory module $(\tilde{a}_3)$ has the index $(\tilde{a}_1, \tilde{a}_2, \tilde{a}_3)$ of the outcome vector which is associated with the element (a_3, a_2, a_1) of the source vector.

Other permutations upon non linear vectors of any length may be implemented with the Benes interconnection network (Del Gallo (1985)).

8. CONCLUSION

We have expounded a parallel memory design well adapted to a vector SIMD architecture. This parallel memory allows conflictless access to linear vectors when
the distance between two consecutive elements of the array is odd. First of all
it is this case that we must optimize, because the unity skip is the most often
encountered. An even distance can appear in two ways, that is to say :

- We do an access into one (or many) dimension with an even step : $R = 2^q n_i r_i$
  where r_i is an integer, n_i is an odd integer.

In this case it is impossible to avoid conflict with a linear storage and a number of memory modules which is a power of two.

- We do an access with non zero ratio following dimension   i with r_i even.

As $r_i = d_{i-1} d_{i-2} \ldots d_o$ where d_j is the number of elements in the jth dimension,
the programmer or the compiler may introduce virtual elements for obtaining an
odd r_i. For example if dj is even we define the array $A(0 : d_0-1;\ldots ;0 : d_j ;$
$\ldots;0 : d_{m-1}-1)$ which avoids access conflicts following the jth dimension.

Our parallel memory is easy to implement since all address calculations except
multiplications and additions are done with power of two.
Consequently we can get a very low access-time especially if all calculations
are done with specialized **circuits**.
Conflicts management requires composition of permutation λ and β

$$\beta^P_{0,0,p-q,0} \circ \lambda^{p-q}_{y-1,0} \circ \lambda^P_{1,-e+j}$$

The $\lambda^P_{1,-e+j}$ permutation is done for each access to a subvector and then can be
pipelined. The two others are performed sequentially. For reducing the number of
data transfers through the omega network, it should be desirable to define a
combinational control for the Benes network to realize the permutation

$$\beta^P_{0,0,p-q,0} \circ \lambda^{p-q}_{y-1,0}$$

which associates the input x with binary representation $(\hat{x}_2,\hat{x}_1)$, with the output
$(\hat{x}_1,\hat{x}_2 \cdot y^{-1})$ where $\hat{x}_2$ contains (p-q) bits and $\hat{x}_1$ contains q bits.

REFERENCES

Barnes (1968) : G.H Barnes and al, ; The Illiac IV computer, IEEE T.C. Vol
C-17 pp 746-757, Aug 1968.

Batcher (1974) : K.E Batcher ; STARAN parallel processor system hardware ;
Proc. Fall Joint Computer Conf. AFIPS Conf. AFIPS Press, vol 43, pp 405-410
1974.

Bather (1976) : K.E Bather ; The multi-dimensional access memory in STARAN ;
Proc. 5th Sagamore Conf. Parallel Processing, Lecture Notes in Computer Science
New York Springer, Vol 24, 1976.

Del Gallo (1985) : Y. Del Gallo ; Etude et réalisation de l'unité de commande
du calculateur vectoriel OPSILA ; Thèse 3è cycle, Université de Nice, Novembre
1985.

Feng (1974) T.Y Feng : Data manipulation functions in parallel processors and
their implementations ; IEEE T.C Vol C-23 pp 309-318, 1974.

Feng (1980) ; T.Y Feng, C. WU ; The reverse exchange interconnection network ;
IEEE T.C vol C29, pp 801-811 1980.

Kuck (1982) ; D.J Kuck, R.A Stokes ; The Buroughs Scientific Processor ; IEEE
T.C Vol C31, pp 363-376, may 1982.

Lawrie (1975) ; D.H Lawrie ; Access and alignment of data in an array processor ;
IEEE T.C Vol C24, pp 1145-1155, déc. 1975.

Lawrie (1982) ; D.H Lawrie, C. Vora ; The prime memory system for array access ;
IEEE T.C vol C31, pp 435-442, may 1982.

Lenfant (1978) : J. Lenfant ; Parallel permutations of data : a Benes network
control algorithm for frequently used permutations ; IEEE T.C vol C27, pp 637-
647, july 1978.

Opferman (1971) : D.G. Opferman, N.T Tsao-Wu ; On a class of rearrangeable switching networks - part 1 control algorithm ; Bell System Techn. journal, Vol 50,
N°5, pp 1572-1600, 1971.

Perrot (1981) : R.H Perrot, D.K Stevenson, User's experience with the ILLIAC IV
system and it's programming languages ; SIGPLA, vol 7, n°16, pp 75-88, 1981.

Tahé (1979) : S. Tahé ; transfert de données sur un calculateur parallèle vectoriel ; Thèse Docteur-Ingénieur, Université de Rennes, Juillet 1979.

HIGHLY PARALLEL COMPUTERS
G.L. Reijns, M.H. Barton (editors)
Elsevier Science Publishers B.V. (North-Holland)
©*IFIP, 1987*

Performance Analysis of a Data-Driven Multiple Vector Processing System

Nigel P. Topham[†]

Department of Computer Science, University of Edinburgh

James Clerk Maxwell Building
The Kings Buildings
Mayfield Road
Edinburgh EH9 3JZ
Scotland

Vector processors containing several vector units are now available commercially. However, these machines are not extensible. Shared memory structures and inefficient processor communications limit the number of vector units that could usefully cooperate within the confines of these architectures. This paper analyses the performance of an *extensible* vector processing architecture. A performance model for the system is presented, and the performance of two different algorithms is predicted. It is shown, that for compute-bound problems, the performance of the system is not limited by memory bandwidth, or by interprocessor communication overheads.

Introduction

The development of practical parallel machines has been dominated by the requirement for very high performance numerical processors. This initially led to the development of vector processing (VP) machines, such as the STAR-100 [Hint72], the CRAY-1 [Russ78] and the CYBER 205 [Linc82]. These first generation vector processors are characterized by their use of pipelined arithmetic and high bandwidth stores. They define a set of instructions, operating on vectors, which enable them to stream vector operands through pipelined arithmetic units at very high rates. Their parallelism is limited, in its extent, by the number of segments in each pipeline and by the number of concurrent vector instructions that can be sustained by a single instruction stream.

Subsequent vector processors incorporate more than one instruction stream, and in theory these machines have the potential for extremely high numerical processing rates. Such machines include the CRAY X-MP [Chen83], the CRAY-2[Cray85] and the ETA Systems GF10 [Eta83]. In a multi-user environment these instruction streams are

---

[†]The research documented in this paper was supported by the U.K. SERC post-doctoral research fellowship scheme.

wholly independent and the maximum performance available to each user is bounded by the performance of a single processor. A far more interesting situation occurs when a single task attempts to exploit the full power of large numbers of vector processors concurrently. The performance of individual VPs must still be optimized, and this has implications for both machine architecture and language design. This topic is discussed later.

This paper is concerned with the performance of cooperating vector processors and with the relationship between the architecture of interprocessor communication mechanisms performance. There are two distinct ways in which interprocessor communications can be implemented.

- A shared memory resource.

- A dedicated communication medium.

The emphasis is placed here on interprocessor communication because this now represents a significant problem in the field of very high performance multiprocessors, especially *vector* processors. The problems associated with interprocessor communications in shared-memory multiprocessors are basically two-fold [Jone80]. Firstly, contention for access to shared memory results in a less than unit increase in performance as processors are added to the system. Secondly, synchronization constraints between processors can further degrade performance. This occurs as a result of two distinct phenomena.

The most common method of implementing process synchronization, via shared memory locations, involves the use of locks. These operate either on critical sections of code, or on shared items of data. This leads to the possibility of performance degradation caused by inefficient algorithms in which a small number of shared locks are referenced excessively. When a processor is locked-out it experiences a performance degradation proportional to the *wait-time* involved. In general wait-times are difficult to predict. However, measurements taken on **Cm*** [Jone80] have shown that a synchronized algorithm may run at less than half the speed of an asynchronous, non-deterministic algorithm. This implies a significant wait-time degradation. These asynchronous algorithms are discused in more detail by Baudet [Baud78].

Only a relatively small class of iterative algorithms can usefully exploit non-determinism, and therefore the emphasis here is placed on obtaining efficient deterministic operation. Wait-times are determined by several factors, the most notable being -

- Parallel decomposition of algorithms.

- The granularity of synchronization.

The parallel decomposition of the algorithm determines where synchronization must be applied, and is a subject of much research [Vrsa85]. The granularity of synchronization is especially important in VPs due to the possibility of large vectors. If synchronization is performed on whole vectors then wait-times will be a function of the average vector length. However, if synchronization is performed on individual vector elements then wait-times will be determined primarily by algorithmic decomposition. For example, linear recurrence relationships between data objects in distinct processors require closely-coupled and data-driven synchronization if they are to be processed concurrently.

The effect of VLSI on supercomputer performance also means that processor communications will become more important. It is now easier, and cheaper, to duplicate a high performance VP than to produce a single processor with twice the performance.

In a previous paper [Ibbe85], the design of a parallel vector processing system, MU6V, was presented. This paper outlined the design of an interprocessor communication strategy, and a virtual vector addressing mechanism, based on a fully distributed memory and the duplication of shared data. It used a broadcast communication protocol incorporating hardware synchronization at the vector-element level. This effectively produced a *data-driven* system, in which process synchronization was governed by the availability of data rather than the sequencing of instructions.

One of the most important features of the MU6V system is the global virtual addressing mechanism. The system is programmed under the assumption that there is a global data-base of shared vectors. This is known as the global vector space. Each VP containes a private set of vector descriptors defining the subset of the global vector space which is to reside in that VP. The distribution of data structures is therefore not confined to a distribution across a partitioned real address space, enabling vectors to be duplicated when required in more than one VP.

Processors only need to communicate when a particular global data item has to be updated. This is performed explicity, and under program control. The mechanism of communication involves one VP broadcasting a packet, containing the global virtual address of the item and the new data value, to all other VPs. Each processor uses it's table of vector descriptors to recognise relevant broadcast addresses, and uses a full/empty bit associated with each data element to implement a global synchronization protocol.

The rest of this paper analyses the performance of such a parallel system in terms of the performance of the communication mechanism, and in terms of the known behaviour of an important class of numerical algorithms.

The Model

The block structure of the vector unit being modelled is shown in Figure 1. Instruction processing is divided into two sections.

- Primary operand processing.

- Stream processing.

Primary operand processing performs the virtual-to-real address translation, and operates on primary operands from two sources. Firstly, operands defined within instructions must be processed, and secondly, incoming vector elements that have been broadcast must also be processed.

In this analysis it is assumed that the primary operand unit consists of a pipeline, accepting new operand requests at a rate of P requests per Second. The actual value of P in a particlular implementation will depend upon the cycle time of the memory in which the vector descriptors are held.

Processed operand descriptors are passed on to the stream unit which is then responsible for streaming the operands through the vector pipe(s). All vector operations are assumed to be *memory-to-memory* operations. For the purpose of this analysis it

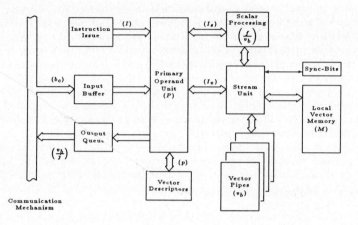

Figure 1: Block Structure of a Single Vector Unit

is also assumed that the absolute maximum numerical processing rate is not limited by the processing rate of the vector pipes.

Some proportion of the incoming global broadcast operations will refer to data held locally within a particular VP, the rest will refer to data that is not used by that VP. This distinction is recognized by the primary operand unit. Let the proportion that is locally relevant be λ, where $0 \leq \lambda \leq 1$. Incoming requests are passed on to the stream unit, once their eligibility has been determined. They cause a cycle to be stolen from the local memory in order that the data synchronization constraint may be tested, and, that the data can be written to the local memory. This requires a single *read-modify-write* cycle.

The instruction set of this machine is assumed to consist of 3-address dyadic and 2-address monadic vector instructions. These require a maximum of three operand translations per vector instruction. The scalar instructions are able to access single elements of vectors, but since many scalar instructions will not access vectors, an arbitrary average of one descriptor access per scalar instruction is assumed.

A further assumption made is that instructions can be issued, at the required rate, to the primary operand unit. Many techniques have been devised in the past to achieve consistently high instruction issue rates in other machines, and any appropriate technique could be employed within the framework of this machine model.

This model is pessimistic in assuming that there is no temporal overlap between the execution of scalar and vector instructions. Existing machines do allow overlap; however, the scalar instructions within this model represent those instructions corresponding to the non-vectorizable and wholly sequential parts of the user's algorithm.

In this respect a *two-state* VP is being modelled [Buzb83]. Each VP is operating in either a scalar *or* a vector mode. This two-state model is characterized by several parameters. The ratio of the performance of the vector pipes to the performance of the scalar unit is denoted by f. Hence, a single scalar instruction can be completed in the time it takes to produce f elemental vector results. The start-up time for a vector operation is measured in terms of arithmetic pipeline beats, and is denoted by s.

The ratio of scalar instructions issued to vector instructions issued is denoted by r, and this depends upon the proportion of elemental operations performed at vector rate, denoted by α $(0 \le \alpha \le 1)$, and the average length of each vector operation, denoted by l. This relationship is given below in Equation 1.

$$r = \frac{l\,(1-\alpha)}{\alpha} \tag{1}$$

The processing rate of the vector pipeline is given by v_b (elemental operations per Second), and hence the average instruction issue rate I can be derived.

$$I = v_b \left[\frac{r+1}{rf+l+s}\right] \tag{2}$$

The corresponding scalar and vector instruction issue rates, I_s and I_v, are given by Equations 3 and 4 respectively.

$$I_s = I \left[\frac{r}{r+1}\right] \tag{3}$$

$$I_v = I \left[\frac{1}{r+1}\right] \tag{4}$$

The rate at which primary operand requests are generated, as a result of instruction processing, can be deduced from these equations. This is denoted here by p.

$$p = I_s + 3I_v = v_b \left[\frac{r+3}{rf+l+s}\right] \tag{5}$$

Another important parameter of the system is the actual global communication rate, denoted by b_c such that $0 \le b_c \le B$, where B is the maximum bandwidth of the global broadcast mechanism. An inherent limit is placed upon the *sustainable* communication bandwidth, since the primary operand unit must process both local operand requests and globally distributed operands. Hence,

$$b_c \le P - p \tag{6}$$

The second constraint on VP performance concerns the bandwidth of the local VP memory, denoted by M. This limitation equates available local memory bandwidth to the requirements of both local vector processing and interprocessor communications.

$$M \ge \lambda b_c + 3 v_b \tag{7}$$

These equations define a simple model of this multiprocessor system in terms of fixed system parameters and in terms of variable *operational* parameters. One of the most important operational parameters is concerned with locality. This system does not attempt to provide sufficient global broadcast bandwidth to allow indiscriminate distribution of shared data. Instead, the known existence of data-locality within numerical algorithms is exploited to the full. The locality of read operands matters little, since the duplication of shared information allows all processors to read the same piece of information at the same time. The local memories can be regarded effectively as local write-back caches, and in this respect it is the rate at which "write-backs" are performed that is important. In this system a write-back consists of a global broadcast operation, performed under program control. The locality, denoted by j, is defined as the average interval between successive broadcasts from a single VP. This is measured in terms of VP minor cycles $\left(\frac{1}{v_b}\right)$.

Hence, the actual quantity of global communication can be expressed in terms of the number of VPs in the system, denoted by q.

$$b_c = q\frac{v_b}{j} \tag{8}$$

From these equations the limitation imposed on the sustainable vector pipeline rate by the local memory bandwidth can be derived, and is given in Equation 9

$$v_b \leq \frac{jM}{3j + \lambda q} \tag{9}$$

The true performance of the system can be modelled by analysing algorithms to determine values for those parameters not fixed by the physical design. This includes values for α, j, l and λ. The performance of the system, assuming total vectorization and no synchronization hold-ups will simply be $q.v_b$, and this is referred to as the *absolute performance A_a*.

$$A_a = \frac{qjM}{3j + \lambda q} \tag{10}$$

However, it is known that each VP is effectively a two-state machine, and therefore the two-state performance is of greater interest. This is denoted by A_t. This function expresses a well-known phenomenon, often referred to as "Amdahl's Law", that frequently occurs in mixed parallel and sequential environments. This equation applies to any vector processor.

$$A_t = \frac{A_a}{(1 - \alpha)f + \alpha + \left(\frac{s\alpha}{l}\right)} \tag{11}$$

A very basic measure of the extensibility of the architecture can be gained from examining how A_a varies with the q. This is particularly important in systems containing large numbers of VPs. The upper bound on A_a is denoted by A_a'.

$$A_a' = \lim_{q\to\infty} A_a = \frac{jM}{\lambda} \tag{12}$$

Equation 12 implies that the performance maximum is bounded-above by the bandwidth of the VP local memory, and cannot therefore grow linearly with the size of the system. However, one of the most important features of this machine is that the intended applications are strictly *compute-bound*.

Definition : *Compute-Bound*

A group of cooperating processes are said to be compute-bound if, and only if, the rate of growth of communication between processes is $O(n^a)$ and the rate of growth of computation in the system is $O(n^b)$ such that $b > a$.

It will be demonstrated later that many two-dimensional (2-D) array algorithms can be partitioned into compute-bound parallel processes. There is, however, a school of thought which says that there is no point in attempting to provide increasingly more powerful processors for problems with such high levels of complexity. The returns are small, in terms of increased problem size or reduced granularity, and that to keep pace with the performance requirements of increased problem sizes requires a correspondingly non-linear growth in performance. Quadratic growths in performance are theoretically possible with 2-D systolic arrays. However, mapping different 2-D algorithms, with different communication requirements, onto a processor array with fixed positional communication structures does not appear to be an attractive proposition.

Conversely, the communication mechanism under discussion provides a simple extension to the current concept of a vector machine. This enables much larger numbers of VPs to cooperate than would be possible through currently used techniques, such as physically shared memory spaces and dedicated point-to-point channels.

In a compute-bound environment the level of locality j becomes a function of the linear problem size N. When the problem is only just compute-bound, i.e. $b = a + 1$ the locality j is proportional to N. Hence, for some constant k, the following will hold.

$$A'_a = N M \left(\frac{k}{\lambda} \right) \tag{13}$$

The maximum number of processors that can be supported by the primary operand unit, denoted by q_{max}, is determined by the level of locality within those processors.

$$q_{max} = j \left[\frac{P - p}{v_b} \right] \tag{14}$$

If the number of processors in the system increases in proportion with the linear problem size then two things may be noted. Firstly, the growth in computational complexity will have been reduced from $O(n^x)$ to $O(n^{x-1})$, and secondly, the amount of global communication will remain constant. For algorithms that are more heavily compute-bound the number of sustainable VPs increases accordingly.

The equations which model this system have been given no numerical values, and no mention has been made of the technological implications of varying their arguments. Some of these arguments are determined by the application of the architecture, particularly j, α, and l. These parameters determine the efficiency with which a particular algorithm is able to exploit the concurrency within this architecture. Parameters such as v_b, M, P and B are fixed by the implementation details of a real machine.

Languages

The semantics of a programming language can be thought of as restricting the programmer not in *what* he may compute, but in *how* he may compute it. This becomes particularly noticeable when a language does not provide the facilities required to obtain reasonable efficiency from a parallel machine, when processing an inherently parallel algorithm. It is therefore not appropriate to express concurrent numerical algorithms in a purely sequential language on the machine model described in this paper. A minimal set of extensions to a standard programming language are described in Ibbett *et al.* [Ibbe85], and these fall into two basic categories.

1. The facility to describe concurrent processes.

2. The facility to express the communications between these asynchronous processes in a succinct manner, reflecting the hardware mechanism dedicated to this task.

The algorithms analysed in the next section were coded in this extended language in order that a reasonably detailed study of their behaviour could be made.

The Applications

In this section the performance of two common algorithms, for obtaining the solution to a set of linear simultaneous equations, is presented. These are the *Gaussian Elimination* and *Gauss-Seidel* algorithms. Figures for the number of operations performed in *Gaussian Elimination* can be derived, since its complexity is deterministic. A slightly different approach is required to analyse the *Gauss-Seidel* algorithm, since this algorithm is iterative.

The *Gaussian Elimination* Algorithm

An important parameter of any parallel version of a standard algorithm is the way in which it is decomposed for parallel execution. The parallel *Gaussian Elimination* algorithm analysed here is decomposed into a set of q processes (one for each VP). The two-dimensional array of coefficients is partitioned into q groups of column vectors. Vectors in each group are separated by $q - 1$ vectors that are held in the other $q - 1$ VPs. Hence, column vectors are distributed in an interleaved manner between VPs. This partitioning strategy avoids excessive under-utilization of processors when nearing the end of the elimination phase.

For a problem with n equations there will be n iterations during the elimination phase. The back-substitution phase is not considered here since it represents only a small proportion of the computation time, and is known to have a complexity of $O(n^2)$.

The ith iteration of the elimination phase comprises five sections.

- Index search.

- Swapping rows.

- Calculating and distributing the vector of multipliers.

- Row elimination.

- Discarding the vector of multipliers.

If the latency between distributing a value from one VP and being able to use that value in another VP is L machine cycles then the total time to perform n iterations of the elimination phase, in parallel over q VPs, will be t_{par}.

$$t_{par} = \frac{n^3}{q} + \frac{n^2}{2q}[3q + 3f + 2s + 5] + n\left[\frac{9q + 9f + 6s + 4}{6q} + 24f + 4s + 2L\right] \quad (15)$$

This algorithm will work for any value of q between 1 and n, and therefore the parallel performance can readily be compared with the sequential performance by setting $q = 1$ in Equation 15. This gives a time, for an equivalent sequential computation, of t_{seq}.

$$t_{seq} = \frac{n^3}{3} + \frac{n^2}{2} [3f + 2s + 2] + n [26f + 5s + 2L + 2] \tag{16}$$

It is clear that the dominant term in both t_{par} and t_{seq} is the n^3 term. Note also that all n^3 terms in t_{par} are divided by q. Hence, the majority of the computations in this algorithm can be processed concurrently.

The version of the *Gaussian Elimination* algorithm used here [Toph85] contains sections of code that are *scalar*, but these scalar sections can be processed in *parallel* when partitioned into processes. In this, and any other algorithm, there are two important metrics of efficiency that can be quantified.

- The efficiency of utilization of the vector processing capability. This is often referred to as the level of vectorization, and corresponds to the parameter α, used earlier.

- The utilization of the processors. This is inversely proportional to the amount of wait-time exhibited during program execution, and is a measure of how well-suited an algorithm is to this particular machine model.

In this algorithm there are m_s scalar operations per processor, i.e. operations that cannot be vectorized.

$$m_s = \frac{2n(n-1)}{q} + 26n \tag{17}$$

There are m_v elemental operations per processor that can be performed at full vector rate.

$$m_v = \frac{n(n+1)}{q} \left[\frac{2n+1}{6} + 3q + 1 \right] \tag{18}$$

The level of vectorization, α, is defined by Equation 19, and therefore the level of vectorization in this algorithm, α_{ge}, is given by Equation 20.

$$\alpha = \frac{m_v}{m_v + m_s} \tag{19}$$

$$\alpha_{ge} = \frac{(n+1)[6(3q+1) + 2n + 1]}{(n+1)[6(3q+1) + 2n + 1] + 12(n-1) + 156q} \tag{20}$$

The relationship between α_{ge} and the problem size, n, can be seen from the graph in Figure 2. This indicates that a high level of vectorization can be achieved for values of n greater than around 100.

The level of vectorization in this algorithm is not sensitive to the value of q. For example, with $q = 32$ we get $\alpha_{ge} = 0.927$, and with $q = 1$ we get $\alpha_{ge} = 0.944$.

In the introduction it was stressed that this paper is concerned with obtaining efficient deterministic operation through the use of a data-driven communication mechanism. The efficiency of operation is characterized by the average level of processor utilization, exhibited during the execution of a particular algorithm. In the *Gaussian*

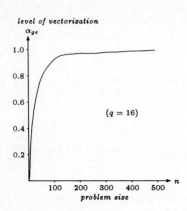

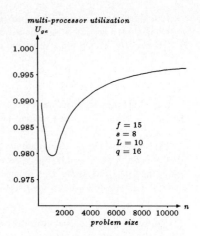

Figure 2: Graph showing how the level of vectorization varies with problem size in the *Gaussian Elimination* algorithm.

Figure 3: Graph showing how processor utilization varies with problem size in the the *Gaussian Elimination* algorithm.

Elimination algorithm the level of utilization is determined by $q - 1$ processors waiting for the values produced by a single processor during the pivoting phase of each iteration.

If each processor spends an amount of time B doing useful computations, and $q - 1$ processors spend an amount of time W being idle whilst a single processor computes a sequential section of code, then the overall utilization factor (during elimination) will be U_q, given by -

$$U_q = \frac{qB + W}{q(B + W)} \tag{21}$$

Equations for B and W, for the *Gaussian Elimination* algorithm, are given below.

$$W = n^2 + 2n(4f + s + L) \tag{22}$$

$$B = \frac{n^3}{3q} + \frac{n^2}{2q}[q + 6f + 4s + 1] + n[3q(32f + 4s + 3) + 6(3f + 2s + 1) + 1] \tag{23}$$

The relationship between U_q and n is shown in Figure 3, and it can be seen that for large values of n, $U_q \to 1$, and that utilization never falls below 0.979.

The two-state performance metric represents the vector-efficiency of a processor when busy. Combining the two-state performance with the utilization factor gives a measure of the actual performance that is *sustainable* for a given configuration. This is represented by φ_{ge}.

$$\varphi_{ge} = \frac{U_q}{f(1 - \alpha_{ge}) + \alpha_{ge}} \tag{24}$$

The value of φ_{ge} represents the proportion of the maximum system burst processing rate that is sustainable when processing this particular problem. Figure 4 shows the relationship between φ_{ge} and the problem size n.

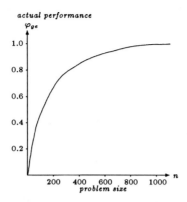

actual performance

φ_{ge}

Figure 4: Graph showing how the predicted actual performance of the *Gaussian Elimination* algorithm varies with problem size.

When comparing the two-state efficiency with the utilization factor it becomes apparent that exploiting multi-process parallelism efficiently is considerably easier than achieving efficient utilization of the machine's vector capability. This problem is only resolved when long vector operations are performed, or when scalar performance is improved (by reducing f).

The *Gauss-Seidel* Algorithm

The *Gaussian Elimination* algorithm is a highly parallel algorithm in which the vector operations do not interact with each other. This is not the case with the *Gauss-Seidel* algorithm, where successive approximations to element i of the solution use some values from the previous iteration (from element i to element n), and some values from the present iteration (from element 1 to element $i - 1$). The computation of n new values for the elements of the solution therefore defines a linear recurrence relation between elemental computations. Conventional vector processors are unable to process element computations in parallel, since they do not allow the synchronized updating of vector elements on an element by element basis.

The synchronized close-coupling of vector processors, in the machine model under examination, enables interacting vector operations in different VPs to overlap their execution as far as elemental data dependencies will permit.

The decomposition of the standard *Gauss-Seidel* algorithm on such a parallel system is achieved in much the same way as for the *Gaussian Elimination* algorithm. The two-dimensional array of coefficients is partitioned into q sets of interleaved row-vectors. Each VP holds a copy of the most up-to-date approximation to the solution, and a copy of the $\underline{b}$ vector (where the equation being solved is of the form $A\underline{x} = \underline{b}$). During each iteration a new value for each element of $\underline{x}$ is broadcast globally. Acceptance of each broadcast element is dependent upon *all* recurrence dependencies being satisfied

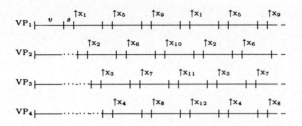

Figure 5: Global Time Graph for the *Gauss-Seidel* Algorithm

for that iteration.

Therefore, a processor computing $x[i]$ will be able to complete this computation as soon as element $x[i-1]$ has been broadcast. The new value for $x[i]$ may then itself be broadcast, permitting the computation of $x[i+1]$ to be completed. If there are more rows of A than processors then each processor will hold more than one row-vector from A, and compute several elements of $\underline{x}$. The sequence of broadcasts is shown in Figure 5, for a system with four VPs and a value of $n = 12$.

Sections marked v represent the scalar product operation between one row from A and $\underline{x}$. The section marked s represents the scalar computations required to calculate a single element of $\underline{x}$. At points marked "$\uparrow X_i$" a value for $x[i]$ is broadcast. The pattern of delays, indicated by "..." in Figure 5, force the system into a self-synchronizing state, after which no further delays occur.

The performance of this algorithm can be analysed by considering the latency that exists between distribution of a new value for $x[i]$ and distribution of a new value for $x[i+1]$. This latency is denoted by Δ. If the length of the scalar product operation is n, the number of scalar steps involved in completing the computation for $x[i]$ is g and the latency of the broadcast mechanism is L, then,

$$\Delta = L + fg + 1 \tag{25}$$

Processors produce results in a continuous sequence, therefore, the shortest time for a single iteration will be t_i

$$t_i = n\Delta \tag{26}$$

During each iteration a single processor computes $\left(\frac{n}{q}\right)$ new values, corresponding to a useful computation time of t_c,

$$t_c = \frac{n}{q}(S + n + fg) \tag{27}$$

A time sequence for these operations is shown in Figure 6. The utilization of each VP is governed by how much time is spent computing in the minimum time for each iteration. Hence, a value of U_q for the *Gauss-Seidel* algorithm is given in Equation 28.

$$U_q = \min\left(1, \frac{t_c}{t_i}\right) \tag{28}$$

Critical utilization occurs when $t_c = t_i$, and at this point the introduction of more VPs will reduce U_q to a value less than 1. Therefore, the maximum number of VPs that

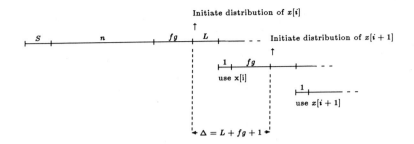

Figure 6: Computation and Distribution Timing in the *Gauss-Seidel* Algorithm.

can cooperate on this algorithm with full utilization is given by q_m,

$$q_m = \frac{n + S + fg}{\Delta} \tag{29}$$

The multi-processor speedup, denoted by π, is $q\,U_q$. Therefore when $q \le q_m$ we get $\pi = q$. Also, when $q > q_m$ we get $\pi = qU_q = q_{max}$.

This algorithm is clearly compute-bound since each row calculation produces a single global result. Therefore, the ratio of computation time to communication time in each processor is $\simeq n$.

These algorithms have been implemented on a microprocessor emulator containing three VP emulators [Toph85]. No observable deviation from linear speedup was observed for up to three processors, and work on larger systems is required in order to verify the predicted speedup for such systems in general.

Conclusions

This paper has presented a theoretical performance model for a parallel vector processor in which interprocessor communications are implemented by global packet broadcasting. This communication mechanism has been shown to possess sufficient bandwidth to enable the system to be linearly extensible when processing compute-bound problems. The performance analysis has also shown that it is significantly easier to obtain efficient multi-process parallelism than it is to obtain efficient pipelined-vector parallelism. This is true even for algorithms such as the *Gaussian Elimination* algorithm, traditionally considered to be highly vectorizable.

Most algorithms currently processed by supercomputers are compute-bound. If they did not have a compute-bound complexity then they would clearly not need the high performance offered by supercomputers.

The provision of process synchronization at the lowest level ensures that the highest possible level of concurrency can be exploited. This results in a closely-coupled data-driven system that is able to operate concurrently even when there are data dependencies between operands and results in different VPs.

The overheads associated with process communications are not expected to grow as the size of the system grows, except for logarithmic increments in transmission delays incurred during broadcasting. This is because the processing of data synchronization constraints is distributed throughout the system, and because the "one-to-many" style of communication requires only a single data transfer operation to communicate a shared value to all interested processors.

References

[Balf79]   Balfour A., Marwick D.H., **Programming in Standard FORTRAN '77**, Heinmann Educational Books Ltd., 1979.

[Bask76]   Basket F. and Smith A.J., "Interference in Multiprocessor Computer Systems and Interleaved Memory", *Comm. of the ACM*, Vol. 19, No. 6, June 1976, pp. 327-334.

[Baud78]   Baudet G.M., "Asynchronous Iterative Methods for Multiprocessors", *Journal of the ACM*, Vol. 25, No. 2, 1978, pp. 226-244.

[Bhan75]   Bhandarkar D.P., "Analysis of Interference in Multiprocessors", *IEEE Trans. on Computers*, Vol. C-24, No. 9, September 1975, pp. 897-908.

[Buzb83]   Buzbee B.L., "The Efficiency of Parallel Processing"; *Los Alamos Science, (conference highlights)*, No. 9, Fall, 1983.

[Chen83]   Chen Steve S., "Large Scale and High-speed Multiprocessor System for Scientific Applications - CRAY X-MP Series", *Proceedings of NATO Advanced Research Workshop on High Speed Computation (ed. J. Kowalik)*, Springer Verlag, Julich, W. Germany, June 1983.

[Cray85]   Cray Research Inc., **The CRAY-2 Computer System**, Pubn. No. MP-0201, Minneapolis, MN, 1985.

[Eta83]   ETA Systems Inc., **Goals, Technologies and Strategies**, St. Paul, Minnesota, September, 1983.

[Hint72]   Hintz R.G., Tate D.P., "Control Data STAR-100 Processor Design", *IEEE COMPCON-72 Digest*, 1972, pp. 1-4.

[Ibbe85]   Ibbett R.N., Capon P.C., Topham N.P., "MU6V : A Parallel Vector Processing System", *Proc. 12th Annual Int. Symp. on Computer Architecture*, 1985, pp. 136-144.

[Jone80]   Jones A. and Schwartz P., "Experience using multiprocessor systems - a status report", *ACM Computing Surveys*, Vol. 12, No. 2, June 1980, pp. 121-165.

[Kung82]   Kung H.T., "Why Systolic Architectures ?", *Computer*, January 1982, pp. 8-24.

[Linc82]   Lincoln N.R., "Technology and Design Tradeoffs in the Creation of a Modern Supercomputer", *IEEE Transactions on Computers*, Vol. C-31, No. 5, May 1982.

[Miur82]   Miura K., Uchida K., **FACOM Vector Processor VP 100/200**, Mainframe Division, Fujitsu Ltd., Kawasaki, Japan, 1982.

[NEC85]   NEC Corporation, **Supercomputer SX-1/SX-2**, NEC Publication No. E51133, Tokyo, 1985.

[Russ78]   Russel R.M., "The CRAY-1 Computer System", *Communications of the ACM*, Vol. 21, No. 1, 1978, pp. 63-72.

[Toph85] Topham N.P., "A Parallel Vector Processing System", Ph.D. thesis, University of Manchester, 1985.

[Vrsa85] Vrsalovic D., Gehringer E.F., Segall Z.Z., Siewiorek D.P., "The Influence of Parallel Decomposition Strategies on the Performance of Multiprocessor Systems", *Proc. 12th. Annual Int. Symp. on Computer Architecture*, June, 1985, pp. 396-405.

HIGHLY PARALLEL COMPUTERS
G.L. Reijns, M.H. Barton (editors)
Elsevier Science Publishers B.V. (North-Holland)
©*IFIP, 1987*

MATCHING PARALLEL ALGORITHMS WITH ARCHITECTURES: A CASE STUDY

M. Cosnard, Y. Robert and M. Tchuente

C.N.R.S. - Laboratoire TIM3-IMAG
I.N.P.G. BP 68
38402 Saint Martin d'Hères Cedex
FRANCE

We study the influence of the architecture on the design of parallel algorithms. As a case study we parallelize a linear system solver: Jordan method, on various parallel architectures. We first recall the sequential implementation, then we derive parallel synchronous and asynchronous versions of the Jordan method for computers with a shared memory guaranteeing conflict free access to the data, and design a systolic implementation on a triangular array of cells.

INTRODUCTION

On parallel architectures, a method can lead to various parallel versions. The number of processors is not the only parameter since the constraints imposed by the architecture of the machine (see the various taxonomies of Flynn [10], Gajski [12], Treleaven [36], the systolic model, Kung [20], ...) can modify the performances of the method.

In this paper, we concentrate on the influence of the architecture on the design of parallel algorithms. As a case study we parallelize a linear system solver: Jordan method, on various parallel architectures. We first recall the sequential implementation, then we derive parallel versions of the Jordan method for SIMD computers, MIMD computers, both with a shared memory guaranteeing conflict free access to the data, and design a systolic implementation on a triangular array of cells.

We evaluate the amount of arithmetic operations which are required by the different algorithms, and we assume that the time needed for data accessing, retrieving and exchanging is the same for all algorithms and can be neglected. We shall assume that the computational cost of each elementary arithmetic operation is the same: this will be our basic unit.

However, for SIMD or MIMD architectures, we shall assume in the following that we can access the elements of the matrix A, either by rows or by columns. Then the two allowed transfer operations will be loading and storing a row or a column. The duplication of a row or a column will have a zero cost, i.e. we assume that it is possible to transfer simultaneously the same data to various processors. In this case, no processor can modify this data.

This work has been supported by the Centre National de la Recherche Scientifique through the GRECO C3

Once the constraints defined, the first step in the parallelization of a method is the definition of the elementary tasks and their precedence graph. This graph shows the temporal dependency of the operations of the algorithm. This warrants the absence of conflict, the temporal integrity of the data and a perfect correspondance between the method and its parallel version. The tasks are then assigned to the available processors according to the precedence graph.

The parallelization of Gaussian elimination has been studied by Lord, Kowalik and Kumar [25] in case of an unbounded number of processors and by Srinivas [35] in case of a fixed number of processors. Parallel algorithms for the QR decomposition have been proposed in case of $\lfloor n/2 \rfloor$ processors ($\lfloor \ \rfloor$ is the floor function) by Cosnard and Robert [5] for square matrices and Cosnard, Muller and Robert [6] in the rectangular case; see also the papers of Modi and Clarke [27] and of Sameh and Kuck [30]. Systolic algorithms for Gaussian elimination have been proposed by Ahmed et al. [1] and by Gentleman and Kung [13]. Some variations can be found in Schreiber [33].

JORDAN METHOD

The well-known Gaussian elimination method is the most commonly used algorithm to solve linear systems of equations on sequential computers. It consists of two distinct steps: triangularizing the matrix, and then solving a triangular system. Another way to proceed is to gather these two steps into a single one: diagonalizing the matrix, usually via the Jordan method. However the Jordan method is more costly than that of Gauss ($n^3 + O(n^2)$ arithmetic operations against $2n^3/3 + O(n^2)$). Most often, pivoting of rows or columns (or both) is used for stability reasons. We shall not consider here the overhead due to pivoting.

In what follows we suppose that we have to solve a dense linear sytems. Hence we shall work with a matrix A of order n by n+1.

```
(* Jordan method *)
For k  <- 1 to n
      (* updating row k *)
      c  <- 1/a_kk
      For j  <- k+1 to n+1
            a_kj  <- a_kj *c
      (* zeroing off-diagonal elements of row k *)
      For i  <- 1 to n , i≠k
            For j  <- k+1 to n+1
                  a_ij  <- a_ij - a_ik* a_kj
```

Data access, by rows or columns, leads to various tasks decompositions of the method. In case of the matrix product and of Gaussian elimination, Dongarra et al [8] have shown a way to derive parallel implementations of the primal algorithm, by interchanging do-loops. Comparing rows and columns implementations of linear systems solvers, Cosnard et al. [7] proved that for Jordan method, the version by rows is more efficient.

```
{ JORDAN by rows }
For k <- 1 to n
    For j <- k+1 to n+1,
        do akj <- akj /akk
    For i <- 1 to n, i≠k
        For j <- k+1 to n+1,
            do aij <- aij - aik* akj
```

We can define the following tasks:

- JR_{kk} : < **For** j <- k+1 **to** n+1,
       do a_{kj} <- a_{kj}/a_{kk} >

- JR_{ki} : < **For** j <- k+1 **to** n+1, i ≠ k
       do a_{ij} <- $a_{ij} - a_{ik}{}^* a_{kj}$ >

JR_{kk} can be processed in n+1-k units and JR_{ki}, i≠k, in 2(n+1-k) units. The precedence constraints are:

(A) $JR_{kk} << JR_{ki}$ for i≠k
(B) $JR_{ki} << JR_{k+1,i}$ for i≠k

which leads to the precedence graph:

```
JR11
JR12        JR13 JR14    ...        JR1,n-1    JR1n      level 1
    ...
JRkk
JRk,k+1     JRk,k+2  ... JRk,n JRk,1  ...  JRk,k JRk,k-1  level k
JRk+1,k+1
    ...
JRn,n
JRn,1 JRn,2          ...                    JRn,n-1  level n

col. 1                                  col. n
```

A SYNCHRONOUS ALGORITHM.

We consider first the case of a SIMD computer. We do not want to derive a specific algorithm for a specific computer, as Lord et al. [25] for the HEP 1. We are concerned by complexity results and the influence of coarse architectutal features on the design of parallel algorithms. For such considerations, Schwarz [34] introduced the concept of Paracomputer. The Paracomputer is a SIMD structure with a non bounded number of processors (the number of processors can increase to infinity). Each processor can access in parallel a shared memory. The organisation is such that no routing delays or memory conflicts due to the hardware can occur. Although not realistic, the paracomputer is a useful concept for studying the inherent parallelism of a given algorithm and the influence of synchronization.

Assuming that we are working on a paracomputer, the data constraints are taken into account by the precedence graph. The only new architectural constraint introduced by the model is that we are searching for a parallel synchronous version of the method.

We call JR_p the complexity of the parallel implementation of Jordan method by rows: it is the execution time of an optimal algorithm. In general a synchronous algorithm will not be optimal. The following theorem addresses the problem of the influence of the number of processors on the goodness of the parallelization. It is an illustration of the two cases: for $p=n-1$ or $p \leq n/2$ there exists an optimal synchronous algorithm, for $n/2<p<n-1$ an optimal algorithm is asynchronous. EJR_p denotes the asymptotic efficiency.

Theorem 1:
   i) If $p=n-1$, $JR_p=3n(n+1)/2$ and $EJR_p=2/3$.

   ii) If $n/2 \leq p=\alpha n \leq n-1$, $JR_p \leq n^2(n+2p)/(2p) + O(n)$

   and $EJR_p \geq 2/(1+2\alpha)$
   iii) If $1 \leq p \leq n/2$, $JR_p=n^3/p + O(n^2/p)$ et $EJR_p=1$.

Proof:
i) The precedence graph implies that it is not necessary to use more than n-1 processors since JR_{kk} must be executed before the n-1 tasks JR_{ki}. Hence the longest path in the graph is:

$$JR_{11} \mapsto JR_{12} \mapsto JR_{22} \mapsto JR_{23} \cdots JR_{k-1k-1} \mapsto JR_{k-1k} \mapsto \cdots JR_{nn} \mapsto JR_{n1}$$

If p=n-1, we deduce from this that:

$$JR_p \geq 3 \sum_{k=1}^{n} (n+1-k) = 3n(n+1)/2$$

Assigning to the first processor the tasks of the longest path and to the n-2 remaining processors the n-2 tasks JR_{ki}, $i \neq k,k+1$, we obtain a synchronous algorithm whose execution time is the preceding lower bound. Hence an optimal algorithm is synchronous.

ii) If $n/2 \leq p=\alpha n < n-1$, it is not possible to execute simultaneously all the tasks JR_{ki}, $i \neq k$. It remains n(n-1-p) non executed tasks. Since the execution time of the tasks JR_{ki} is twice this of JR_{kk}, an optimal algorithm is asynchronous. In the following we derive a synchronous algorithm.

This algorithm is based on the following remarks:

- JR_{kk} must be executed as soon as possible in order that the execution of JR_{k+1i} be not delayed by the precedence constraints

- we do not begin immediately the n-p-1 non executed tasks of a given level, but gather the non executed tasks until their number is greater than p-1. Then we assign these tasks to the p-1 free processors during the execution of $JR_{k'k'}$.

In order to describe this algorithm, we set N=n(n-1) and r=n-p-1. Remark that $1 \le r < n/2-1$. Define $\{e_k\}$ as:

$$e_k = (kr/(p-1)) - \sum_{j=1}^{k-1} e_j$$

e_k takes values 0 or 1: it is 0 if the number of non executed tasks in levels less than or equal to k is less than p-1 and it is 1 otherwise. We number the tasks JR_{ki} in the following way:

$$T_{(k-1)(n-1)+j} = JR_{k((k+j-1)MOD\ n)+1} \quad \text{avec } 1 \le j \le n-1.$$

The algorithm is:

```
(* synchronous JORDAN by rows *)
      compt <- 1 ;
      P1 executes JR_11 ;
      P2, P3, ..., Pn are free ;
(* we process the n-1 levels *)
      for k <- 1 to n-1 do
            P1, ..., Pp execute T_compt, ..., T_compt+p-1 ;
            compt <- compt+p ;
(* the number of non executed tasks is less than p-1 *)
            if e_k equals 0 then
                  P1 executes JR_k+1,k+1 ;
                  P2, P3, ..., Pn are free ;
            end if ;
(* the number of non executed tasks is greater than p-1 *)
            if e_k equals 1 then
                  P1 executes JR_k+1,k+1 ;
                  P2, ..., Pp execute T_compt, ..., T_compt+p-2 ;
                  compt <- compt+p-1 ;
            end if ;
      end for ;
(* execution of the remaining tasks *)
      while compt ≤ N do
            P1, ..., Pp execute T_compt, ..., T_compt+p-1 ;
            compt <- compt+p ;
      end while ;
      end .
```

We illustrate the behaviour of the algorithm in the case of a matrix of size 9 with 5 processors. ij in column Ps means that Ps executes JR_{ij}.

	n=9	p=5	r=3	
k	1 2 3 4 5 6 7 8			
e_k	0 1 1 1 0 1 1 1			

	P1	P2	P3	P4	P5
	11				
k=1	12	13	14	15	16
e_1=0	22				
k=2	17	18	19	23	24
e_2=1	33	25	26	27	28
k=3	29	21	34	35	36
e_3=1	44	37	38	39	31
k=4	32	45	46	47	48
e_4=1	55	49	41	42	43
k=5	56	57	58	59	51
e_5=0	66				
k=6	52	53	54	67	68
e_6=1	77	69	61	62	63
k=7	64	65	78	79	71
e_7=1	88	72	73	74	75
k=8	76	89	81	82	83
e_8=1	99	84	85	86	87
k=9	91	92	93	94	95
	96	97	98		

Let us first prove that this algorithm satisfies the precedence constraints. For this we show that:
- no JR_{ki} can be executed before JR_{kk}, which is equivalent to

$$\text{nb } JR_{ki} \text{ algo} = (k-1)p + (p-1)\sum_{j=1}^{k-2} e_j \leq (k-1)(n-1) = \text{max nb possible} JR_{ki}$$

- $JR_{k-1,k}$ is executed before JR_{kk}, which is equivalent to

$$\text{rank } JR_{k-1,k} = (k-2)(n-1)+1 \leq (k-1)p + (p-1)\sum_{j=1}^{k-2} e_j$$

In order to show the first inequality, we remark that:

$$\sum_{j=1}^{k-2} e_j = ((k-1)r/(p-1)) - e_{k-1} \le (k-1)r/(p-1)$$

hence

$$(k-1)p + (p-1)\sum_{j=1}^{k-2} e_j \le (k-1)p + (k-1)r \le (k-1)(n-1) .$$

The second inequality is equivalent to:

$$(p-1)\sum_{j=1}^{k-2} e_j \ge (k-1)r - (p-1) -r$$

hence

$$\sum_{j=1}^{k-2} e_j \ge (k-2)r/(p-1) - 1$$

which can be deduced from:

$$\sum_{j=1}^{k-2} e_j = ((k-2)r/(p-1))$$

In order to evaluate the execution time A of this algorithm, we have to determine, at each step the maximal execution time of the tasks to be process. The preceding inequalities show that at the kth step, the algorithm terminates the (k-1)th level of the tasks JR_{ki}, begins the kth level, and executes $JR_{k+1,k+1}$. We obtain:

$$A \le n + \sum_{k=1, e_k=0}^{n-1} [(n-k) + 2(n+1-k)] + \sum_{k=1, e_k=1}^{n-1} [2(n+1-k) + 2(n+1-k)] + 2$$

$$\le n+3 + \sum_{k=1}^{n-1} 3(n+1-k) + \sum_{k=1}^{n-1} e_k(n+1-k)$$

We first compute the part of the sum that contains e_k:

$$\sum_{k=1}^{n-1} ke_k = \sum_{j=1}^{n-1} \sum_{k=j}^{n-1} e_k = \sum_{j=1}^{n-1} (\sum_{k=1}^{n-1} e_k - \sum_{k=1}^{j-1} e_k)$$

$$= (n-1) \sum_{k=1}^{n-1} e_k - \sum_{j=1}^{n-1} \sum_{k=1}^{j-1} e_k$$

hence:

$$\sum_{k=1}^{n-1} e_k (n+1-k) = 2 \sum_{k=1}^{n-1} e_k + \sum_{j=1}^{n-1} \sum_{k=1}^{j-1} e_k$$

$$= 2((n-1)r/(p-1)) + \sum_{j=1}^{n-1} ((j-1)r/(p-1))$$

$$\leq (n-1)(1+n/2) \, r/(p-1)$$

We deduce the value of A:

$$A \leq n+3 + 3(n-1)(1+n/2) + (n-1)(1+n/2) \, r/(p-1)$$

$$\leq n+3 + (n-1)(1+n/2)(2+(n-2)/(p-1))$$

iii) If the number p of processors is between 1 and n/2, we have to dispach the processors so that they have an optimal execution time. We call the p processors P1, P2, ... , Pp, k the number of yet processed levels, and l the number of executed tasks at the beginning of step k.

```
(* initialisation *)
P1 executes JR₁₁ ;
for k <- 1 to n do
        (* we process the kth level *)
        if l=0 then
            P1, P2, ... , Pp  process JR_{k+1,k} ... JR_{k+p,k}
        end if ;
        P1 executes JR_{k+1,k+1},
        and P2, ... , Pp execute JR_{k+1+l,k} ... JR_{k+l+p-1 MOD n,k} ;
        while the kth level is not finished do
            execute p tasks in the order of the precedence graph ;
            l <- number of executed tasks at level k+1 ;
end.
```

We can verify easily that the algorithm satisfy the precedence constraints. Indeed, the relation $p < n/2$ implies that $JR_{k+1,k+1}$ is executed after $JR_{k+1,k}$ and before $JR_{j,k+1}$ for $j \neq k+1$. The execution time of the algorithm is:

$$JR_p \leq n + \lceil n/p \rceil \sum_{i=1}^{n} 2(n+1-i)$$

$$\leq n^3/p + O(n^2)$$

hence, $EJR_p \geq 1$ which shows that the algorithm is asymptotically optimal: $JR_p = n^3/p + O(n^2)$ and $EJR_p = 1$.

AN ASYNCHRONOUS ALGORITHM.

We now derive an asynchronous optimal algorithm for the Jordan method in case $n/2 < p < n-1$. We can no longer consider the Paracomputer as our model since it is basically a synchronous machine. However, we shall modify this model to derive a MIMD computer. We consider a computing structure with a non bounded number of processors (the number of processors can increase to infinity). As in the paracomputer each processor can access in parallel a shared memory but in an asynchronous way. Moreover these processors execute independently their own instructions set, hence process the data asynchronously. The organisation is such that no routing delays or memory conflicts due to the hardware can occur. Once again this provides with a useful concept for studying the inherent parallelism of a given algorithm and the influence of synchronization.

We call JR_{opt} the minimal execution time of Jordan method by rows when considering a number of processors less than or equal to n.

Theorem 2 :

    (i) $JR_{opt} = 3n^2/2$

    (ii) $EJR_{n-1} = 2/3$

    (iii)   for $p \le 2n/3$, $p = \alpha.n$, there exists an asymptotically optimal algorithm of efficiency 1; its execution time is n^2/α.

    (iv)   the minimal value of a in order to obtain an algorithm of time JR_{opt} is

        $\alpha = 2/3$.

    (v)   for $p \ge 2n/3$, $p = \alpha.n$, $EJR_p = 2/3\alpha$.

Proof:

    i) computation of JR_{opt}

The longest path in the graph is:

$$\{ JR_{11}, JR_{12}, JR_{22}, JR_{23}, ..., JR_{kk}, JR_{k,k+1}, ..., JR_{n,n}, JR_{n,1} \}$$

and hence $JR_{opt} = 3n(n+1)/2$.

    ii) asymptotic efficiency with n-1 processors

It is easy to construct an algorithm using $p = D = n-1$ processors in time JR_{opt}. The asymptotic efficiency is then

    $EJR_{n-1} = n^3/n(3n^2/2) = 2/3$

    iii) $p \le (2n/3)$

We assume that $p = \alpha.n$, avec $\alpha \le 2/3$. We introduce an asymptotically optimal algorithm and evaluate its execution time. Without loss of generality we set $p = 2q+1$.

We assign all the tasks of the longest path to the first processor which processes them as soon as possible. Then we divide the remaining tasks into q blocks of $r = (n-2)/q$ consecutive columns and we assign their execution to a pair of processors. For example, processors 2 and 3 process the tasks corresponding to columns 1 to r and processors 2i and 2i+1 the tasks of columns (i-1)r+1, (i-1)r+2, ... , ir.

We shall present the scheduling of the first pair of processors. The remaining pairs operate in a similar way, using a simple change of indices. P2 and P3 process columns 1 to r. For simplicity, we assume that r=3s.

For s=1 (which corresponds to $\alpha = 2/3$), the processors operate along the following scheme (ij in column Ps means that processor Ps processes the task JR_{ij}):

P1	P2	P3	allocated time
11			
12	13	-	n+1
12	13	14	n
22	15	14	n
23	15	24	n
23	25	24	n-1
33	25	26	n-1
34	35	26	n-1
34	35	36	n-2
44	37	36	n-2
45	37	46	n-2
45	47	46	n-3
55	47	48	n-3
56	57	48	n-3
...	...	...	...

Since the execution time of JR_{ki} is twice that of JR_{kk}, we divided (conceptually) their execution into two parts. Hence the algorithm is clearly asynchronous. Remark that P1, P2 and P3 are unemployed during at most one time unit when they process a task. More precisely, we loose 3 time units every two levels with respect to an algorithm using JR_{opt}. We deduce that the execution time is:

$$JR_{alg} = JR_{opt} + \lceil 2n/3 \rceil.$$

Hence this algorithm is asymptotically optimal and its efficiency is:

$$EJR_{2n/3} = n^3/(2n/3).(3n^2/2) = 1$$

For any s, P2 and P3 begin processing the same tasks in levels 1 and 2 as precedently, but before processing levels 3 and 4, they finish the execution of the tasks of levels 1 and 2, by blocks of 3 columns, as indicated in the following example for s=2.

P1	P2	P3	allocated time
11			
12	13	-	n+1
12	13	14	n
22	15	14	n
23	15	24	n
23	25	24	n-1
33	25	26	n-1
-	16	26	n+1
-	16	17	n
-	18	17	n
-	18	27	n
-	28	27	n-1
-	28	29	n-1
34	35	29	n-1
34	35	36	n-2
44	37	36	n-2
45	37	46	n-2
45	47	46	n-3
55	47	48	n-3
-	38	48	n-1
-	38	39	n-2
-	3,10	39	n-2
-	3,10	49	n-2
-	4,10	49	n-3
-	4,10	4,11	n-3
56	57	4,11	n-3
...	...	...	...

The execution rate of the processors (except P1) is asymptotically equal to 1, which shows that the algorithm is of efficiency 1 and hence optimal. Its execution time is now equal to s times JR_{alg}:

$$s.\ JR_{alg} = (2n/3p).\ (3n^2/2) = n^3/p = n^2/\alpha$$

Remark that it is not interesting to use more than $2n/3$ processors: there exists an algorithm of time T_{opt} using only $2n/3$ processors. Indeed, we know that $\alpha = 2/3$ is the minimal value in order to obtain an algorithm of time equivalent to T_{opt} using $p = \alpha.n$ processors: for $\alpha < 2/3$, the execution time of an optimal algorithm is n^2/α.

Moreover, since the algorithms are asymptotically optimal, the various evaluations of the efficiency are complexity results on the parallelisation of this method.

SYSTOLIC IMPLEMENTATION

Systolic arrays have been proposed to triangularize a dense matrix by Gaussian elimination [1], [13]. However, there remains a triangular system to be solved. Kung and Leiserson have proposed a systolic triangular system solver, but the data has to be stored in the host and reordered by diagonals before entering this second systolic array. We present here another method which consists of directly diagonalizing the matrix by use of the Jordan elimination method.

General description of the algorithm

We proceed in two phases as follows:

phase 1 : The first phase corresponds to the scheme introduced by Gentleman and Kung [13], for the Gaussian elimination (see the figure below); it transforms the system
$$(1) \ Ax = b$$
into an equivalent triangular system
$$(2) \ Tx = b'$$

The coefficients of the matrix (A,b) are input to the array row by row. The first row is stored in the upper row of the array, and, as any row numbered $i \geq 1$ is read by the array, it is combined with the first one in order to put to zero the element a_{i1}; this combination corresponds to a transformation of the form

$$
\begin{bmatrix} a_{11} , a_{12} , \dots , a_{1n} , b_1 \\ a_{i1} , a_{i2} , \dots , a_{in} , b_i \end{bmatrix} := M_{i1} \begin{bmatrix} a_{11} , a_{12} , \dots , a_{1n} , b_1 \\ a_{i1} , a_{i2} , \dots , a_{in} , b_i \end{bmatrix}
$$

The 2x2 matrix M_{i1} is computed by the cell at the upper left corner at time $t = i$, and sent to the other cells of the first row; more precisely, the cell at position (1,j) performs the transformation

$$(a_{1j}, a_{ij})^t := M_{i1} \cdot (a_{1j}, a_{ij})^t \ \text{at time } t = i+j-1.$$

Similarly, if

$$
(A^{(k)}, b^{(k)}) = \begin{pmatrix} a_{11}^{(k)} \underline{\hspace{2cm}} a_{1n}^{(k)} \ b_1^{(k)} \\ \\ 0 \quad a_{kk}^{(k)} \underline{\hspace{1cm}} a_{kn}^{(k)} \ b_k^{(k)} \\ \\ a_{nk}^{(k)} \underline{\hspace{1cm}} a_{nn}^{(k)} \ b_n^{(k)} \end{pmatrix}
$$

denotes the matrix obtained from (A,b) after the elimination of the elements at positions (i,j) such that i>j, j = 1, ... ,k-1, then ($a_{kk}^{(k)}, \dots , a_{kn}^{(k)}$, $b_k^{(k)}$) is stored in the k-th row of the array, and, when $(a_{ik}^{(k)}, ..., a_{in}^{(k)}, b_i^{(k)})$, $i > k$ is read by this row of cells, it is combined with $(a_{kk}^{(k)}, ..., a_{kn}^{(k)}, b_k^{(k)})$ in order to set $a_{ik}^{(k)}$ to zero .

At the end of this phase the matrix (T,b') is stored in the array as follows:

$$t_{11} \quad t_{12} \quad t_{13} \quad t_{14} \quad b'_1$$
$$t_{22} \quad t_{23} \quad t_{24} \quad b'_2$$
$$t_{33} \quad t_{34} \quad b'_3$$
$$t_{44} \quad b'_4$$

phase 2 : during this phase, the solution of the triangular system is computed as follows:

First of all, the lines of the triangular system $Tx = b'$ are normalized from top to bottom. This is simply done by letting any diagonal cell generate the matrix

$$Dkk = \begin{bmatrix} 0 & 0 \\ 1/c & 0 \end{bmatrix}, \text{ where } c = t_{kk} \text{ is the content of its internal register.}$$

It is easily seen that any cell at position (k,j) which receives the matrix

$$Dkk = \begin{bmatrix} 1/c & 0 \\ 0 & 0 \end{bmatrix} \text{ where } c = 1/t_{kk} ,$$

sends t_{kj}/t_{kk} downwards and transmits Dkk to the right.

As the row $(t_{k,k+1}, t_{k,k+2}, ..., t_{k,n}, b'_k)$ goes downwards during this phase, it is successively combined with the rows numbered k+1, k+2, ... , n, in order to eliminate successively $t_{k,k+1}, t_{k,k+2}, ..., t_{k,n}$. Clearly, at the end of the process, we obtain a linear system associated with a diagonal matrix.

As a consequence, the elements $b'_1, b'_2, ..., b'_n$ which are output in this order from the cell at the bottom right corner, correspond to the solution of $Ax = b$. Moreover, the internal registers of all the cells are set to zero, hence, the array is ready for the solution of a new system.

Structure of the basic cells

We need three types of cells.

Diagonal cell. The diagonal cell at position (k,k) works as follows: its first non zero entry a_{kk}, is stored in its internal register; this corresponds to the input (Init, a_{kk}) and to the generation of the matrix

$$M = \begin{bmatrix} 0 & 1 \\ 0 & 0 \end{bmatrix}$$

Afterwards, when it receives a_{jk} for $j > k$, together with the signal T, the transformation M_{jk} which combines the lines numbered k and j in order to annihilate a_{jk}, is computed and sent to the right.

This shows that, during each cycle, it performs three operations:
- it computes a 2x2 matrix M and sends it to the right.
- if (c,a_{in}) denotes the couple consisting of the current value of its internal register, and the input variable from matrix (A,b), then $(c',c'')^t = M.(c,a_{in})^t$ is computed;
- the new value of c is 0 if the control signal on its upper input port is Div, and c' otherwise.
- the input control signal u is transformed into v and sent downwards as follows:
    if (u = Diag) and (c ≠ 0) then v := Nil { the signal diag is destroyed }
    else   v := T;

square cell. During each cycle, it computes $(c',a_{out})^t = M.(c,a_{in})^t$ where c is the content of its internal register, and a_{in} is the upper input variable. Then c' is assigned to c, and a_{out} is sent downwards.

delay cell. During each cycle, it just transmits its imput variable.

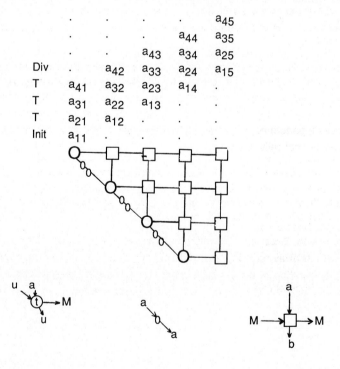

$$\begin{bmatrix} t \\ b \end{bmatrix} := M \begin{bmatrix} t \\ a \end{bmatrix}$$

if u = Init **then** {the incoming coefficient must be stored}

$$M := \begin{bmatrix} O & 1 \\ O & O \end{bmatrix}$$

if u = T **then** { triangularization phase}

$$M := \begin{bmatrix} 1 & -c/a_{in} \\ 0 & 1 \end{bmatrix};$$ { a_{in} is the upper input variable }

if u = Div **then** {row normalization}

$$M := \begin{bmatrix} 1/t & 0 \\ 0 & 0 \end{bmatrix};$$

Timing constraints. Since there are two delay cells between two diagonal cells, it is easily verified that the control signal **Init** meets any diagonal element a_{kk} in the diagonal cell at position (k,k). As a consequence the timing constraints of the triangularization phase are verified.

On the other hand, let us assume that, in the second phase of the algorithm, the cell at position (k,k) receives the signal **Diag** at time t. The coefficients a_{kk} and $a_{k,k+1}$ must be normalized at times $t+1$ and $t+2$, and the coefficient $a_{k,k+1}$ must be combined with $a_{k+1,k+1}$ at time $t+2$ in order to be eliminated. As a consequence, the normalization of $a_{k+1,k+1}$ can be performed at time $t+3$; this is possible, since there are two delay cells between two diagonal cells of the array.

Macro-pipelining. Clearly, the two phases of the algorithm can be pipelined. That is to say, phase 2 can be started as soon as the matrix M_{n1} has been generated by the cell at the upper left corner, and sent to the right. This macro-pipelining is the essential feature of our systolic implementation.

Time performance. Since the last coefficient b'_n corresponding to the solution of $Ax = b$, is output from the array one step after the normalization of a_{nn} , we have obtained a systolic implementation of the Gauss-Jordan algorithm, which works in time $4n$ on a triangular array of order $n \times n$.

REFERENCES

[1] H.M. Ahmed, J.M. Delosme, M. Morf, Highly concurrent computing structures for matrix arithmetic and signal processing, Computer Magazine, 1982, 65-82

[2] R.P. Brent, H.T. Kung, F.T. Luk, Some linear-time algorithms for systolic arrays, Technical Report TR CS 82-541 (1982), Cornell University Department of Computer Science

[3] A. Bojanczyk, R.P. Brent, H.T. Kung, Numerically stable solution of dense systems of linear equations using mesh-connected processors, Preprint CMU, 1981

[4] M. Cosnard, Y. Robert, Complexité de la décomposition QR en parallèle, C.R. Acad. Sc. Paris 297, A, 1983, 549-552

[5] M. Cosnard, Y. Robert, Complexity of parallel QR factorization, to appear in Journal of ACM

[6] M. Cosnard, J.M Muller and Y. Robert, Parallel QR decomposition of a rectangular matrix, Numer. Math. 48, 1986, 239-249

[7] M. Cosnard, Y. Robert and D. Trystram, Résolution parallèle de systèmes linéaires denses par diagonalisation, Bulletin Electricité de France, D.E.R., Série C, to appear

[8] J.J. Dongarra,F.G. Gustavson and A. Karp, Implementing linear algebra algorithms for dense matrices on a vector pipeline machine, SIAM Review, 26,1, 1984, 91-112

[9] M. Feilmeier, Parallel computers - Parallel mathematics, IMACS North Holland, 1977

[10] M.J. Flynn, Very high-speed computing systems, Proc. IEEE 54, 1966, 1901-1909

[11] M.J. Foster, H.T. Kung, The design of special-purpose VLSI chips, IEEE Computer 13, 1, 1980, 26-40

[12] D.D. Gajski, J.K. Peir, Parallel processing : problems and solutions, Preprint Univ. Illinois, 1984

[13] W.M. Gentleman, H.T. Kung, Matrix triangularisation by systolic arrays, Proc SPIE 298, Real-time Signal Processing IV, San Diego, California, 1981

[14] D. Heller, A survey of parallel algorithms in numerical linear algebra, SIAM Review 20, 1978, 740-777

[15] D. Heller, I. Ipsen, Systolic networks for orthogonal equivalence transformations and their applications, Proc. 1982 Conf. Advanced Research in VLSI, p 113-122, MIT 1982

[16] R.W. Hockney and C.R. Jesshope, Parallel computers, Adam Hilger, Bristol, 1981

[17] P. Huard, La méthode Simplex sans inverse explicite, bulletin EDF, 1979, 79-98

[18] K. Hwang and F. Briggs, Parallel processing and computer architec- ture, MC Graw Hill, 1984

[19] D.J. Kuck, The structure of computers and computations, J. Wiley & Sons, New York, 1978

[20] H.T. Kung, The structure of parallel algorithms, Advances in Computers 19, 1980, 65-112

[21] H.T. Kung, Why systolic architectures, IEEE Computer 15, 1, 1982, 37-46

[22] H.T. Kung, Programmable systolic chip, NATO Advanced Study Institute on Microarchitecture of VLSI computers, Sogesta, Italy, July 9-20, 1984

[23] H.T. Kung, C.E. Leiserson, Systolic arrays for (VLSI), in Proc. of the Symposium on Sparse Matrices Computations, I.S. Duff and G.W. Stewart eds, Knoxville, Tenn., 1978, 256-282

[24] H.T. Kung, W.T. Lin, An algebra for VLSI algorithmic design, Technical Report, Carnegie Mellon University, April 1983

[25] R.E. Lord, J.S. Kowalik, S.P. Kumar, Solving linear algebraic equations on an MIMD computer, J. ACM 30 (1), 1983, 103-117

[26] J. Misklosko et V. Kotov, Algorithms, software and hardware of parallel computers, Springer Verlag

[27] J.J. Modi et M.R.B. Clarke, An alternative Givens ordering, Numer.Math. 43, 1984, 83-90

[28] Y. Robert, Block LU decomposition of a band matrix on a systolic array, Int. J. Computer Math., 17, 1985, 295-315

[29] Y. Robert, M. Tchuente, Resolution systolique de systemes lineaires denses, RAIRO Modélisation et Analyse Numérique, 19,2,1985, 315-326

[30] A. Sameh et D.J. Kuck, On stable parallel linear system solvers, J. ACM 25 (1), 1978, 81-91

[31] A. Sameh, An overview of parallel algorithms, Bulletin EDF, 1983, 129-134

[32] U. Schendel, Introduction to numerical methods for parallel computers Ellis Horwood Series, J. Wiley & Sons, New York, 1984

[33] R. Schreiber, Systolic arrays: high performance parallel machines for matrix computation, Proc. Elliptic problem solvers II, Academic Press 1984, 187-194

[34] J.T. Schwarz, Ultracomputers, A.C.M. Trans. Lang. Syst. 2, 1980, 484-521

[35] M. Srinivas, Optimal parallel scheduling of Gaussian elimination DAG's, IEEE T.C. 32,1983,1109-1117

[36] P.C. Treleaven et D.R. Brownbridge, R.P. Hopkins, Data-driven and Demand-driven computers, ACM computing surveys, 14, 1982, 93-143

HIGHLY PARALLEL COMPUTERS
G.L. Reijns, M.H. Barton (editors)
Elsevier Science Publishers B.V. (North-Holland)
©IFIP, 1987

145

A LINEAR SYSTOLIC ARRAY FOR ROMBERG INTEGRATION

D.J. Evans

Department of Computer Studies
Loughborough University of Technology
Loughborough, Leicestershire,
U.K.

A systolic array is presented to improve numerical approximations to integrals using the Richardson's extrapolation
procedure in the form of Romberg integration. A design is
presented which is an intuitive linear systolic array which
has a computation time of 3n cycles, which is a significant
improvement on the $O(n^2)$ steps required to construct the
extrapolation table sequentially.

INTRODUCTION

The use of systolic arrays to date has largely been applied to fundamental
problems in Matrix and Linear Algebra. These problems, i.e. the solution of
B.V. problems, as well as signal and image processing applications account for
approximately 70% of Numeric Computation. Apart from various sorting and
searching systolic algorithms, little application has been made to other
computational areas. Research in [5], has been aimed at developing new
algorithm classifications such as hard, soft and hybrid systolic algorithms in
order to define other areas capable of exploiting systolic algorithm design
principles.

In this report we focus attention on the area of interpolation and extrapolation,
where McKeown [1] has shown that Aitken's Iterated Interpolation algorithm can
be performed by a systolic array in $O(n)$ time. Here we discuss the extrapolation procedure in the Romberg Integration algorithm.

Interpolation and extrapolation techniques also have wide uses in Numerical
Computation and often result in tables of a triangular form. The triangular
form and the manner in which the table is formed indicates that systolic
techniques used for matrix type algorithms such as the back-substitution
process and matrix vector multiplication [6], may also be applicable to interpolation and extrapolation algorithms.

THE ROMBERG INTEGRATION ALGORITHM

The Romberg Algorithm is well-known, and is based on the Newton-Cotes formula
(see [2],[3] for definitions). We use the particular Newton-Cotes formula
known as the Trapezoidal method, which is one of the easiest to use, but which
is usually not so accurate. The Romberg algorithm is widely applicable, using
this easy-to-apply formula to obtain initial approximations followed by
Richardson's extrapolation to improve these approximations to gain a required
accuracy.

Thus, to evaluate the integral $I = \int_a^b f(x)\,dx$, we select an integer n>0 followed
by the procedure

INPUT endpoints a,b; integer n.
OUTPUT an array R. (R_{nn} is the approximation to I. Computed by rows; only 2
rows are saved in storage).

Step 1:   Set h=b-a
$$R_{1,1} = \frac{h}{2}\{f(a) + f(b)\}$$

Step 2:   OUTPUT $(R_{1,1})$

Step 3:   For i=2(1)n DO steps 4-8

       Step 4:   Set $R_{2,1} = \frac{1}{2}[R_{1,1} + h \sum\limits_{k=1}^{2^{i-2}} f(a+(k-0.5)h)]$

               (Approximation using Trapezoidal method)

       Step 5:   For j=2(1)i

              Set $R_{2,j} = \dfrac{4^{j-1}R_{2,j-1} - R_{1,j-1}}{4^{j-1}-1}$ (Extrapolation)

       Step 6:   OUTPUT $(R_{2,j}$ for j=1,2,...,i)

       Step 7:   Step h = h/2

       Step 8:   For j=1(1)i

              Set $R_{1,j}=R_{2,j}$ (update row 1 of R)

Step 9:   STOP

As a start for our systolic algorithm we re-state these two basic steps:

(i)   Approximate using the Trapezoidal rule with
$m_1=1$, $m_2=2$, $m_3=4,\ldots,m_n=2^{n-1}$ for integer n>0
and step size $h_k=(b-a)/m_k=(b-a)/2^{k-1}$ and use $R_{k,1}$ for the approximation k=1(1)n, neglecting the error terms $O(h_k^2)$.

(ii)   By using Richardson's Extrapolation procedure we speed-up the
convergence
$$R_{k,2} = \frac{4R_{k,1} - R_{k-1,1}}{3}$$ for next approximation k=2(1)n

      Generally,
$$R_{ij} = \frac{4^{j-1}R_{i,j-1} - R_{i-1,j-1}}{4^{j-1}-1} \qquad \begin{array}{l} i=2(1)n \\ j=2(1)i \end{array}$$

This results in the triangular table of approximations given by,

$$
\begin{array}{llll}
R_{11} & & & \\
R_{21} & R_{22} & & \\
R_{31} & R_{32} & R_{33} & \\
R_{41} & R_{42} & R_{43} & R_{44} \\
\vdots & \vdots & \vdots & \\
R_{n1} & R_{n2} & R_{n3} & \cdots\cdots R_{nn}
\end{array}
$$

                             Romberg Extrapolation Table

Where the elements for the first column $R_{i,1}$, i=1(1)n are produced by step (i),
and the diagonal entries $R_{i,i}$, i=1(1)n are the terms that converge to the
correct value of the integral. In general, the diagonal terms $\{R_{ii}\}_{i=1}^{\infty}$ of the
array converge much faster than $\{R_{m,1}\}_{m=1}^{\infty}$ and we stop when $|R_{n-1,n-1}| <$
tol=required accuracy.

In the above algorithm we have constructed a table of size n, and take R_{nn} as
the approximation regardless of whether the method has converged (before R_{nn})

or not after the table has been constructed. For the systolic array this has important consequences, firstly we must have a fixed number of cells, in order to fabricate the design, and secondly we have to decide the number of cells to ensure that approximations are sufficiently accurate. As in the algorithm above, we construct a finite sized table of n rows, but allow the systolic array to close down if convergence has been achieved before the full table is constructed. In order to achieve accurate results we can choose n as large as possible subject to chip area restrictions.

Next we note the important point that although only the last row of the Romberg Triangle, and the $R_{i,1}$ value of the next row is required to construct row i, the parallel evaluation of the triangle terms as discussed in [1] can still be applied, i.e.,

$$
\text{Precomputed}
\left\{
\begin{array}{llllllll}
R_{11} \\
R_{21} & R'_{22} \\
R_{31} & R'_{32} & R'_{33} \\
R_{41} & R'_{42} & R'_{43} & R'_{44} \\
R_{51} & R'_{52} & R'_{53} & R'_{54} & R'_{55} \\
R_{61} & R'_{62} & R'_{63} & R'_{64} & R'_{65} & R'_{66} \\
R_{71} & R'_{72} & R'_{73} & R'_{74} & R_{75} & R'_{76} & R'_{77} \\
R_{81} & R'_{82} & R'_{83} & R'_{84} & R'_{85} & R'_{86} & R'_{87} & R'_{88}
\end{array}
\right.
$$

-------- elements on same line can be computed in parallel

The extrapolation calculations are simpler than those given in [1] and result in simpler basic cells and input output techniques.

SYSTOLIC ARRAY COMPUTATION

The two basic steps defined above provide us with a natural partitioning of the computation between the host machine and the systolic array.

(i)   The host computes $R_{k,1}$, k=1(1)m, for m≤n, before waking the array.

      (Note n is the maximum sized table, but we can compute a smaller one on the size n array).

(ii) The systolic array computes R_{ij}, i=2(1)m, j=2(1)i (i.e. construct the table by extrapolation).

This division is natural because (i) involves evaluating the function f(x), and since f(x) can be arbitrary (within the constraints of integration, continuous, etc.) including it as part of the array would require an arbitrary number of complex basic array cells, which is not a desirable nor practical approach to the design.

For step (ii) we first consider a set of linearly connected cells, i.e., the basic cells implement the Richardson Extrapolation Procedure (REP), hence are called REP cells. The array consists of n-1 REP cells, each with two inputs and three outputs, two outputs are inputs to the adjacent cell to the right, the third connects to a Fanin network, for filtering out the results.

The Fanin network is used as only the R_{ii}, i=2(1)n values are required to decide convergence, and as each REP cell will compute a column of the triangle, with cell i computing the i+2th column. Each cell will output only one diagonal value, and if c is the latency of the REP cell, outputs from cells will occur at c, 2c, 3c, respectively, on the fanin network line, thus no values will be confused and only one output wire is sufficient for our needs.

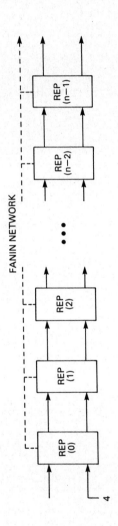

Romberg Linear Systolic Array

The REP Cell

The Richardson Extrapolation cell is shown in Fig. 1. It consists of i ips, a multiplier, subtractor and divider, this seems complex but later we show that this is acceptable. The latency of the cell is c=3, taking into account all the delays through arithmetic elements and delay registers. The cell performs Richardson's extrapolation procedure, and that each cell computes the power 4^j for the next cell, hence the two input and two output lines. The leftmost cell accepts the elements $R_{11}, R_{21}, \ldots, R_{n1}$ on one input line and the second input is hardwired to the value 4 (using a permanently register stored value). This allows the construction of the powers of 4 systolically, rather than sequentially by the host, although the multiplier seems extravagent because we could precompute and then load them into each cell before starting the array (i.e. replace the multiplier by a register). Later we show that the computation of the powers of 4 systolically using the extra multiplier in the REP cell can be justified.

The operation of the REP cell is simple to understand, and a one-bit control line is added which is associated with the R_{ii} values i=1(1)m, such that,

$$\text{control} = \begin{cases} 1\text{-send result of cell on Fanin network} \\ \quad \text{as well as normal output.} \\ 0\text{-normal output only.} \end{cases}$$

The control value moves systolically with the results from cell to cell, ensuring that all the R_{ii} values will be placed on the Fanin network back to the host, and no other values will use it (i.e. only true approximations). Fig. 2 shows the first 7 steps of an array with n=6. The total time for the array is thus given by,

$$T = \text{(cell latency)} * \text{(number of cells)} = 3(n-1) = 3n-3$$

where T is the time to construct the complete table. If we converge before all rows of the table are computed we can just stop inputting and reading output results, essentially closing down the array and no explicit commands are needed as the cells do not retain any values. Likewise if we run out of R_{kl} values, k=1(1)m for m<n inputting a suitable dummy element (δ), zero for instance, will not affect the construction of the first m rows of the triangle, already being computed along the array, hence smaller triangles can be constructed with time,

$$T = 3(m-1) < 3(n-1) .$$

Finally, we remark that a time cycle is equivalent to a single ips step, and that each REP cell has area equivalent to 2.5 ips cells.

Further, a systolic ring architecture for Romberg integration has been developed (Evans & Megson [4]) in which only 1/3 n REP cells are required together with certain other advantages, [5],[6].

CONCLUSIONS

A linear systolic array has been presented which will compute the Romberg integral table in a time 3n. This is significantly faster than the $O(n^2)$ operations required by the algorithm performed on a sequential machine.

Finally, a numerical example is given in Appendix 1 and the OCCAM program which simulates the given linear systolic array is presented in Appendix 2.

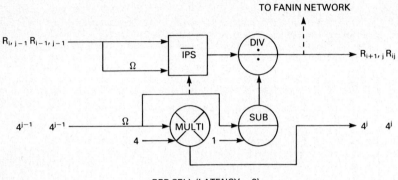

REP CELL (LATENCY = 3)

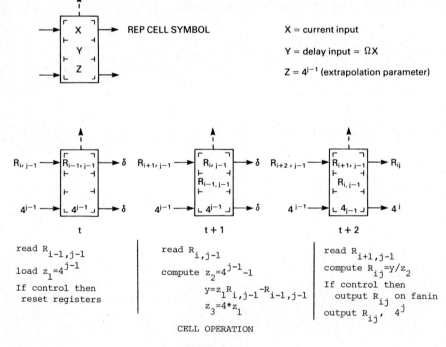

CELL OPERATION

FIGURE 1

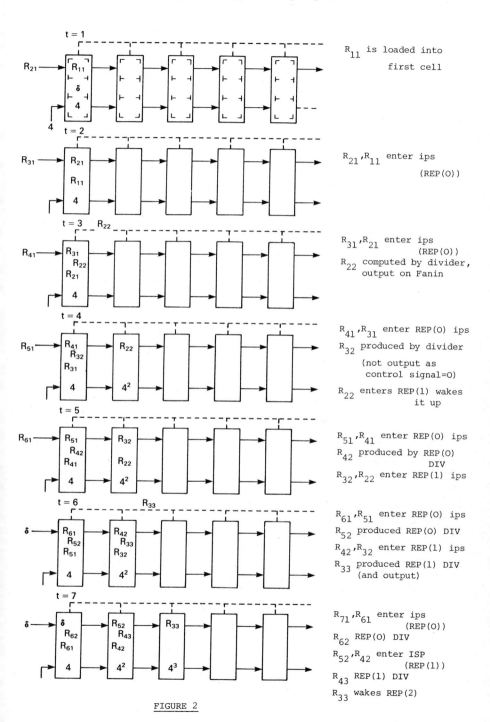

FIGURE 2

REFERENCES

[1] G.P. McKeown, "Iterated Interpolation Using a Systolic Array", Internal
     Report CSA/21/1984, UEA, Norwich.

[2] Burden, Faires and Reynolds; Publisher Prindle, Weber & Schmidt 2nd Ed.
     "Numerical Analysis", Ch. 3, Ch. 4.

[3] L.W. Johnson, R.D. Reiss, "Numerical Analysis", Addison Wesley, 1977,
     Ch.5.

[4] D.J. Evans & G.M. Megson, "Romberg Integration Using Systolic Arrays",
     Parallel Computing, Vol.3, 1986.

[5] G.M. Megson & D.J. Evans, "Design and Simulation of Systolic Arrays",
     Internal Report 230, Computer Studies Dept., Loughborough University of
     Technology, May 1985.

[6] Mead & Conway, (eds.), "Introduction to VLSI Design", Addison-Wesley,
     1980, pp.271-292.

APPENDIX 1

Test example:

$$\int_0^\pi \sin x \, dx \quad N=6$$

ROMBERG TABLE

```
     0
     1.57079633    2.09439511
     1.89611890    2.00455976    1.99857073
     1.97423160    2.00026917    1.99998313    2.00000555
     1.99357034    2.00001659    1.99999975    2.00000001    1.99999999
     1.99839336    2.00000103    2.00000000    2.00000000    2.00000000   2.0
```

LINEAR SYSTOLIC ARRAY (no. of REP CELLS = 5)

STARTING VALUES	DIAGONAL ENTRIES (FANIN)
R[0]=0.000000	2.094395
R[1]=1.570796	1.998571
R[2]=1.896119	2.000005
R[3]=1.974232	2.000000
R[4]=1.993570	2.000000
R[5]=1.998393	

APPENDIX 2 - LINEAR SYSTOLIC ARRAY FOR ROMBERG INTEGRATION - OCCAM PROGRAM

```
-- program
-- Systolic Array: To construct the extrapolation table in Romberg's
                   Integration algorithm.
-- The basic cell is the REP or Richardson's Extrapolation cell
-- which computes the extrapolation values
-- Table size
def n = 5:
-- library routines
EXTERNAL Proc str.to.screen(value s[]) :
EXTERNAL Proc num.to.screen(value n) :
EXTERNAL Proc fp.num.to.screen(Value float f):
EXTERNAL Proc fp.num.from.keyboard(Var float f) :

Proc REP(Chan inl, outl, in2, out2, out3, cntrlin, cntrlout ) =
  --
  -- Richardsons extrapolation cell
  --
  var float tl, t2, p.4, p.res, rnew, rold, res :
  var switch, running, toggle, c.fifo[4] :
  seq
    -- initialisation
    p.res := 0.0
    rold := 0.0
    res := 0.0
    tl := 0.0
    t2 := 1.0
    seq i =[0 for 3 ]
      c.fifo[i] := 0
    switch := true
    running := true
    toggle := true
    -- cell
    while running
      seq
        -- control input
        if
          switch
            cntrlin?c.fifo[0]
        -- decide on input/output
        if
          (c.fifo[0] = 6 ) and switch
            switch := false
          c.fifo[3] = 6
            -- destroy cell
            running := false
        cntrlout!c.fifo[3]
        -- i/o
        if
          switch
            par
              inl?rnew
              in2?p.4
        if
          running
            par
              outl!res
              out2!(p.res)
              -- output to fanin network
              if
```

```
                        c.fifo[3] = 1
                          seq
                            toggle := false
                            out3!res
                        toggle
                          out3!0
              -- extrapolation formula
              res := t1/t2
              t1 := (p.4*rnew)- rold
              t2 := p.4- 1.0
              rold := rnew
              p.res := p.4 * 4.0
              -- shift control fifo
              seq i =[ 0 for 3]
                c.fifo[3-i] := c.fifo[(3-i)-1]
              if
                c.fifo[0] = 6
                  c.fifo[0] := 0 :
proc fnet(chan gather[], var float vec[], var k ) =
  --
  -- fanin network: primitive routine to collect values
  --
  seq
    par j =[0 for n]
      -- check all processes
      seq
        if
          j > k
            -- those still to output
            gather [j]?any
          j = k
            var float tmp :
            -- current output
            seq
              gather[k]?tmp
              if
                tmp <> 0.0
                  seq
                    vec[k] := tmp
                    k := k + 1 :
proc getdata( chan out1,out2, cntrl ) =
  --
  -- read starting values, and pump into
     array then closedown array systolically
  var float four, vec[n+1] :
  seq
    four := 4.0
    str.to.screen("*nEnter Romberg Starting values")
    seq i=[0 for (n+1)]
      seq
        str.to.screen("*nR[")
        num.to.screen(i)
        str.to.screen("] =")
        fp.num.from.keyboard(vec[i])
        fp.num.to.screen(vec[i])
    str.to.screen("*n*n*n")
    -- start pumping
    seq i=[0 for (n+1)]
      par
        if
          i = 0
```

```
              cntrl!1
          true
              cntrl!0
          out1!vec[i]
          out2!four
      -- close down
      cntrl!6 :

proc putdata( chan in1, in2, fanin[], cntrl ) =
    --
    -- collect garbage falling off array, and
    -- call fanin to collect next result and print out
    -- diagonal entries
    --
    var float vec[n] :
    var running, cl, k :
    seq
      k := 0
      running := true
      -- collect results until stopped
      while running
        seq
          cntrl?cl
          if
            cl = 6
              running := false
            true
              par
                in1?any
                in2?any
                fnet(fanin, vec, k)
      -- output diagonal approximations.
      str.to.screen("*n*n Diagonal Table Entries")
      seq i =[0 for n]
        seq
          str.to.screen("*n")
          fp.num.to.screen(vec[i]) :

-- main
--
-- The Romberg array
chan in1[n+1], in2[n+1], fanin[n], cntrl[n+1] :

par
  getdata(in1[0], in2[0], cntrl[0])
  par i =[1 for n]
    REP(in1[i-1], in1[i], in2[i-1], in2[i], fanin[i-1], cntrl[i-1], cntrl[i])
  putdata(in2[n], in1[n], fanin, cntrl[n])
```

HIGHLY PARALLEL COMPUTERS
G.L. Reijns, M.H. Barton (editors)
Elsevier Science Publishers B.V. (North-Holland)
©IFIP, 1987

ON THE SYNTHESIS OF SYSTOLIC STRUCTURES

Hristo N. Djidjev

Institute of Mathematics
Bulgarian Academy of Sciences
Sofia 1090, P.O. Box 373
BULGARIA

A constructive methodology for automatic
synthesis of systolic structures with
good performance is proposed that combines both processes of algorithm and system developement. As a result of the
analysis a systolic design is derived
that has a regular, modular structure
and correctly implements the corresponding algorithm.

INTRODUCTION

A most suitable architecture for VLSI implementation, that is
under intensive investigation in the last few years, are the systolic arrays. Their simple communication structure, the use of
simple and uniform processing elements and low I/O requirements
are features that make them so attractive from the viewpoint of
current technology [4]. A number of systolic designs have been
proposed for problems in linear algebra, discrete transformations
and signal processing, for combinatorial problems and others [3].
One interesting question that is not sufficiently well answered
is connected with the correctness, verification, and the developement of a methodology for automatically deriving systolic designs
from an algorithm specification. Approaches to this problem include trasformations to systems of recursive equations [1,5,6,8]
and to optimization problems [5], the wavefront method [7], design transformations by symbols pushing [2], and others. A
drawback of the existing approaches is their unsufficient utilization of the regularity of both algorithms and hardware and the
need to operate with unnecessary big representation structures.

Our method incorporates both processes of algorithm and hardware design. Graph theory notation is used for description of the
two types of structures which simplifies the transition from algorithm to hardware.

In the first part of the paper techniques are presented for
formal description of algorithms, computing structures, and hardware implementation of algorithms, some of their basic properties,
and a number of criteria for performance evaluation. On this basis
a methodology is developed for the synthesis of systolic structures implementing a given algorithm. The time for this analysis is
independent of the real problems's size (the problem's parameters)
and depend only of the size of the algorithm description. As a result of the analysis a description of the system can be derived,
together with an evaluation of performance characteristics. Examples are provided illustrating the methodology for the matrix
multiplication problem.

PROGRAM GRAPHS

To analyze the properties of a given sequential algorithm a
proper way to represent the dependencies between the computations
have to be used. For this purpose a graph called a program graph
is constructed that contains all the essential information about
the flow of data.

We begin by some basic definitions and notations from graph
theory. A graph G is an ordered pair (V,E) of sets, where V is a
set of vertices and E is a set of edges. We shall denote those two
sets by $V(G)$ and $E(G)$ respectively. Each edge e is an ordered pair
(v,w) of vertices (i.e. the graphs in this paper will be only directed), the vertices v and w are adjacent and e is incident with
both v and w. The number of edges incident with some vertex v is
the degree of v. A path p with length k is a sequence $(v_1,\ldots,v_k)$
of vertices such that $(v_i,v_{i+1}) \in E$ for $1 \leq i \leq k-1$. If $v_1 = v_k$,
then p is a cycle. If H contains no cycles, then G is acyclic. Two
graphs G and G' are isomorphical, if there exists a one-to-one map
$M: V(G) \rightarrow V(G')$, such that for any couple v, w of vertices of G (v,w)
is an edge of G iff $(M(v),M(w))$ is an edge of G.

DEFINITION 1. A coloured flow graph, or simply a flow graph,
we call a directed acyclic graph G with colours and labels on its
edges and colours on its vertices with the following properties:
    1) Edges with the same label have the same colour;
    2) For each label l there exists a path beginning and ending
at vertices with degree 1 and containing all edges with label 1 and
only them;
    3) For each colour c and each vertex v there is at most one
edge with colour c that enters v.

When a flow graph is used to represent an algorithm, vertices
correspond to operations on data and edges - to data transfers. In
this case we call the graph a program graph. The colours and labels
of the edges are used to characterize the different data flows,
while the colours of the vertices correspond to the kind of data
operation each vertex represents.

A difference between our definition of a flow graph and the
traditional definition of a program graph is that in the first case

the number of the edges that enter some vertex equals the number
of the vertices that leave the same vertex. A computaion in this
case is viewed as a process in which certain elements of data
meet, interact and (possibly) change, and are used later as an
input of other computation (i.e. leave for other destinations).
Thus the flow graph representation is more suitable for investigating systolic structures. There is a number of obvious ways
for transforming program graphs into flow ones and we will not
discuss that problem here.

Since G is acyclic, then a partial ordering "$\leq$" between the
vertices of G can be defined so that $v \leq w$ iff there exists a path
from v to w. The minimal elements with respect to this ordering
are input vertices and the maximal elements are output vertices.
All the input and output vertices form the set of the terminal
vertices. From the definition of G the degree of any terminal vertex is one. The edges incident to the terminal vertices are called
terminal and input or output edges respectively.

LEMMA 1. If an edge with label 1 enters/leaves the nonterminal vertex v, then an unique edge with label 1 leaves/enters v.

LEMMA 2. For each label 1 there exists exactly one input and
exactly one output edge with label 1.

Further we shall use the following denotations: if $e = (v,w)\epsilon$
$E(G)$, then $lab(e) = lab(v,w)$ will be the label of e and $col(e) =$
$= col(v,w)$ will be the colour of e; if $v\epsilon V(G)$ then $col(v)$ will be
the colour of v.

EXAMPLE 1. Consider the following algorithm for finding the
product C of two 2x2 matrices A and B.

Each computation is of the form

$$[a(i,k,j-1), b(k,j,i-1), c(i,j,k-1)]$$
$$\rightarrow [a(i,k,j), b(k,j,i), c(i,j,k)],$$

where

$$a(i,k,j) = a(i,k,j-1),$$
$$b(k,j,i) = b(k,j,i-1),$$
$$c(i,j,k) = c(i,j,k-1) + a(i,k,j-1)*b(k,j,i-1);$$

$a(i,j,0), b(i,j,0)$ - elements of A and B,
$c(i,j,0) = 0,$
$c(i,j,2)$ - elements of the matrix C.

The program graph of this algorithm is illustrated on Figure 1.
The vertices with degree 1 are terminal vertices. The edges used
for routing the elements of A, B, C have colours 1, 2, 3 respectively. With each terminal vertex a pair (c,1) of numbers is associated, where c denotes a colour and 1 - a label. The path joining the
couple of input and output vertices both marked with (c,1) will
contain only the edges with colour c and label 1.

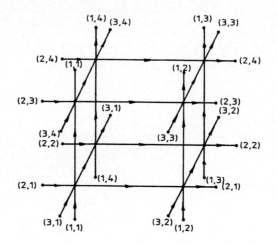

Figure 1
The flow graph of the algrorithm in Example 1

HARDWARE GRAPHS

To analize the properties of complex computing systems or to
map a given algorithm onto a system with a fixed structure, it is
most convenient to use a graph representation of the structure,
Thus a flow graph is constructed, called a hardware graph, whose
vertices represent the processing elements and whose edges - the
links between adjacent elements. The terminal edges of the graph
correspond to the input and the output ports (Figure 2 (a)).

Thus each flow graph may be viewed as a program or as a hardware graph, depending on the interpretation.

If we direct our attention towards VLSI systems, we must conform to the restrictions imposed by the current technology. We
shall consider the following properties usually required from the
hardware graphs suitable for direct VLSI implementation: planarity,
location of the I/O ports on the boundary of the embedding, regularity.

A graph is planar if it can be embedded in the plane so that
the curves corresponding to its edges do not intersect except at
the endpoints. The planarity restriction on the VLSI systems requires that the hardware graph be planar. According to the type of
the problem considered, we distinguish the following cases: (i) a
VLSI system with a fixed structure (which is supposed to be planar)
is investigated; and (ii) an algorithm (a problem) is investigated

and as a result a suitable VLSI systems is designed. In the first case we examine the hardware graph of the system together with the embedding of the graph in the plane induced by the original system's embedding. In the second case we may have the choice between different embeddings of a planar hardware graph, in which case the choice of an embedding may influence the effectiveness of the system.

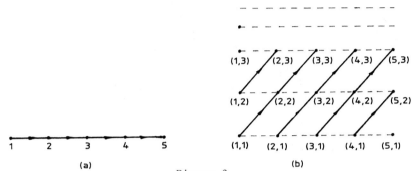

Figure 2

A hardware graph and its space-time graph

Each planar embedding of a graph G divides the plane into connected regions called faces. Exactly one of the faces is unbounded, the outer face. All vertices and edges that are incident or lie in this face form a graph which we call a boundary. A natural restriction on the location of the terminal edges (i.e. the input and output ports) is that they must lie on the boundary of the hardware graph (with regard to a given embedding).

To be easily embeddable on a chip, a VLSI design must have a regular structure. Most often this is achieved by connecting each processing element with its neibourghs in a fixed manner. This natural requirement restricts severely the number of possible VLSI designs with a given size, but such a restriction will be an advantage in our task of finding optimal systolic implementations, since it reduces the search space. A more formal treatment of the problem of presenting a regularity requirement into the design specifications will be given in the next sections.

HARDWARE IMPLEMENTATION

Let G be a hardware graph. Denote $V' = V(G) \times \{1,2,\ldots\}$, $E' = \{(w_1,w_2): w_1 = (v_1, t_1) \in V', w_2 = (v_2,t_2) \in V', (v_1,v_2) \in E(G), t_2 = t_1+1\}$, $col\ (w_1,w_2) = col\ (v_1,v_2)$, $lab(w_1,w_2) = lab(v_1,v_2)$, $col((v,t)) = col(v)$, where $(v,t) \in V'$. The graph $G' = (V',E')$ is a space-time graph of G (Figure 2 (b)).

If $v' = (v,j)$ is a vertex of V', then the numbers v and j will be called a projection and a level of v' and denoted by $pr(v')$ and $lev(v')$ respectively.

The space-time graph is directed and acyclic. It represents an infinite sequence of computations performed on the hardware graph. The goal of our research is to investigate ways of mapping a program graph onto a space-time graph of a given hardware graph.

DEFINITION 2. A hardware implementation of a program graph G is an embedding $M: V(G) \to V(G')$, where G' is a space-time graph of some hardware graph H, if the following conditions are satisfied:
1) If $v,w \in V(G)$, $v \neq w$, then $M(v) \neq M(w)$.
2) If $(v,w) \in E(G)$, then $(M(v),M(w)) \in E(G')$.
According to this property M defines an embedding of E(G) on E(G'), which will be denoted by M too, such that $M((v,w)) = (M(v), M(w))$.
3) If $v \in V(G)$ and $e \in E(G)$, then $col(M(v)) = col(v)$, $col(M(e)) = col(e)$, $lab(M(e)) = lab(e)$.
This condition requires that M preserves colours and labels.

The hardware implementation M is systolic, if M satisfies the following additional requirements.
4) If v is a terminal vertex of G, then $pr(M(v))$ is a terminal vertex of H.
5) If $(v',w') \in E(G')$ and there exists $v \in V(G): v' = M(v)$, then there exists $w \in V(G): w' = M(w)$.
This property states that once a processing element is activated, it activates in the next step all its successors.

It will be more convenient to represent an embedding M as a pair of embeddings $M = (S,T)$, where for any vertex v $S(v) = pr(M(v))$, $T(v) = lev(M(v))$.

From the definition we obtain the following properties of the hardware implementations.

LEMMA 3. Let G be a program graph, H - a hardware graph and G' - the space-time graph of H. A necessary and sufficient condition for an embedding $M = (S,T): V(G) \to V(G')$ to preserve the adjacence relation between the vertices is for any edge $(v,w) \in E(G)$
1) $(S(v), S(w)) \in E(H)$,
2) $T(w) = T(v) + 1$.

The next statement is in some sense the reverse of condition 5) of Definition 2. It states that if some processing element has ever been activated, then each its ancestor would have been activated too.

LEMMA 4. Let G be a program graph, G' - a space-time graph and M be a hardware implementation of G on G'. If $(v',w') \in E(G')$ and $w' = M(w)$, where $w \in V(G)$, there exists $v \in V(G): v' = M(v)$.

Proof. Let $l = lab(v',w')$. Consider the following 2 cases.

a) w' is a terminal (output) vertex of G'. Then by Definition 2, w is a terminal vertex of G and consequently there exists exactly one edge (v,w) incident with w. Then $(M(v), M(w))$ will be an edge in G' incident with w' = M(w). Since w' is terminal, then only one edge is incident with w', whence (M(v),w') = (v',w') and M(v) = v'.

b) w' is not a terminal vertex. Then there exists u'∈V(G'): (w',u')∈E(G') and lab(w',u') = 1. By requirement 5) of Definition 2 there exists u∈V(G): M(u) = u'. Then lab(w,u) = lab(w',u') = 1. Then there exists an (unique) edge (v,w) in G such that lab(v,w)=1. Since M(w) = w', then lab(v',w') = 1 = lab(M(v), M(w)), whence v' = M(v).

LEMMA 5. Let G be a program graph and M be a hardware implementation of G on some space-time graph. Then for any $v,w \in V(G)$, $v \leq w$, lev(M(v)) = lev(M(w)) equals the distance between v and w.

Let G be an n_1 vertex program graph, H be an n_2 vertex hardware graph and M be a hardware implementation of G on the space-time graph of H. For comparing the properties of possible hardware implementations, a number of characteristics are used. The most important of them are the following.

i) The time T of the implementation M is

(1) $T = \max \{lev(M(v)): v \in V(G)\}$;

ii) The number of processors is n_2;

iii) The speedup S_p is

(2) $S_p = n_1/T$;

iv) The processors utilization U is

(3) $U = S_p/n_2$.

Obviously the inequalities

$$T \geq n_1/n_2, \quad S_p \leq n_2, \quad U \leq 1$$

hold for any hardware implementation of G.

RECURSIVE SEQUENCES OF GRAPHS

An important feature of systolic architectures is their regularity. Because of the close link between the structure of the hardware graph and the algorithm implemented on it, only algorithms with simple structures can be embedded effectively on a systolic array. Describing classes of graphs with regular structure that include natural classes of program and hardware graphs will enable us to develope a methodology for constructing hardware implementations with good characteristics.

DEFINITION 3. Let G be a flow graph, let $Q = \{G_i\}$ be a set of flow graphs, $V' = U\ V(G_i)$, $E' = U\ E(G_i)$, and M be an embedding of V' onto $V(G)$. The pair (Q,M) is a covering of G, if the following conditions are satisfied:
1) If $(v,w) \in E'$, then $(M(v), M(w)) \in E(G)$.
According to this property M defines a map of E' on $E(G)$, which will be denoted for convenience by M too, such that $M((v,w)) = (M(v),M(w))$.
2) If $v \in V'$ and $e \in E'$, then $col(v) = col(M(v))$, $col(e) = col(M(e))$, $lab(e) = lab(M(e))$.
3) M induces a one-to-one correspondence between the nonterminal vertices of V' and V.

EXAMPLE 3. On Figure 3 is illustrated a covering of a flow graph G by 3 flow graphs G_1, G_2, G_3. All vertices and edges are assumed to have the same colour and label. Dotted lines represent terminal edges.

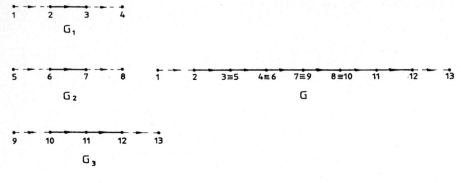

Figure 3
A covering of a graph

From Definition 3 we obtain easily:

LEMMA 6. Let (Q,M) be a covering of the flow graph G and let V', E' be respectively the set of the vertices and the set of the edges of the covering graphs. Let e be any edge in G and let $M^{-1}(e)$ be the set of all edges of E' whose image is e. Then all possible cases are the following:
a) e is terminal, $|M^{-1}(e)| = 1$ and the edge in $M^{-1}(e)$ is terminal;
b) e is nonterminal, $|M^{-1}(e)| = 1$ and the edge in $M^{-1}(e)$ is nonterminal;
c) e is nonterminal, $|M^{-1}(e)| = 2$ and the edges in $M^{-1}(e)$ are terminal.

DEFINITION 4. A sequence $G_0, G_1, \ldots$ of flow graphs is recursive, if the graphs are connected and for all $i \geq 1$ there exist integers $p(i) < i$ and $q(i) < i$ such that
1) There exists a covering (Q_i, M_i) of G_i, where Q_i is a set of graphs isomorphical to $G_{p(i)}$;
2) Shrinking in G_i the set of all nonterminal vertices in each image of graph from Q_i and replacing each set of same coloured adjacent edges by a single edge with the same colour results in a graph isomorphical to $G_{q(i)}$.

DEFINITION 5. If the sequence $G_0, G_1, \ldots$ is recursive with $p(i) = 0$ and $q(i) = i-1$ for all i, then it is a regular recursive sequence.

Each regular recursive sequense is completely determined (up to an isomorphism) by its first element G_0.

In this paper mostly regular recursive sequences will be considered, so if not stated otherwise recursive sequences will always be assumed regular hereafter.

EXAMPLE 3. The flow graph G_0 on Figure 4 (a) may be viewed as a hardware graph of a mesh of processors with size 2x2. The pairs of numbers associated with the vertices have the same interpretation as in Example 1. The graph on Figure 4 (b) represents a mesh of processors with size 4x4, which graph is the second element G_1 of the regular recursive sequence induced by G_0.

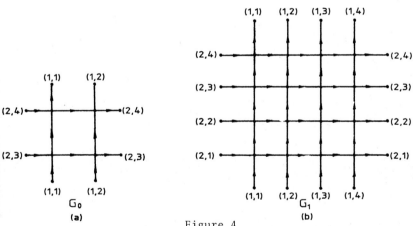

Figure 4
Recursive sequence of 2 graphs

The following statements about recursive sequences are obtained from Definitions 4 and 5.

LEMMA 7. Let $G_0, G_1, \ldots$ be a recursive sequence of flow graphs and let $i \geq 1$. Let (Q_i, M_i) be a covering of G_i and let x be any nonterminal vertex of G_i. Denote by G_0' the isomorphical to G_0 graph from Q_i whose image contains x, by $v_1(x)$ the vertex in G_{i-1} to which G_0' is shrinked, and by $v_2(x)$ the corresponding to x vertex in G_0'. Then the map $v = (v_1, v_2)$ that maps to any x the couple $(v_1(x); v_2(x))$ is a one-to-one map of $V'(G_i)$ onto $V'(G_{i-1}) \times V'(G_0)$, where $V'(G)$ denotes the set of nonterminal vertices of G.

COROLLARY 1. There exists a one-to-one map between $V(G_i)$ and $V(G_0)^{i+1}$.

LEMMA 8. Let $G_0, G_1, \ldots$ be a recursive sequence of flow graphs, v be any vertex in G_0, and c be any colour in G_0. Then there exists an edge with colour c incident with v.

Our next task will be to investigate when the graphs in a given recursive sequence are planar.

Let H be a planar hardware graph embedded in the plane so that all its terminal edges are contained in the outside (unbounded) region. The embedding induces a (cyclic) permutation p of the set of its terminal edges.

DEFINITION 6. H satisfies Property A, if for any colour c
1) all input edges with colour c are consecutive in p;
2) all output edges with colour c are consecutive in p.

LEMMA 9. If H satisfies Property A and $(l_1, \ldots, l_k)$ is the induced sequence of labels of input edges with colour c in p, then $(l_k, \ldots l_1)$ will be the corresponding sequence of output edges (Figure 5).

Proof. Follows from Lemma 1 and the topology of the plane.

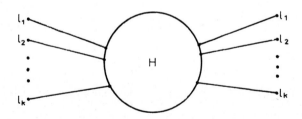

Figure 5
An illustration of Lemma 9

THEOREM 1. Let $H_0, H_1, \ldots$ be a recursive sequence of hardware graphs. If H_0 is planar and satisfies Property A, then each graph in the sequence is planar.

Proof. Suppose that for some $i \geq 1$ G_{i-1} is planar. Embed G_{i-1} in the plane. Substitute each vertex by a small circle so that no 2 circles surround common region. Draw G_0 in each circle and unite the curves corresponding to appropriate pairs of same labeled edges in each couple of adjacent circles into a single curve (see Lemma 9). Thus an embedding of G_i is obtained. The correctness of the theorem follows by an induction.

From the proof of Theorem 1 the nest statement follows.

COROLLARY 2. Let $H_0, H_1, \ldots$ be a sequence of hardware graphs. If H_0 is planar and satisfies Property A, then there exist embeddings of $H_0, H_1, \ldots$ in the plane such that if the vertices v' $\in V(H_{i-1})$ and $v_i \in V(H_0)$ lie on the peripheries of the corresponding embeddings, then the vertex $(v'; v_i)$ also lies on the periphery.

Theorem 1 and its corollary show that if a hardware graph H_0 is planar and its embedding in the plane satisfies Property A, then the graphs in the sequence of graphs induced by H_0 will possess the required properties of the structures suitable for VLSI implementation: planarity, location of the input/output ports on the boundary of the embedding, and regularity.

The next problem we treat is connected with developement of a methodology for finding hardware implementations with good characteristics. We begin with a closer examination of the properties of the recursive sequences.

Let G be a flow graph.

DEFINITION 7. A regular path with label 1 will be called any path in G whose edges have a same label 1. A maximal regular path in G is a regular path that connects a couple of terminal vertices.

DEFINITION 8. The diameter of G is the maximum length of a maximal regular path in G.

The next statements concern links between the consecutive elements in a recursive sequence of graphs.

LEMMA 10. Let $G_0, G_1, \ldots$ be a recursive sequence of flow graphs and $(v,w) \in E(G_i)$ for some $i \geq 1$, let $v = (v'; v_i)$, $w = (w'; w_i)$, $1 = lab(v,w)$, and let d be the maximum length of a maximal regular path with label 1 in G_0 minus one. Then all possible cases are the following:
a) $v' = w'$, $(v_i, w_i) \in E(G_0)$, $lab(v_i, w_i) = 1$;
b) $(v', w') \in E(G_{i-1})$, $lab(v', w') = 1$, there exists a regular path with label 1 and lenth d-1 between w_i and v_i.

168   *H.N. Djidjev*

LEMMA 11. Let $G_0,G_1,\ldots$ be a recursive sequence of flow graphs and let $p = (v_1,\ldots,v_k)$ be a maximal regular path in G_0. Then if (x,y) is any edge in G_{i-1} with the same colour as p, then $((x; v_{k-1}), (y; v_2)) \in E(G_i)$.

Let $G_0,G_1,\ldots$ and $H_0,H_1,\ldots$ be recursive sequences of flow graphs, G_i' be the space-time graph of H_i, $i \geq 0$, and M be a hardware implementation of G_0 on G_0'. Define recursively a sequence of embeddings $M_0,M_1,\ldots$; $M_i = (S_i,T_i): G_i \to G_i'$ by

(3) $S_i((v';v_i)) = (S_{i-1}(v'); S_0(v_i))$,

(4) $T_i((v';v_i)) = (T_{i-1}(v')-1)d + T_0(v_i)$,

where $v' \in V(G_{i-1})$, $v_i \in V(G_0)$, $i \geq 1$, and d is the diameter of G_0 minus one.

DEFINITION 9. The embedding M_0 is systolically expandable to the sequences $G_0,G_1,\ldots$ and $G_0',G_1',\ldots$ if for all $i \geq 0$ M_i is a systolic implementation of G_0 of G_1'. The sequence $M_0,M_1,\ldots$ is induced by M_0.

DEFINITION 10. Let $H_0,H_1,\ldots$ be a recursive sequence of hardware graphs. The sequence of space-time graphs $G_0,G_1,\ldots$, where G_i is the space-time graph of H_i, is induced by G_0.

LEMMA 12. Let $G_0,G_1,\ldots$ and $H_0,H_1,\ldots$ be recursive sequences of program and hardware graphs respectively, G_i' be the space-time graph of H_i, $i \geq 0$, and $H_i = (S_i,T_i)$ be a hardware implementation of G_i on G_i', where S_i is defined by (3) and $T_i (v'; v_i) = f_i(T_{i-1}(v'), T (v_i))$, where f_i is some function. Then for any vertex v in G_1 all regular maximal paths containing v in G_0 have equal lengths.

Proof. Let x be any vertex in G_0, $p = (v_1,\ldots,v_i = v,\ldots,v_k)$ be a maximal regular path with label 1 and colour c in G_0 and (x,y) be any edge with colour c in G_0 (see Lemma 8). By Lemma 11 $((x; v_1),\ldots,(x; v_{k-1}) = (y; v_1),\ldots,(y; v_k))$ will be a regular path with label 1 in G_1. Its subpath $p_2 = ((x; v_i), (x; v_{i+1}),\ldots, (y; v_i))$ has a length

$$T_1((y; v_i)) - T_1((x; v_i)) = f_1(T_0(y),T_0(v)) - f_1(T_0(x),T_0(v)) =$$
$$= f_1(T_0(x)+1,T_0(v)) - f_1(T_0(x),T_0(v)) = f_1^*(x,v).$$

Since p_2 has a length $k-1 = f_1^*(x,v)$, p_1 is arbitrary and p_1 has a length k, then the claim of the elmma is true.

COROLLARY 3. Let G_0 be the graph from Lemma 12, v_1 and v_2 be vertices belonging to the same component of G_0, and p_1 and p_2 be arbitrary maximal regular paths in G_0 containing v_1 and v_2 respectively. Then p_1 and p_2 have equal lengths.

COROLLARY 4. Let the graph G_0 from Lemma 12 be connected. Then the diameter d of G_0 equals the length of an arbitrary maximal regular path in G_0.

Nonconnected flow graphs represent algorithms and computing structures that can be decomposed into completely independent parts and each such part can be examined independently. Then without a loss of generality we assume that all flow graphs considered hereafter are connected.

LEMMA 13. Let $G_0, G_1, \ldots$ be a recursive sequence of program graphs, $H_0, H_1, \ldots$ be a recursive sequence of hardware graphs, G_i' be the space-time graph of H_i for $i \geq 0$, and $M_0, \ldots, M_{i-1}$ be a sequence of systolic embeddings, $M_j \colon V(G_j) \to V(G_j')$. If the embedding $M_i \colon V(G_i) \to V(G_i')$ is defined by the equalities (3) - (4) and $(v,w) \in E(G_i)$, then $(M_i(v), M_i(w)) \in E(G_i')$ and $lab(v,w) = lab(M_i(v), M_i(w))$, $col(v,w) = col(M_i(v), M_i(w))$.

Proof. Let $e = (v,w)$ be any edge in G_i. By Lemma 3 we have to prove that

(5) $(S_i(v), S_i(w)) \in E(H_i)$,

(6) $T_i(w) = T_i(v) + 1$.

Let d be the diameter of G_0 minus one, $v = (v'; v_i)$, $w = (w'; w_i)$, where $v', w' \in V(G_{i-1})$, $v_i, w_i \in V(G_0)$. According to Lemma 10 the following cases exist.

a) $v' = w'$. Then $(v_i, w_i) \in E(G_0)$ and consequently $(S_0(v_i), S_0(w_i)) \in E(H_0)$, whence

$$(S_i(v), S_i(w)) = ((S_{i-1}(v'); S_0(v_i)), (S_{i-1}(w'); S_0(w_i)) \in E(H_i).$$

Then (5) holds.

Further, since v_i and w_i belong to the same component of G_0, by Lemma 10

$$T_i(w) - T_i(v) = T_{i-1}(w'-1) . d + T_0(w_i)$$

$$- ((T_{i-1}(v')-1) . d + T_0(v_i)) = T_0(w_i) - T_0(v_i) = 1.$$

Finally determine the label and the colour of the edge $(M(v), M(w))$ by

$$lab(v,w) = lab(v_i, w_i) = lab(S_0(v_i), S_0(w_i))$$

$$= lab(S_i(v), S_i(w)) = lab(M_i(v), M_i(w)),$$

whence $lab(v,w) = lab(M_i(v), M_i(w))$ and $col(v,w) = col(M_i(v), M_i(w))$,

b) $v' \neq w'$. Denote $v^* = (S_{i-1}(v'))$, $w^* = S_{i-1}(w')$, $c = col(e)$, $l = lab(e)$,

$$V(H_i, v^*) = \{(v^*; x) \in V(H_i): x \in V(H_0)\},$$

$$V(H_i, w^*) = \{(w^*; x) \in V(H_i): x \in V(H_0)\}.$$

Since there is an unique edge in H_{i-1} that goes out from v^* and has colour c (namely the edge (v^*, w^*)), then by Definition 4 all edges with colour c going out from $V(H_i, v^*)$ enter into $V(H_i, w^*)$.

On the other hand, $v = (v'; v_i)$ and the label of $e = (v,w)$ is 1, whence there is an edge with label 1 starting from v_i and consequently an edge e' with label 1 starting from $(S_{i-1}(v')$; $S_0(v_i)) = (v^*; S_0(v_i))$. From the above arguments, the second vertex of this edge must be in $V(H_i, w^*)$, i.e.

(7) $e' = ((v^*; S_0(v_i)), x)$, $x \in V(H_i, w^*)$.

Similarly, there exists an edge e'' in H_i with label 1, second vertex $(w^*; S_0(w_i))$ and first vertex in $V(H_i, v^*)$, i.e.

(8) $e'' = (y, (w^*; S_0(v_i)))$, $y \in V(H_i, v^*)$.

Since there can be at most one output edge with label 1 in H , there is in H_i at most one edge with label 1 starting from $V(H_i, v^*)$. Then from (7) and (8)

$$e' = e'' = ((v^*; S_0(v_i)), (w^*; S_0(w_i)))$$

$$= ((S_{i-1}(x'); S_0(v_i)), (S_{i-1}(w'); S_0(w_i))) = (S_i(v), S_i(w))$$

and consequently (5) is satisfied.

From Lemma 10 $T_{i-1}(w') = T_{i-1}(v') + 1$ and $T(v_i) - T(w_i) = d-1$, whence

$$T_i(w) - T_i(v) = (T_{i-1}(w') - 1) \cdot d + T_0(w_i)$$

$$- ((T_{i-1}(v') - 1) \cdot d + T_0(v_i)) = d - (d-1) = 1.$$

Then from Lemma 3 $(M_i(v), M_i(w)) \in E(G_i')$.

Moreover $lab(M_i(v), M_i(w)) = lab(v,w)$ and $col(M_i(v), M_i(w)) = col(v,w)$.

The next statement gives a necessary and sufficient condition for a systolic embedding to be extendable on recursive sequences of graphs.

THEOREM 2. Let $G_0, G_1, \dots$ be a recursive sequence of connected program graphs, $H_0, H_1, \dots$ be a recursive sequence of hardware graphs, G_i' be the space-time graph of H_i for $i \geq 0$, and M_0 be a hardware implementation of G_0 on G_0'. M is systolically expandable to the sequences $\{G_i\}$ and $\{G'_i\}$ iff M_0 is a systolic implementation.

Proof. The necessity of the claim is obvious.

We shall prove the sufficiency by an induction on i. Let $M_0, M_1, \ldots$ be the sequence of embeddings defined by the formulae (3)-(4) and suppose that for some $i \geq 1$ M_{i-1} is a systolic implementation of G_{i-1} on G'_{i-1}. To prove that M_i is also a systolic implementation, we have to check whether the requirements 1)-5) from Definition 2 are satisfied. Condition 1) obviously holds, conditions 2) and 3) follow from Lemma 13.

Consider now the condition 4). Let $v = (v^*; v_i)$ be a terminal (say input) vertex of G_i. We have to prove that $pr(M(v))$ is a terminal vertex of H_i. Obviously v^* and v_i will be input vertices of G_{i-1} and G_0 respectively. From the inductive assumption $S_{i-1}(v^*)$ and $S_0(v_i)$ will be input vertices of H_{i-1} and H_0 respectively, whence $S_i(v) = (S_{i-1}(v^*); S_0(v_i))$ will be an input vertex of H_i.

Let $(v^*,w^*) \in E(G'_i)$ and let $v \in V(G_i)$ exists such that $v^* = M_i(v)$. Property 5) requires to prove that there exists $w \in V(G_i)$ such that $w^* = M_i(w)$. Denote

$$pr(v^*) = (v''; v''_i), \quad pr(w^*) = (w''; w''_i), \quad v = (v'; v'_i).$$

The following cases exist.

a) $v'' = w''$. Then by Lemma 10 $(v''_i, w''_i) \in E(H_{})$. Since $v''_i = S_0(v'_i)$, then $w''_i = S_0(w'_i)$, where $w_i \in V(G_0)$. Moreover $T_0(w'_i) = lev(M_0(w'_i)) = lev(M_0(v'_i)) + 1 = T_0(v'_i)+1$.

Thus

$$pr(w^*) = (S_{i-1}(v'); S_0(w'_i)) = S_i((v';w'_i)),$$

$$lev(w^*) = lev(v^*) + 1 = T_i((v'; v'_i)) + 1 = T_i((v'; w'_i)).$$

b) $v'' \neq w''$. Then by Lemma 10 $(v'', w'') \in E(H_{i-1})$ and the distance between v''_i and w''_i equals $d-1$.

Since $v'' = S_{i-1}(c')$, then $w'' = S_{i-1}(w')$ for some $w' \in V(G_{i-1})$, $T_{i-1}(w') = T_{i-1}(v') + 1$.

Furthermore $v''_i = S_0(v'_i)$. By Lemma 4 $w''_i = S_0(w'_i)$ for some $w_i \in V(G_0)$, $T_0(v'_i) - T_0(w'_i) = d-1$. Therefore

$$pr(w^*) = (w'', w''_i) = (S_{i-1}(w'); S_0(w'_i)) = S_i((w'; w'_i));$$

$$lev(w^*) = lev(v^*) + 1 = (T_{i-1}(v') - 1) \cdot d + T_0(v'_i) + 1$$

$$= (T_{i-1}(w') - 2) \cdot d + T_0(w'_i) + d - 1 + 1 = T_i(w', w'_i)).$$

Then all conditions from Definition 2 are satisfied and the claim is true.

EXAMPLE 4. Consider the algorithm from Example 1 for finding the product C of two 2x2 matrices A and B. Its program graph (Figure 1) induces a recursive sequence $G_0, G_1, \ldots$ of program graphs, where G corresponds to an algorithm for multiplying two $2^{i+1} \times 2^{i+1}$ matrices.

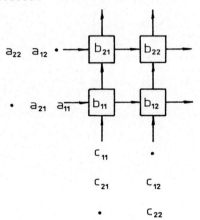

Figure 6
An expandable systolic implementation

Consider now the hardware graph illustrated on Figure 4 (a) that induces a sequence $H_0, H_1, \ldots$ of hardware graphs. A possible hardware implementations of G_0 on the space-time graph of H_0 is illustrated on Figure 6. Each time-cycle the next element from the queue of elements waiting on the corresponding input port enters the system; points in the figure represent an absence of elements on that position (such a representation of the hardware implementation seems more convenient for illustrating the hardware implementation in our case). Each square of the figure represents a processing element performing the operation c:= c+a*b and each processing element contains an element of the matrix B that stays there during the computation process. It can be shown that this implementation is systolic one and by Theorem 2 it induces a sequence of systolic implementations whose i-th element of the sequence represents a well known systolic structure for matrix multiplication.

We have obtained hardware implementations for this and other problems some characteristics of which are better compared with the existing designs. A detailed description of some of these designs will be included in a future publication.

IMPLEMENTATION ANALYSIS

Given the graphs G_0 and H_0 from Theorem 2 and an expandable implementation M_0, one can construct G_i, H_i and a systolic hardware implementation of G_i on the space-time graph of H_i. It is natural to expect that the characteristic of that embedding will depend on G_0, H_0 and M_0 only. The following statements give the explicit form of that dependence.

Let $G_0, G_1, \ldots$, $H_0, H_1, \ldots$, and $G_0', G_1', \ldots$ be recursive sequences of program graphs, hardware graphs, and the space-time graphs of the hardware graphs respectively, let M_0 be an expandable systolic hardware implementation of G_0 on G_0', and let $M_0, M_1, \ldots$ be the sequence induced by M_0.

LEMMA 14. The following relations between implementation characteristics hold:

(9) $\quad |V(G_i)| = |V(G_0)|^{i+1}$,

(10) $\quad |V(H_i)| = |V(H_0)|^{i+1}$,

(11) $\quad l_i = (l_0-1) \cdot (d^{i+1}-1)/(d-1)+1$,

where $l_i = \max\{\text{lev}(M_i(v)): v \in V(G_i)\}$ and d is the diameter of G_0 minus one.

Proof. Induction of i.

THEOREM 3. Let T_i, N_i, Sp_i, U_i, and Seq_i be the time, the number of processors, the speedup and the cell utilization of M_i, and the number of vertices (operations) in G_i respectively. Then

(12) $\quad T_i = (T_0-1) \cdot (d^{i+1}-1)/(d-1)+1;$

(13) $\quad N_i = N_0^{i+1};$

(14) $\quad Seq_i = Seq_0^{i+1};$

(15) $\quad Sp_i = Seq_0^{i+1}/ (T_0-1) \cdot (d^{i+1}+1)/(d-1)+1 ;$

(16) $\quad U_i = (Seq_0/N_0)^{i+1}/ (T_0-1) \cdot (d^{i+1}-1)/(d-1)+1 .$

Proof. Follows from (9)-(11) and Lemma 14.

The results from this paper may be used as a basis for developement of a computer system for synthesis of systolic designs. Such a system, that will make use of other novel ideas to be comented in future papers, is now under an developement.

REFERENCES

1. M.C. Chen, C.A. Mead, "Concurrent algorithms as space-time recursion equations", Proc. USC workshop on VLSI and modern signal processing, Nov. 1982, pp. 31-52.

2. H.T. Kung, W.T. Lin, "An algebra for systolic computation", Elliptic Problems Solvers II, Academic Press, 1984, pp. 141-160.

3. H.T. Kung, "The structure of parallel algorithsm", Advances in Computers, v. 19, 1980, pp. 65-112.

4. H.T. Kung "Why systolic architectures", Computer, Jan. 1982, pp. 37-46.

5. G.-J. Li, B.W. Wah, "The design of optimal systolic arrays", IEEE Trans. Comp., Jan. 1985, pp. 66-77.

6. R.G. Melhem, W.C. Rheinboldt, "A mathematical model for the verification of systolic networks", Techn. Rep. ICMA-82-47, Univ. of Pitsburg, 1983.

7. D.I. Moldovan, "On the analysis and synthesis of VLSI algorithms", IEEE Trans. Comp., Nov. 1982, pp. 1121-1126.

8. P. Quinton, "Automatic synthesis of systolic arrays from uniform recurrent equations", SIGARCH Newsletter, v. 12, 1984, n. 3, pp. 208-214.

HIGHLY PARALLEL COMPUTERS
G.L. Reijns, M.H. Barton (editors)
Elsevier Science Publishers B.V. (North-Holland)
©IFIP, 1987

THE SOLUTION OF ORDINARY DIFFERENTIAL EQUATIONS
BY SYSTOLIC ARRAY EXTRAPOLATION TABLES

D.J. Evans

Department of Computer Studies
Loughborough University of Technology
Loughborough, Leicestershire,
U.K.

We consider here the systolic array construction of extrapolation tables used in the solution of Ordinary Differential
Equations (ODE's) associated with initial value type problems.
The technique is examined first for a low order formula, i.e.
Euler's method which is combined with extrapolation to improve
the estimates of the solution i.e. Gragg's method. A generic
form is also given to systolic arrays for the construction of
extrapolation tables.

INTRODUCTION

The construction of extrapolation and difference tables has a form very similar
to the operations in certain matrix equations. This similarity can be
exploited to produce systolic arrays to construct the tables. In [1],[8],
Romberg integration was solved using a systolic array with these matrix
properties, while [2] solved Aitken's iterated interpolation algorithm on a
systolic array. In this paper certain similarities to matrix computations and
extrapolation tables are indicated giving a generic definition of an extrapolation systolic array. This correspondence is developed and combined with
the solution of initial-value problems associated with ODE's of the form

$$y' = f(t,y) \text{ , } a \leqslant t \leqslant b \text{ with initial condition } y(a) = \alpha \qquad (1)$$

Before the development of systolic arrays for any application two fundamental
points must be considered:

(i)   The systolic array can only be applied to existing initial value ODE
      algorithms by constructing the extrapolation tables.

(ii) As the array must be of fixed size, a limit to the number of levels
      or step divisions must be made, so that the table size is of fixed
      size and manageable.

The first point indicates that the evaluation of $f(t,y)$ or any part of the
algorithm that involves the evaluation of $f(t,y)$ must be placed outside the
systolic array. The evaluation of $f(t,y)$ in general can be arbitrary as long
as it is integrable and a systolic array would also become arbitrarily complex
if it was included in the array. Together with this is the fact that all the
function values which are used to estimate a point $y(t)$ at every level must be
evaluated before the array can be used. This appears to defeat the object of
the extrapolation idea as we will normally stop when convergence is reached,
ignoring the computation at a lower level of step division, and moving on to
the next point.

Extrapolation algorithms can be applied in two situations, where the function f
is approximated by either polynomials or rational functions. The latter are
usually better as they allow larger stepsizes to be used. Also, the use of
extrapolation in ODE's is beneficial as the ODE solution is related to finding
an indefinite integral and so extrapolation techniques allow the ODE methods to

compete with algorithms like ROMBERG integration[1].

EXTRAPOLATION METHODS

We now show how an extrapolation procedure can be incorporated into the solution to ODE's using an algorithm attributed to Gragg as this will provide a suitable vehicle by which to illustrate the points (i) and (ii) above and also relate extrapolation techniques to matrix computations.

Consider the initial value problem (1) using Euler's method and stepsize h>0, then,

$$w_0 = \alpha$$
$$w_{i+1} = w_i + hf(t_i, w_i), \quad i=0(1)n-1 \tag{1.1}$$

Put $N = (b-a)/h$ and $t_i = a+ih$, $i=0(1)n-1$.   (1.2)

The error $y(t_i) - w_i$ leads to a function $\delta(t)$ such that,

$$y(t_i) = w_i + h\delta(t_i) + O(h^2), \qquad i=1(1)n \tag{1.3}$$

To apply extrapolation we need approximations of $y(t_i)$ for different stepsizes. Put $w(t,h) \equiv$ approximation of $y(t)$ with stepsize h.   As an example choose two step levels h_0 and h_1 ($<h_0$). Now consider evaluating $y(b)$ and put,

$$q_0 = (b-a)/h_0 \text{ and } q_1 = (b-a)/h_1 .$$

Now apply (1.1),(1.2) and (1.3) twice once with $h=h_0$ and once with $h=h_1$ giving

$$y(b) = w(b,h_0) + h_0\delta(b) + O(h_0^2) , \tag{1.4a}$$
$$y(b) = w(b,h_1) + h_1\delta(b) + O(h_1^2) . \tag{1.4b}$$

Elementary manipulation of (1.4a) and (1.4b) results in,

$$y(b) = \frac{h_0 w(b,h_1) - h_1 w(b,h_0)}{h_0 - h_1} + O(h_0^2) \tag{1.5}$$

If the difference method has a particular type of error expansion [3] it can be generalised to construct an extrapolation table, with diagonal elements converging to a good (accurate) approximation to $y(t)$. e.g. using three levels (or stepsizes) h_0, h_1, h_2 we obtain,

$$y_{1,1} = w(t,h_0)$$

$$y_{2,1} = w(t,h_1) \qquad y_{2,2} = \frac{h_0^2 y_{2,1} - h_1^2 y_{1,1}}{h_0^2 - h_1^2}$$

$$y_{3,1} = w(t,h_2), \qquad y_{3,2} = \frac{h_1^2 y_{3,1} - h_2^2 y_{2,1}}{h_1^2 - h_2^2}, \quad y_{3,3} = \frac{h_0^2 y_{3,2} - h_2^2 y_{2,2}}{h_0^2 - h_2^2}$$

We begin to relate this to matrix computation, as the extrapolation table is a lower triangular matrix of values for the above example,

$$Y = \begin{bmatrix} y_{11} & & \\ y_{21} & y_{22} & O \\ y_{31} & y_{22} & y_{23} \end{bmatrix} \tag{1.6}$$

From [3] we define Gragg's extrapolation algorithm for solving ODE's:

Approximate the initial value problem

$$y' = f(t,y) \quad a \leq t \leq b, \quad y(a) = \alpha$$

local array with given tolerance

INPUT: endpoints a,b, initial condition α, tolerance TOL, level limit $p \leq 8$
         maximum stepsize (h_{max}), minimum stepsize (h_{min})

OUTPUT: T,W,h where W approximates y(t) and stepsize h was used or a message when the minimum stepsize exceeded.

STEP1:   Initialise array NK=(2,3,4,6,8,12,16,18)

STEP2:   Set $T_0 = a$
         $W_0 = \alpha$
         $h = h_{max}$

STEP3:   For i=1(1)7
             For j=1(1)i
             $Q_{i,j} = (NK_{i+1}/NK_j)^2$ $(Q_{ij} = h_j^2/h_{i+1}^2)$

STEP4:   While ($T_0 < b$) do

         STEP5:   K=1
                  FLAG=0   (Boolean accuracy test)

         STEP6:   While (K$\leq$P AND FLAG=0) do

             STEP7:   HK=h/NK$_k$
                      $T = t_0$
                      $w_2 = w_0$
                      $w_3 = w_2 + HK*f(T,w_2)$ (Euler step)
                      $T = t_0 + HK$

             STEP8:   For j=1(1)NK-1
                      $w_1 = w_2$
                      $w_2 = w_3$
                      $w_3 = w_1 + 2*HK*f(T,w_2)$
                      $T = T_0 + (j+1)*HK$ (mid-point method)

             STEP9: $y_k = [w_3 + w_2 + HK*f(T,w_3)]/2$
                      (smooth for $y_{k,1}$)

             STEP10: If K$\geq$2 then
                 STEP11: j=k
                          $v = y_1$ (save y_{k-1} η_{k-1})
                 STEP12: While (j$\geq$2) do

                          $y_{j-1} = y_j + \dfrac{y_j - y_{j-1}}{Q_{k-1,j-1} - 1}$ (extrapolation) $y_{k,k-j+2}$

                          j=j-1

                 STEP13: If $|y_1 - v| \leq$ TOL then FLAG=1
                          (accept y_1 as new w)

             STEP14: K=K+1

         STEP15: K=K-1
         STEP16: If FLAG=0 then

$$h=h/2 \qquad \text{(w rejected, decrease h)}$$

If $h<h_{min}$ then OUTPUT 'minimum h exceeded fail'

STOP

ELSE

$w_0 = y_1$

$T_0 = T_0 + h$

OUTPUT (t_0, w_0, h)

If $(k \leqslant 3)$ and $(h < h_{max}/2)$ then $h=2h$

(increase h if possible)

STEP17:   STOP

Now STEP3, provides the next matrix link, the general version of (1.5), can be simplified to give the form in STEP12, with $Q_{k-1,j-1}$ the ratio of the two step sizes squared. STEP3 defines a constant matrix for the algorithm of dimension p*p of the form,

$$Q = \begin{bmatrix} Q_{11} \\ Q_{21} \\ \vdots \\ \vdots \\ Q_{P,1} \quad - - - - - \quad Q_{PP} \end{bmatrix} \qquad (1.7)$$

Now define E_p as the extrapolation operator, then the extrapolation table is given by,

$$Q(E_p)y_1 = Y , \qquad (1.8)$$

$$y_1 = (y_{1,1}, y_{2,1}, \ldots, y_{P,1})^t ,$$

e.g.

$$(Q_{11}, \ldots, 0) \begin{bmatrix} y_{11} \\ y_{21} \\ \vdots \\ \vdots \\ y_{p1} \end{bmatrix} = \begin{bmatrix} y'_{11} \\ y_{21} \\ \vdots \\ \vdots \\ y_{p1} \end{bmatrix} \quad \text{or} \quad y'_{11} = \frac{h_0^2 y_{21} - h_1^2 y_{11}}{h_0^2 - h_1^2} = y_{21} + \frac{y_{21} - y_{11}}{Q_{11} - 1}$$

and

$$(Q_{21}, Q_{22}, \ldots, 0) \begin{bmatrix} y'_{11} \\ y_{21} \\ \vdots \\ \vdots \\ y_{p1} \end{bmatrix} = \begin{bmatrix} y''_{11} \\ y'_{21} \\ \vdots \\ \vdots \\ y_{p1} \end{bmatrix} \quad \text{or} \quad y'_{21} = y_{31} + \frac{y_{31} - y_{21}}{Q_{22} - 1} \quad \text{and}$$

$$y''_{11} = y'_{21} + \frac{y'_{21} - y'_{11}}{Q_{21} - 1}$$

... etc.

This can be interpreted as a matrix vector type computation

$$Q_1 y_1^{(1)} = y_1^{(2)} , \quad Q_2 y_1^{(2)} = y_1^{(3)} , \ldots, Q_p y_1^{(p)} = y_1^{(p+1)} , \qquad (1.9)$$

with Q_i=row i of Q.

$$y_1^{(1)} = y_1, \quad y_1^{(2)} = (y'_{11} y_{21}, \ldots, y_{p1})^t, \quad y_1^{(3)} = (y''_{11}, y'_{21}, \ldots, y_{p1})$$

$$(2.0)$$

In the derivation of equations (1.9) and (2.0) we have used only the operations used in setting up the extrapolation table, and not on relating the stepsize in the equation (1.5). Thus, we have a generic recurrence structure, where E_p is the extrapolation formula used and Q calculates the multiplicative factors relating the estimates together. The recurrence structure leads to the array in Figure 1.

Now taking the p step levels $h_0, h_1, \ldots, h_{p-1}$ such that,

$$h_1 = \frac{h_0}{2} \, , \; h_2 = \frac{h_0}{4} \, , \; h_3 = \frac{h_0}{8} \, , \; \ldots \, , \; h_{p-1} = \frac{h_0}{2^{p-1}}$$

then Q becomes,

$$Q = \begin{bmatrix} (2)^2 & & & & & \\ (4)^2 & & & & \bigcirc & \\ | & & & & & \\ | & & & & & \\ 2^{2(P-2)} & & & & & \\ 2^{2(P-1)} & 2^{2(P-2)} & - & - & - & (4)^2 & (2)^2 \end{bmatrix} \qquad (2.1)$$

The array in Fig. 1 can now be simplified to give Fig. 2a, where the multipliers are preloaded into the cells before the computation starts and must be calculated by the host machine. To save preloading and host computation of the $Q_{i,j}$ factors we can feed them systolically around the cells, computing the 'factors on the fly' and augmenting the cells with extra hardware to form the power required by the next cell. The number of cells is reduced to $m = \lceil p/c \rceil$ and by using two-level pipelining it is possible to input a value to each cell every cycle even though the latency of the cells is c. This produces the systolic ring Fig. 2b, after mc cycles the last (mth cell) outputs a value and the first cell reads in $y_{p,1}$. (Evans & Megson, [1]).

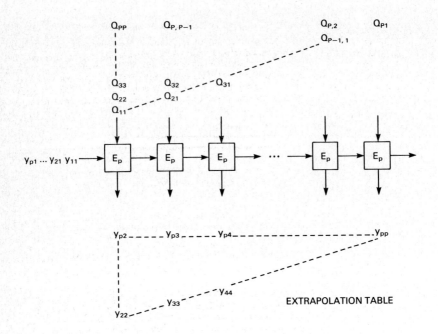

Ep ≡ extrapolation cell, computes extrapolation procedure

Time unit = latency (cost of) extrapolation computation
for cell

Total time = $(P - 1)\,C$

P = number of step levels

C = latency of Ep cells

FIGURE 1: Generic Extrapolation Array

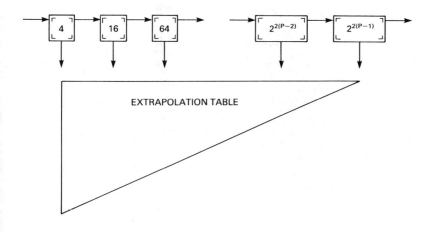

FIGURE 2a: Extrapolation Array for $h_0, h_1 = \dfrac{h_0}{2}$, $h_2 = \dfrac{h_0}{4}$ ...

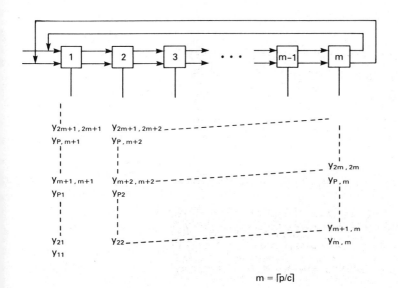

$$m = \lceil p/c \rceil$$

FIGURE 2b: Systolic Ring Computation of Extrapolation Table

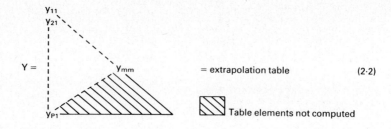

Thus, the systolic ring now overlaps the computation of the remaining elements, with cell 1 starting the systolic construction of the extrapolation table from $y_{m+1,m+1}$ using the values from the mth cell $y_{m,m}, y_{m+1,m}, \ldots, y_{P,m}$, this is repeated on successive cycles.

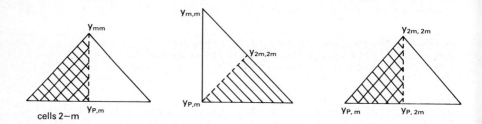

Cycles in Systolic Ring

In [1] a very efficient layout was achieved for the Romberg integration algorithms and it can now be seen that this array can be easily derived from arrays presented here. In [1] we assumed that only the diagonal table entries were required (as they are the ones used to decide convergence). Fig. 2b can also be made into an efficient layout if the output links are made into fanin links and only diagonal values are read in by the host. Thus, we can always produce an array with O(p) E_p-cell area, where p=size of table, as we need only p cells, and with a systolic ring m cells. If the latency c of each cell is equivalent to the number of ips equivalent elements used to implement it then the systolic ring requires area proportional to O(p) ips cells.

EP CELLS

The overall structure of an extrapolation array has been given and for different extrapolation procedures, the EP cell changes complexity. In [1] the cell was defined for the Romberg integration algorithm using the Richardson's extrapolation procedure. For the algorithm presented above we define our EP cell to compute Step 12 while loop body. The E_p cell is given as,

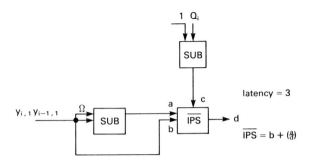

FIGURE 3: The EP Cell

Thus, c=3 and counting sub-cells as equivalent to $\overline{IPS}$ the systolic ring requires O(P) $\overline{IPS}$ area.
Computation time of array T=3(P-1).

We have seen earlier that the extrapolation is easily performed on a systolic array with EP cells for performing Gragg's algorithm and the Bulirsch & Stoer procedure [4] is given by Evans and Megson [7]. Fig. 4 shows the generic extrapolation array amended for the Bulirsch and Stoer scheme. · Note the two horizontal channels between cells. However, recalling the points (i) and (ii) from the introduction, we notice the restrictions on the use of the systolic arrays on ODE's. The evaluation of the starting values in both schemes, using the different step levels, ensures that the computation of next level starting value is:

a)   dependent upon the arbitrary complexity of the function f(t,y)

b)   the number of additional f(t,y) evaluations to complete the difference approximation at that level.

True systolic movement overall the algorithm could be achieved if the following two constraints are observed:

a)   All the Q_{ij} were pre-calculated at the start of the algorithm, up to and including the deepest step level.

b)   The cost of successive level starting values could be computed in the interval between inputs to the systolic array (i.e. the periodicity).

Clearly, these conditions cannot be satisfied except under contrived situations, for instance with trivial ODE functions and a very small number of levels. All the Q_{ij} can be precomputed as can be trivially observed from the algorithm above. However if we consider an arbitrary ODE function, the periodicity of the array is equivalent to the cycle time of one IPS cell = (mult time + add time), which is the periodicity of the array. Clearly our ODE function must be computable within this time period, if not we must precompute all the starting values then pump them into the array.

If the ODE function is simple enough to be computed within the periodicity time, successive lower levels will require more and more function evaluations and ultimately the number of function evaluations to compute the next starting

STEPSIZE MULTIPLIERS

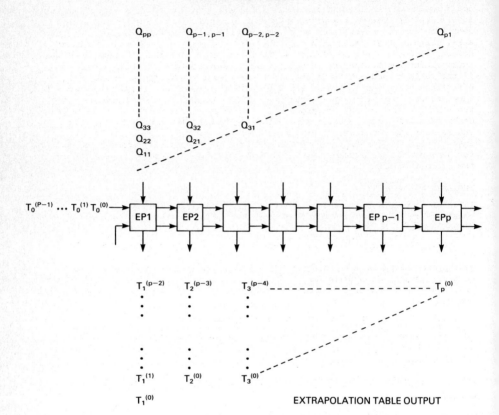

EXTRAPOLATION TABLE OUTPUT

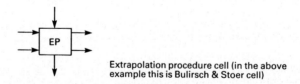

Extrapolation procedure cell (in the above
example this is Bulirsch & Stoer cell)

FIGURE 4: General Structure of Systolic Array to generate the Bulirsch
         & Stoer Extrapolation Table

value will require a time greater than the periodicity, and the array would
not function correctly. As a result of the arbitrary function and the changing
levels, we are forced to evaluate the starting values before using the array,
resulting in the construction of a finite table of predetermined size. If the
array contains P EP cells then any table of size p'<p can also be constructed.
However we do not know how large the table has to be for the convergence of the
extrapolated result, and so we would have to precompute p starting values even
if the table turned out to be only of level size p'. Clearly we would gain
efficiency as on the next point in the overall interval one could construct a
table of size p' with only p' starting values. A problem occurs however, if on
the next interval point, convergence is not obtained for the table of size p'.
Other than producing more starting values and re-constructing a larger table
and re-running, the array p' cannot be improved. Murphy & Evans [5] has
investigated the construction of a more flexible table construction algorithm
for a sequential algorithm. Later we show that these ideas can be adopted in
the systolic design.

IMPLEMENTATION DETAILS

In order to understand how the flexibility in [5] can be utilised we must
consider how the array will be implemented. The step levels can be considered
as sequences

$$\{h_0, h_0/2, h_0/4, h_0/8, \ldots, h_0/2^{p-1}\} \text{ or } \{h_0, h_0/2, h_0/3, h_0/4, h_0/6, h_0/8 \ldots\}$$

We suppose that p is the number of EP cells on a chip, then we have to provide
vertical inputs and outputs for the Q_{ij} and table outputs. However this is not
practical due to the high pin count. However precomputing the Q_{ij} and control
the chip as:

(i)   Load Q_{ij} into the chip (using chip storage)

(ii) Compute the table using the array (using chip storage to hold the
      table)

(iii) Output the tableau.

This clearly requires extra storage and control in addition to the systolic
array.

Fig. 5a shows a possible arrangement for the chip using the systolic array
connections to preload the Q_{ij} input to the chip memory. The memory is also
shown in Fig. 5b with the control signals required. The feedback loops are
added to allow the Q_{ij} to circulate once they are loaded. Thus, the array can
be used for successive points over the interval h=h_0, without having to preload
Q_{ij} for every table. Notice that the table has the same structure as the Q_{ij}
and so the same method can be used for reading out the table at the end of
computation, too.

Clearly, we should try to make p small to fit the design on a single chip, and
to ensure that latch mistimings, etc., cannot occur with the feedback
connection [6].

ADAPTIVE SYSTOLIC EXTRAPOLATION ARRAY

The adaptive systolic array attempts to reduce the number of function evaluations needed to compute the starting values required, so that a convergent
table can be constructed. We noted earlier that all the function values for a
certain sized table must be computed before the array is used, changing to a
larger table while it is being computed using the current array is not possible.
Also, a prediction of a smaller table would mean that some starting values were
calculated and not used. For choice of a large table this is wasteful. We
describe now how to implement the flexibility of the algorithm in Murphy & Evans

a)

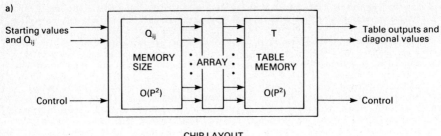

Starting values
and Q_{ij} → →

| | Q_{ij} | | | T | | Table outputs and |
| | MEMORY SIZE | ARRAY | | TABLE MEMORY | | diagonal values |

Control →   → Control

CHIP LAYOUT

b)

Loading Q_{ij} with simple shifts

```
 •    •    •    •    Q₁₁  •    •    •       Q₂₁  •    •    •
 •    •    •    •     •    •    •            Q₁₁  •    •
 •    •    •          •    •                 •    •
 •                    •                      •
                    Input                  Shift down and input
Q₂₂  Q₂₁  •    •    Q₃₁  •    •    •       Q₃₂  Q₃₁  •    •
Q₁₁  •    •         Q₂₂  Q₂₁  •            Q₂₂  Q₂₁  •
 •    •             Q₁₁  •                 Q₁₁  •
 •                   •
Shift left          Shift down and input   Shift left
Q₃₃  Q₃₂  Q₃₁  •   Q₄₁  •    •    •       Q₄₂  Q₄₁  •    •
Q₂₂  Q₂₁  •         Q₃₃  Q₃₂  Q₃₁          Q₃₃  Q₃₂  Q₃₁  etc.
Q₁₁  •             Q₂₂  Q₂₁                Q₂₂  Q₂₁
 •                 Q₁₁                     Q₁₁
Shift left          Shift down and input   Shift left
```

c)   Memory structure

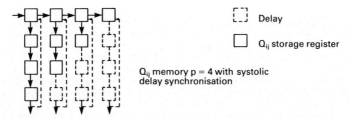

⌐ ⌐ Delay
∟_⌐

▢ Q_{ij} storage register

Q_{ij} memory p = 4 with systolic
delay synchronisation

Control		Action	
0	0	Shift down	Load Q_{ij}
0	1	Shift right	
1	0	Shift left	
1	1	Shift up	Read T

FIGURE 5

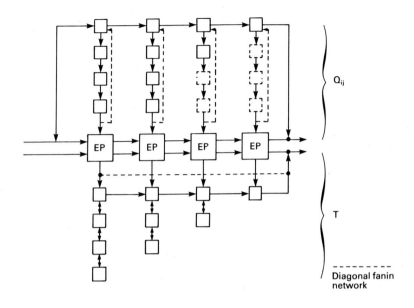

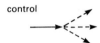

FIGURE 6: Internal Memory Extrapolation Array

[5], to produce what we shall call the 'adaptive array'. The array is based on
the idea of the systolic priority queue for keeping real time order statistics
such as max, min, see [6]. The idea is that the host inputs values to the array
at intermittent intervals, with the array having no knowledge of when the next
input will arrive. On the cycles between inputs, the cells of the systolic
array continue to compute the remaining order of the list, with the max or min
value always remaining in the host array interface cell. We suggest a
modified form of an array like the priority queue for this. The extrapolation
array performs no computation between inputs delays by a significant time. We
define two measures of time, array time and host time. If we compute p'
starting values we can compute a table of size p' and array time identical to
host time. Now if we compute $p''<p'$ starting values we can compute the table
of size p''. Then if we realise that the table will not be big enough to
satisfy convergence to a certain accuracy, then before all the p'' inputs have
entered the array, we can freeze the array, compute the remaining $p'-p''$
starting values and start up the array continuing as normal. Now we have
enough values to compute the table of size p'. The array total time $= 3(p'-1)$
while the host time = (array time) + (freeze time). Essentially the systolic
array is insensitive to the time elapsed by the host to compute extra starting
values (i.e. while it is frozen). Assuming that all the registers in the cells
and memory of the chip described allow a value to be stored indefinitely, the
freeze command can be achieved simply by gating the array clock signal with a

convergence condition (which signifies more values are required). Normally, the practice of gating the clock signal is bad practice, but as it is gated only once before it restarts the rest of the array it will have a global effect and can be accepted.

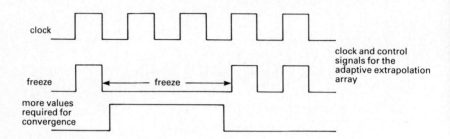

clock and control signals for the adaptive extrapolation array

FIGURE 7: Clock and control signals for the adaptive extrapolation array

Since $\overline{\text{FREEZE}}$ = (CLOCK) and (CONVERGENCE), convergence can be computed using Murphy & Evans [5], which defines whether in the table the diagonal values are smoothly converging or not. The fact that we output diagonal results while also constructing the table can be used by the host to decide convergence criteria and:

(i)   The detection of smooth convergence which by decreasing errors can decide:

   a)   whether to abandon the table because it is not converging

   b)   that the array will converge using only the already computed starting values

   c)   the size of the table required to provide convergence using extra starting values

(ii) If (i) provides an incorrect prediction to the convergence we decide:

   a)   whether to change the stepsize h_0 (increase or decrease)

   b)   to re-run the array with the same stepsize, but with more starting values.

(iii) Whether to close down the array because convergence has already been achieved with a table smaller than p' (=no. of starting values).

(iv) Raise an exception that no more cells can be used as the maximum number in the array are already in use, i.e. no more starting values can be included.

It should be noted that the freeze command will allow the larger tables to be constructed, and that the original array allowed any table smaller than the available starting values to be constructed. This leaves only (iia) to be described, clearly if the stepsize is altered the Q_{ij} must be recalculated and loaded into the chip again, which of course requires that the array be closed down and re-started.

Clearly for large tables the results can be constructed by alternating the freeze/computation phases, so that we compute the minimum number of starting values and do not waste function evaluations to fit the restrictions of the non-adaptive array. A final warning to the practicality of the adaptive array is given as follows, we must be able to collect enough diagonal estimations to perform a prediction.

A way to reduce the throughput of the array is to build a cell without two-level pipelining (then two inputs would be required for each diagonal element). This was avoided previously as the cost of the overall computation is increased due to reduced throughput.

REFERENCES

[1]   D.J. Evans & G.M. Megson, "Romberg Integration Using Systolic Arrays", Parallel Computing, Vol.3, 1986.

[2]   G.P. McKeown, "Iterated Interpolation Using Systolic Arrays", UEA Norwich, Internal Report CSA/21/1984.

[3]   Burden, Fiares and Reynolds, "Numerical Analysis 2nd Ed.", Prindle, Weber and Schmidt, 1978.

[4]   R. Bulirsch & J. Stoer, "Numerical Treatment of Ordinary Differential Equations by Extrapolation Methods", Numerische Mathematik 8, 1-13 (1966).

[5]   C.P. Murphy and D.J. Evans, "A Flexible Variable Order Extrapolation Technique for Solving Non-Stiff Ordinary Differential Equations", Int.J. Comp.Math. 10 (1981), pp.63-75.

[6]   C.E. Leiserson, "Area-Efficient VLSI Computation", Ph.D. Thesis, Carnegie Mellon University, Oct. 1981.

[7]   D.J. Evans & G.M. Megson, "Construction of Extrapolation Tables by Systolic Arrays for Solving Ordinary Differential Equations", Parallel Computing, Vol.3, 1986.

[8]   D.J. Evans, "Linear Systolic Array for Romberg Integration", in Highly Parallel Computers for Numerical and Signal Processing Applications IFIPS Conference, Nice (1986).

HIGHLY PARALLEL COMPUTERS
G.L. Reijns, M.H. Barton (editors)
Elsevier Science Publishers B.V. (North-Holland)
©IFIP, 1987

THE UTILISATION OF BIT LEVEL
SYSTOLIC ARRAYS IN WORD LEVEL SYSTEMS

Dr J V McCanny

Department of Electrical and Electronic Engineering
The Queen's University
Belfast   BT9 5AH
N Ireland

ABSTRACT
Bit level systolic array structures for computing
sums of products are studied in detail. It is shown
that these can be sub-divided into two classes and
that, within each class, architectures can be
described in terms of a set of constraint equations.
It is further demonstrated that high performance
system level functions with attractive VLSI
properties can be constructed by matching data flow
geometries in bit level and word level architectures.

1   INTRODUCTION

Considerable advances have been made in recent years in the
development of algorithms and architectures which can exploit the
potential computational power of VLSI. One area where progress has
been rapid has been in the field of digital signal processing,
reflecting the fact that typical operations tend to be highly
structured and involve matrix type computations. An important
contribution to this area has been the emergence of systolic arrays.
Architectures of this type have now been developed for a number of
important real time computations, such as the solution of linear
systems of equations and least squares minimisation, and hardware
systems based on these ideas have been implemented in a number of
laboratories (1). The systolic approach can also be exploited at the
bit level in the design of high performance VLSI chips and two such
chips have now been successfully produced as a result of a
collaborative research programme in the UK involving RSRE and the GEC
Hirst Research Centre (2,3).

Given the success of the word and the bit level systolic array
approaches to system and chip level design respectively, the question
arises as to how one might marry the two techniques. The motivation
here is to have system level systolic arrays constructed form chips
which are themselves systolic arrays at the bit level. The purpose of
this paper is to examine how this can be achieved for functions which
are suited to bit level implementation, namely those involving sums of
products. For the purposes of illustration we will concentrate most
of our attention on matrix multiplication. However, as is discussed
later, the ideas which emerge are directly applicable to other
functions.

The first half of the paper concentrates on bit level systolic arrays
for computing sums of products and shows how these can be described
using a systematic design approach. The second half of the paper
describes how these architectures can be exploited in various word
level systolic arrays, and a number of examples are given.

2   COMPUTATION OF INNER PRODUCTS AT BIT LEVEL

2.1   Alternative approaches

The inner product of two vectors $a = \{a_k\}$ and $b = \{b_k\}$ ($k = 0,1...$ $N - 1$) is defined as

$$C = \sum_{k=0}^{N-1} a_k \, b_k \qquad (1)$$

If $a_k = a_{kq}$ ($q = 0..m - 1$) and $b_k = b_{kr}$ ($r = 0...n - 1$) are m and n bit binary words, respectively, then the pth bit of the result, C_p, ($0 \le p \le m+n-2$) can be written as

$$C_p = 2^p \sum_{k=0}^{N-1} \sum_{q=0}^{m-1} a_{kq} \, b_{kp-q} + \text{carries} \qquad (2)$$

It follows from equation (2) that there are two approaches which can be adopted for deriving bit level systolic arrays for computing inner products. As will be shown, these correspond to two different classes of architecture. One can derive circuits in which the summation over q is performed first followed by the summation k. This corresponds to the pipelined multiplication and accumulation of words a_k and b_k. Alternatively, one can design arrays in which partial products of the form $a_{kq} b_{kp-q}$ are first formed by summing over k and all partial products of the same significance are then accumulated by summing over q. The latter approach is one which we have adopted in a number of systolic circuits (3,4). Within each class of architecture many bit level systolic designs can be generated, including ones with bit parallel and bit serial data organisations. However, as will be discussed in section 2.3 and 2.4 these are closely interrelated and can be derived using a systematic design approach. We shall first examine pipelined multiplier circuits before considering arrays which involve the summing of equivalent partial products.

2.2   Pipelined multipliers

The pth bit, c_{kp}, of the product of two binary words a_k and b_k can be represented using the recurrence

$$c_{kp}^q = c_{kp}^{q-1} + 2^p a_{kq} \, b_{kp-q} + \text{carries} \; (0 \le p \le m+n-2) \qquad (3)$$

where $c_{kp}^o = 0$. If we assume that this computation is to be carried out on a systolic array of bit level processors and that any carries generated can be added simply to bits of higher significance (as is usually the case) then equation (3) states that in such a circuit the bits of the word a_k must be convolved with the bits of the word b_k to form bits in the product word c_k. To achieve this, the relative movement of the two bit streams must be co-linear so that all the bits in a_k interact with all the bits in b_k. The motion of a bit c_{kp} must be such that, having accumulated the partial product $a_{kq-1} b_{kp-q-1}$ on the q-1 th stage of the computation it must move to encounter the partial product $a_{kq} b_{kp-q}$ on the qth stage. This puts fundamental constraints on systolic architectures which one can derive for pipelined multiplication.

In a recent paper Li and Wah (5) have described a formal design
technique for deriving systolic array architectures. They have
shown that for a given computation one can write down a set of
vector constraint equations which must be satisfied in any
functionally correct design. These particular equations relate
periods of computation, times of data access, data distribution and
data velocities. If we define the velocities of data bits in
equation (3) to be $\underline{a}_v$, $\underline{b}_v$ and $\underline{c}_v$ respectively and define $\underline{a}_{qs}$
and $\underline{a}_{ks}$ as the directional displacements between bits a_{kq} and
a_{kq+1} and between a_{kq} and a_{k+1q} respectively (with similar
definitions for $\underline{b}_{qs}$, $\underline{c}_{ps}$, $\underline{b}_{ks}$ and $\underline{c}_{ks}$) then following the
approach referred to (5) one can derive the following constraint
equations which describe all systolic for pipelined multipliers (6).

$$t_{qa} \, \underline{a}_v + \underline{a}_{qs} = t_{qa} \, \underline{c}_v$$

$$t_{qb} \, \underline{b}_v + \underline{b}_{qs} = t_{qb} \, \underline{c}_v$$

$$t_p \, \underline{b}_v + \underline{b}_{ps} = t_p \, \underline{c}_v + \underline{c}_{ps} = t_p \, \underline{a}_v$$

$$(4)$$

$$t_k \, \underline{a}_v + \underline{a}_{ks} = t_k \, \underline{b}_v + \underline{b}_{ks} = t_k \, \underline{c}_v + \underline{c}_{ks} = 0$$

subject to $t_{qa} = -t_{qb}$ and $|t_{qa}| = |t_{qb}| = t_q$

In the above t_{qa} and t_{qb} represent times between accessing a_{kq}
and a_{kq+1} and b_{kq} and b_{kq+1} respectively. The time between

computing c_{kp}^q and c_{kp+1}^q is represented by t_p whilst the time

between computing c_{kp}^q and c_{kp}^{q+1} is represented by t_q. Since
the a and b bits required at successive computations must be
accessed on each time slot t_q it follows that $|t_{qa}| = |t_{qb}| =$
t_q. However, the bits a_{kq} and b_{kp-q} are accessed in opposite
order (one in ascending the other in descending order). Hence the
additional constraint that $t_{qa} = -t_{qb}$ has been added to the
equations given above.

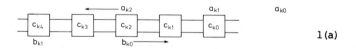

1(a)

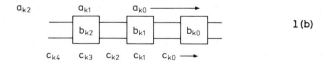

1(b)

Figure 1   Examples of bit serial multipliers

The equations given in (4) apply to both serial and bit parallel
systolic multipliers. The reasons for this are as follows. The
data interactions required for both types of multiplier are
identical in that the relative movement of data bits representing
a_k and b_k must be co-linear. Whilst this is readily achieved on
a linear array with a bit serial organisation, it can also be
achieved by adding identical components of velocity perpendicular to
two serial interacting streams. This is what happens in a two
dimensional multiplier with parallel input data. The input of new
words a_k and b_k to such a structure in a pipelined fashion,
whether every n cycles in a bit serial array or every cycle in a
bit parallel array, is taken care of by the fourth of the above set
of equations. The remaining three relate data velocities, data
distributions and access times.

Some examples of systolic structures which comply with the equations
given in (4) are shown in figure 1 (bit serial arrays) and figure 2
(bit parallel arrays). In both cases the processing elements shown
are assumed to represent gated full adders. In the circuit in
figure 2(a) the bits representing a_k and b_k move in opposite
directions whilst the results are formed on fixed sites. In figure
1(b) the bits representing b_k remain fixed whilst the bits a_{kq}
and c_{kp} move from left to right, with the latter moving at half
the speed of the former. This particular architecture forms the
basis of the circuit proposed by Lyon (7).

The parallel multiplier shown in figure 2(a) is the one proposed by
McCanny and McWhirter (8). It is interesting to observe that the
data flow in this structure is identical to that in figure 1(a)
except that a vertical velocity has been added to all data streams.
An alternative bit parallel multiplier (9) is shown in figure 2(b)
and again this can be described in terms of co-linear interacting
data streams. The main difference between this and figure 2(a) is
that both the words a_k and b_k enter least significant bit first
whereas in figure 1(a) one enters least significant bit first and
the other most significant bit first.

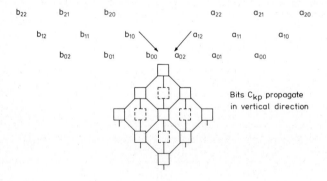

Figure 2a

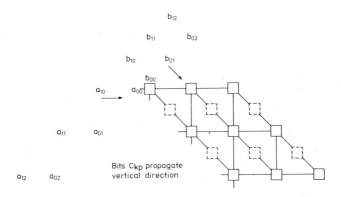

Figure 2b

Figures 2a & b   Examples of bit paralell multipliers

2.3   Circuits for summing equivalent partial products

The alternative approach to computing inner products (equation (2))
is to keep p and q constant and to sum over k. As a result, one
must derive architectures for computing the recurrence

$$C_{q\,p-q}^{k} = C_{q\,p-q}^{k-1} + 2^{p}\,a_{kq}\,b_{kp-q} + \text{carries} \qquad (5)$$

where $C_{q,\,p-q}$ is the sum over k of all partial products
involving bits a_{kq} and b_{kp-q} amd where $C_{q\,p-q} = 0$. The main
difference in circuits based on this approach and those based on
section 2.2 lies in the movement of accumulating partial products
$C_{q\,p-q}$. It follows from equation (5) that on successive
computation steps $C_{q,\,p-q}$ must move so that it encounters partial
products of the form $a_{k-1q}\,b_{k-1p-q}$, $a_{kq}\,b_{kp-q}$ etc. As a
result, the constraint equations which apply to circuits based on
equation (5) differ in some respects from those given by equation (4).
As is shown in detail elsewhere (6), these take the form

$$t_{ka}\,\underline{a}_{v} + \underline{a}_{qs} = t_{ka}\,\underline{c}_{v}$$

$$t_{kb}\,\underline{b}_{v} + \underline{b}_{ks} = t_{kb}\,\underline{c}_{v}$$

$$t_{q}\,\underline{a}_{v} + \underline{a}_{qs} = t_{q}\,\underline{c}_{v} + \underline{c}_{qs} = t_{q}\underline{b}_{v} \qquad (6)$$

$$t_{p}\,\underline{b}_{v} + \underline{b}_{ps} = t_{p}\,\underline{c}_{v} + \underline{c}_{ps} = t_{p}\underline{a}_{v}$$

In this case bits in a_{k} and b_{k} can be accessed in either order.
Hence the only timing constraint which need apply is
$t_{k} = |t_{ka}| = |t_{kb}|$.

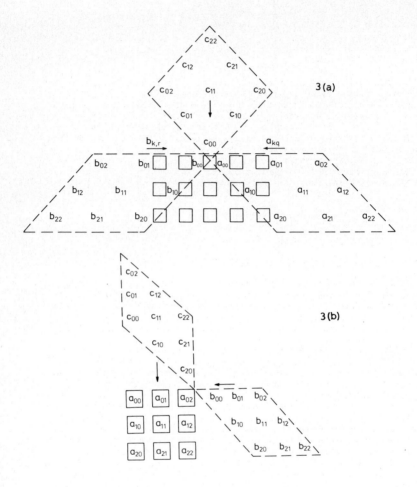

Figure 3   Examples of bit level arrays for
inner product computation

Figure 3 shows two circuits which satisfy these equations. Figure
3(a) is one which we have used in a number of circuits (3,4) and
consists of two sets of contraflowing bit serial streams a_k and
b_k moving across an orthogonal array. Figure 3(b) is derived form
Urqhart and Wood (10) and is quite similar except that one set of
data bits remain on fixed sites. In both arrays the movement of one
set of bits across the other results in the formation of
"interaction regions" of accumulating partial products of the form
C_{qp-q} which propagate down through the array. Final results are
then formed using a separate accumulator array at the bottom of
these circuits (not shown).

Space does not permit us to describe bit parallel structures in any
detail. However, simple examples can be generated by adding
identical vertical components of velocity to all data streams in
figures 3(a) and 3(b).

It should be noted that in common with the circuits described in
section 2.2 the above represent only a few examples of circuits
which can be used for computing inner products. Many other useful
architectures can be generated and as will be discussed in the
following sections the choice of a particular architecture is
heavily dependent on the word or system level problem for which it
is required. It should also be pointed out that the circuits
described represent "base architectures" rather that detailed
designs, in that they omit carry bits and means for handling
negative numbers. However, techniques for handling these are well
established and require no further elaboration here.

3   UTILISATION OF BIT LEVEL STRUCTURES IN WORD LEVEL ARRAYS

3.1   Application to matrix multiplication

We now turn our attention to word level systolic arrays and examine
how the circuits described in section 2 can be utilised either as
building blocks or as processing elements in such circuits. The
main motivations for this are to achieve
      (a)   the high throughput rates which are attainable at the bit
            level and
      (b)   modularity and regularity at all levels within the circuit.

Both of these attributes are highly desirable from the point of view
of VLSI design. Typical functions which are well suited to
implementation using bit level arrays include matrix multiplication,
matrix vector transforms, convolution, correlation and polynomial
multiplication. A wide number of word level systolic arrays have
been proposed for these operations but these are subject to the same
type of constraints discussed in section 2 (5). Typical systolic
structures for matrix multiplication are illustrated figure 4. The
circuit in figure 4(a) is for full matrices and here the elements of
one matrix are associated with fixed processor sites. The second
circuit (figure 4(b)) is best suited to the multiplicaton of banded
matrices (11).

Figure 4a

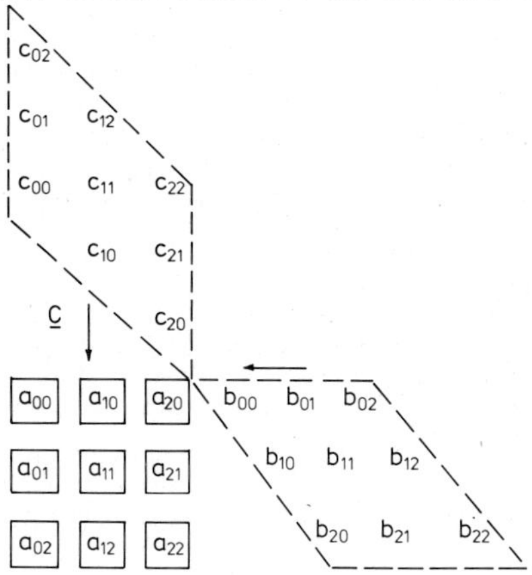

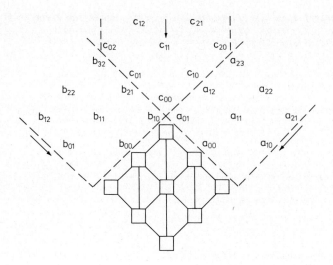

Figure 4b

Figures 4a & b   Examples of matrix x matrix multipliers

The above examples exhibit well defined data interactions. These
circuits can only be efficiently mapped on to bit level arrays
providing the timing of data interactions is correctly maintained
and providing the geometries of data flow at both the word level and
bit level are compatible. In a recent paper Kung and Lam (12) have
studied "two level" pipelining in systolic arrays and have made a
number of observations which are directly relevant here. Firstly,
they have shown that in a unidirectional linear array one can add
the same number of delays to all edges in a cut through that array
and still obtain a functionally correct design. Secondly, if one
adds delays to any edges in a two dimensional array one will obtain
a functionally equivalent design if the total delay added to all
paths between any two nodes is the same. The importance of these
observations to the work here is that one can insert delays in word
level data flows to introduce pipelining at the bit level. If at
the same time one desires highly regular circuits then this can be
achieved by having similar data flow geometries at both word and bit
level. The problem of mapping a given system level function onto
bit systolic level arrays then becomes one of matching potential
word level architectures with available bit level arrays.

A good example of the marriage of bit level and word level systolic
architectures can be derived from figures 4(a) and 3(b). If one
replaces each column of processors in figure 4(a) with the bit level
circuit in figure 3(b) one will obtain an extremely regular VLSI
array (10). Similar ideas can be applied to figure 3(a) if one uses
a matrix multiplier which has an analogous structure at word level
(4).

An important point which is directly relevant here is that if one
ignores then generation of carry bits then one can interpret the
structures such as figures 3(a) and 3(b) as circuits which multiply

matrices of bits representing the words a_k and b_k. Moreover, the constraints equations which apply to these circuits also apply to word level matrix multipliers (5). This then means that for every word level structure which can be designed for matrix multiplication there exists an equivalent bit level array, thus providing a considerable degree of flexibility in implementing such circuits.

Another example of matching architectures can be derived from figure 4(b) (banded matrix multiplication) and figure 2(a) (pipelined multiplication). One will observe that both arrays are similar. As a result one can replace each processing element in figure 4(b) with the circuit in figure 2(a) to give a circuit with equivalent microscopic and macroscopic features. This assumes that additional delays are included between processors to maintain correct timing.

The pipelined multipliers in figures 2(a) and 2(b) can also be used in the array of figure 4(a) despite apparent differences in data flow. However, as one of the data streams in the word level circuit is fixed, it is only a matter of matching two sets of data streams. This can be achieved with either multiplier. Further details of these and other important implementations will be given in a future publication (6).

3.2 Application to other functions

The design techniques described above can be applied to other functions and we will consider these briefly. Given that the recurrence relation for bit level multipliers closely resembles that for convolution/correlation and polynomial multiplication, it is hardly surprising that there are direct analogues between word level arrays for these functions and those for pipelined multiplication. Good examples are the convolution/correlation designs described by Kung (13). As before, one can implement these circuits using processing elements with an equivalent bit level structure, again with the proviso that an appropriate number of delays are included between elements to ensure correct data synchronisation. By the reverse argument, one can also design highly parallel structures for polynomial multiplication or FIR filtering using a word level architecture based on the multipliers in figure 2, for example. The processing element can then be based on the appropriate multiplier. It is interesting to note that Cappello (14) has recently described a high regular FIR filter structure in which processing elements are constructed from the pipelined multiplier shown in figure 2(a). In this case the word level and bit level architectures used are different but they allow compatible data flows. This is another example of how the techniques described above can be exploited.

4 CONCLUSION

In this paper we have investigated how system level functions can be mapped efficiently onto bit level systolic arrays. For computations involving sums of products we have shown that two classes of bit level architectures exist and that all architectures within each class must comply with a set of design constraint equations. We have then demonstrated that highly regular high performance VLSI structures can be generated matching bit level and word level systolic architectures. The results presented can be used as the basis of a technique for automatically mapping problems on to bit level systolic arrays.

REFERENCES

1   Kung, S.Y. "VLSI Array Processors" IEEE ASSP Magazine July
     1984, pp4-22.

2   Corry, A.G. and Patel, K. "Architecture of a CMOS Correlator"
     Proc. IEEE Symp. on Circuits and Systems 1983, pp522-525.

3   Evans, R.A., McCanny, J.V., McWhirter, J.G., McCabe, A.P.H.,
     Wood, D. and Wood, K.W. "A CMOS Implementation of a Multi-bit
     Convolver Chip" VLSI '83 pp227-235.

4   McCanny, J.V., Wood, K.W., McWhirter, J.G. amd Oliver, C.J.
     "The Relationship between word and bit level Systolic arrays as
     applied to matrix x matrix multiplication" Proc. SPIE Tech.
     Symp. Real Time Sig. Proc. VI, August 1983.

5   Li, G.J. and Wah, B.W. "The Design of Optimal Systolic Arrays"
     IEEE trans. computers, C-34, no 1, 1985 pp66-77.

6   McCanny, J.V. to be published.

7   Lyon, R.F. "Two's Complement Pipeline Multipliers' IEEE trans.
     on Comms. Com-24, 0976, pp418-424.

8   McCanny, J.V. and McWhirter, J.G. "Completely iterative
     pipelined multiplier array suitable for VLSI" IEE Proc. G, vol
     129, pp40-46, 1982.

9   Hoekstra, J. "Systolic Multiplier" Electronics Letts Vol 20 no
     24 pp995-996.

10   Urqhart, R.B. and Wood, D. "Systolic Matrix and Vector
     multiplication methods for Signal Processing" IEE Proc. F, vol
     131, no 6, October 1984, pp623-631.

11   Weiser, U. and Davis, A. "A Wavefront Notation Tool for VLSI
     Array Design" CMU conf. on VLSI Systems and Computations 1981
     pp226-234.

12   Kung, H.T. and Lam., M. "Fault Tolerance and Two Level
     Pipelining in VLSI Systolic Arrays" MIT conf. on Advanced
     Research in VLSI, January 1984, pp74-83.

13   Kung, H.T. "Why Systolic Architectures" Computer January 1982,
     pp37-46.

14   Capello, P. "Towards an FIR filter tissue" Proc. ICASSP '85
     pp276-279.

HIGHLY PARALLEL COMPUTERS
G.L. Reijns, M.H. Barton (editors)
Elsevier Science Publishers B.V. (North-Holland)
©*IFIP, 1987*

MIMD MACHINES AND SPARSE LINEAR EQUATIONS

Frans J. Peters

Philips, Corp. CAD Centre
5600 MD Eindhoven, Netherlands

There exist problems not well suited for vector
processors that may be solved efficiently on MIMD
computers. The direct solution of sparse linear
equations is such a problem that is difficult to
vectorize. By combining the techniques of
- nested dissection,
- parallel pivoting of sparse matrices
- parallel solution of dense sets of linear equations
it is possible to obtain for the solution of this
problem with MIMD computers an efficiency of close to
100%.

INTRODUCTION

Supercomputers of to-day are of the vector processing type. They are most
efficiently used if the problem to be solved can be phrased in terms of
operations on long vectors. There exist problems not well suited for vector
processors. The direct solution of sparse linear equations is such a
problem. It is difficult to vectorize; [Duff undated] reported on
experiments yielding speeds of 10 - 20 MFLOPS on a machine which achieves
150 MFLOPS for ordinary matrix multiplication. That is to say the machine
then is used with an efficiency of 7 - 14 % only. We will show that an
MIMD multiprocessor is more suited to solve sparse sets of linear equations.

As far as direct solution of sparse sets of linear equations is concerned
two types of parallelism may be distinguished [Peters 1985]: parallelism
resulting from the sparseness of the equations and parallelism inherent in
the computation of vector products. Both types of parallelism can be
exploited. By combining the techniques of
- nested dissection [George and Liu 1978],
- parallel pivoting of sparse matrices [Peters 1984]
- parallel solution of dense sets of linear equations [O'Leary and Stewart
  1985]
it is possible to obtain for the solution of this problem with MIMD
computers an efficiency of close to 100%. Here we define the efficiency E
in the usual way:

$$E = \frac{T1}{Tp * p}$$

where T1 is the execution time on a single processor and Tp the execution time (inclusive of communication overhead) on a system consisting of p processors.

In papers dealing with complexity it is not uncommon to assume that multiprocessors contain sufficiently many processors. For large sets of equations that assumption is however not very realistic. We will therefore assume that the number of processors is fixed.

The rest of this paper is organised as follows. In the next section we will present the well known formulae for LU-decomposition. In section 2 parallel pivoting of sparse matrices is discussed and in section 3 results of parallel decomposition of dense matrices are given. In section 4 (the heart of the paper) we discuss parallel nested dissection and show the main result. Finally section 5 contains some concluding remarks.

1. LU-DECOMPOSITION

Consider the set of linear equations

$$Qx = y \tag{1}$$

to be solved by some form of Gaussian elimination or LU-decomposition, i.e. a lower triangular matrix L and an upper triangular matrix U are to be computed such that Q = LU. The solution of (1) can then be obtained by forward substitution, i.e. solving y' from Ly' = y, followed by backward substitution, i.e. solving x from Ux = y'. Let q[i,j], l[i,j] and u[i,j] (1 <= i,j <= n) denote the coefficients of Q, L and U respectively. The following relations hold [Wilkinson 1965]:

$$l[j,j]\, u[j,j] = q[j,j] - \sum_{t=1}^{j-1} l[j,t]\, u[t,j] \qquad (1 <= j <= n)$$

$$l[i,j] = \left(q[i,j] - \sum_{t=1}^{j-1} l[i,t]\, u[t,j] \right) . u[j,j]^{-1}$$
$$(1 <= j < i <= n)$$

$$u[j,i] = l[j,j]^{-1} . \left(q[j,i] - \sum_{t=1}^{j-1} l[j,t]\, u[t,i] \right)$$

The coefficients of L and U must obviously be computed in a certain (partially prescribed) order. To compute for instance l[i,j] (i>=j) the values of l[i,t] and u[t,j] (1<=t<j) must be known.

The computation of L and U may be thought of to be composed of the processing of pivots. If the first k-1 pivots have been processed, then "processing the k-th pivot" denotes the following actions:
   - for k<=i<=n compute l[i,k] and u[k,i] (this step consists only of divide operations and in case of Cholesky decompostion moreover of a square root computation);
   - for k<i,j<=n subtract the products l[i,k] u[k,j] from the partially updated matrix coefficient q[i,j] .
The computation of L and U then consists of the processing of the n pivots of Q.

2. PARALLEL PIVOTING OF SPARSE MATRICES

A matrix is called sparse if many of its coefficients are zero. It is well-known that a sparse matrix usually suffers fill-in, that is to say the matrix L + U contains more nonzeros than Q. It is equally well known that the amount of fill-in depends upon the ordering of rows and columns of Q. Instead of solving (1) one usually selects a permutation matrix to rearrange the equations and variables; that permutation matrix is then chosen so as to minimize fill-in. For details the reader is referred to for instance [Rose and Tarjan 1975] or [George and Liu 1981].

By its very nature it is convenient to view a sparse matrix as a graph [Parter 1961], [Rose 1971]. The use of graph theoretic terminology in the context of sparse matrices has now become customary. All definitions of graph theoretic notions as used in this paper may be found in [Peters 1984]. Here we confine ourselves to point out that the connection graph associated with a sparse matrix represents its zero/nonzero structure, whereas the elimination graph represents the zero/nonzero structure of a matrix from which one or more rows and columns have been deleted during the LU-decomposition (pivots that have been processed are eliminated from the graph).

As mentioned above the order in which the pivots are processed is of importance. Not only the fill-in, but also the numerical stability depends upon the ordering chosen. However, if the matrix is sufficiently sparse then the the prescribed pivot order may be lessened without affecting the fill-in

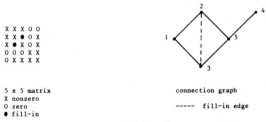

```
X X X O O
X X ● O X
X ● X O X
O O O X X
O X X X X
```

5 x 5 matrix
X nonzero
O zero
● fill-in

connection graph

----- fill-in edge

Figure 1

or the numerical stability. See for instance the connection graph in figure
1. That graph has one fill-in edge. The nodes are numbered according to the
prescribed pivot order. By inspection of the matrix it can be seen that in
order to process pivot 4 none of the values computed by processing pivot 1
are required. Hence, the order of processing pivots 1 and 4 is irrelevant;
they may be processed simultaneously. In order to process pivot 3, results
of processing pivot 1 are required, but because of fill-in results of
processing pivot 2 are needed as well. Hence processing pivot 3 must wait
until the processing of pivots 1 and 2 is finished. It may be proven in
general (see [Peters 1984]) that with parallel processing a pivot may be
processed if it is not connected with pivots of a lower number. Hence, when
pivot 1 is being processed, pivot 4 may be processed as well.

Only if the matrix is sparse some pivots may be processed in parallel. If
all coefficients of the matrix are non-zero then in order to process -say-
pivot j, results of the processing of pivots 1 to j-1 are needed. Hence in a
dense matrix all pivots must be processed strictly sequentially. After
processing the pivots 1 and 4 in the example of figure 1, the elimination
graph as shown in figure 2 remains. It is a complete graph and hence the
remaining pivots have to be processed one after the other.

This often is the case with sparse matrices; after processing a relative few
pivots a dense matrix remains, the pivots of which have to be processed
sequentially. This is precisely the reason why parallel pivoting yields only
modest speed-ups: usually no more than a factor five (no matter how many
processors are available); see [Peters 1985]. Hence we have to take another
approach in order to speed-up sparse LU-decomposition.

With parallel pivoting a pivot may be processed as soon as the following two
requirements are met:
i) a processor is available
ii) the pivot is not connected (in the elimination graph) with pivots of a

Figure 2: elimination graph after processing
pivots 1 and 4 from Figure1

Figure 3.

lower number.
If parallel pivoting is arranged in such a way that requirement ii is met
then parallel processing yields exactly the same fill-in and the same
numerical stability as sequential processing (in the prescribed order). A
rigorous proof may be found in [Peters 1984].

Now consider the matrix Q, such that

$$
Q = \begin{matrix}
Q[1,1] & 0 & 0 & 0 & Q[1,5] \\
0 & Q[2,2] & 0 & 0 & Q[2,5] \\
0 & 0 & Q[3,3] & 0 & Q[3,5] \\
0 & 0 & 0 & Q[4,4] & Q[4,5] \\
Q[5,1] & Q[5,2] & Q[5,3] & Q[5,4] & Q[5,5]
\end{matrix}
$$

where $Q[I,I]$ ($I=1$, ..., 5) are square submatrices. If all submatrices are
considered to be elemental then the associated connection graph is shown in
figure 3. Pivots 1, 2, 3, and 4 may all be processed simultaneously;
processing of pivot 5 however must wait untill the processing of all other
pivots is finished.

More generally, if the submatrices $Q[I,I]$ consist of more than one
element, then all the pivots of $Q[I,I]$ ($I=1,2,3,4$) may be processed
simultaneously with the pivots of $Q[J,J]$ provided that J differs from I and
5. Whether two pivots from $Q[I,I]$ may be processed simultaneously depends
upon the sparseness structure of $Q[I,I]$. If all submatrices are dense then
we may employ at most four processors concurrently and the LU-decomposition
consists of two stages. In the first stage pivots $Q[I,I]$ ($I=1$, ..., 4) are
processed and in the second stage those from $Q[5,5]$. In the first stage at
most four pivots may be processed in parallel, whereas in the second stage
all pivots are processed sequentially.

3. PARALLEL ALGORITHMS FOR DENSE MATRICES

In the preceding section we made the remark that exploitation of the
parallelism due to the sparseness of the equations yields only modest speedup. The processing of a pivot however consists of the computation of a
vector product. Therefore a larger speed-up may be obtained by employing
parallelism to compute vector products or by algorithms to factor dense
matrices in a parallel way.

[O'leary and Stewart 1985] discusses the problem of factoring a dense n x n
matrix on an MIMD network consisting of P processors. It is assumed that the
network is smaller than the number elements in the matrix (i.e. $P < n*n$).
Various ways to assign vertices of the computation graph to the nodes of the
processor network are discussed. Time complexities of the algorithm are

analysed under the assumption that the vertices are scheduled for execution under a round-robin or least-recently-executed regime. Lower bounds are derived for the time it takes to run the algorithm on a linear array of processors and on a square grid of processors respectively.

There are two natural ways to distribute the vertices of the computation graph associated with LU decomposition on the processors of a network. The matrix may be partitioned into blocks and blocks can next be assigned to processors. If the network however is a torus then the matrix coefficients may be wrapped around the torus. In the general case the matrix is partitioned into not too large blocks, and then blocks are wrapped. Although [O'Leary and Stewart 1985] presents formulae for the general case, we will only present results in case the coefficients themselves are wrapped without any blocking. Moreover we will only give the results for a linear array of processors.

Let D be the time it takes to update one matrix element. i.e. to execute a statement of the form:

a := a - an * aw,

then it is shown that a lower bound TD for the time required by the processor of the linear array that takes the longest time equals

$$TD = (n^3 / 3P) D$$

Note that TD is a lower bound, but except for small P that bound is nearly attained by the scheduling algorithm given. TD does not include transmission overhead.

Let R be the additional time required to receive a value coming from another processor and let TR be the time spent by the above mentioned processor receiving values, then the following may be derived

$$TR = (n^2 / 2) R.$$

4. PARALLEL NESTED DISSECTION

In this section we will determine the speed-up that may be achieved if not only parallel pivoting, but also parallel algorithms to factor dense matrices are applied.

Consider the graph Gn, the nodes of which may be thought of as being arranged in a regular grid of n rows and n columns, each node being connected to its four neighbours in the grid. See figure 4 which shows G5. It is well known that for sequential processing the nested dissection ordering of Gn is asymptotically optimal [George 1973]. Nested dissection ordering algorithms are essentially divide and conquer algorithms.

One such algorithm is as follows. Consider S, the 2n-1 nodes that together form a cross such that if they together with their incoming edges are removed, four (nearly) equal subgraphs C1, C2, C3 and C4 remain. Then suppose we number the nodes of Gn so that those in Ci are numbered consecutively (i=1,2,3,4) followed by those in S. Then the associated matrix Q will have the following structure.

$$
Q = \begin{matrix}
Q[1,1] & 0 & 0 & 0 & Q[1,5] \\
0 & Q[2,2] & 0 & 0 & Q[2,5] \\
0 & 0 & Q[3,3] & 0 & Q[3,5] \\
0 & 0 & 0 & Q[4,4] & Q[4,5] \\
Q[5,1] & Q[5,2] & Q[5,3] & Q[5,4] & Q[5,5]
\end{matrix}
$$

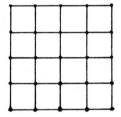

Figure 4:   G5 a regular 5 x 5 grid

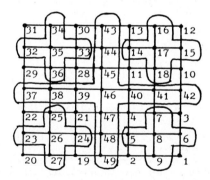

Figure 5:   G7 a regular 7 x 7 grid with a
nested dissection ordering

Obviously we can apply the algorithm recursively to the subgraphs C1, C2, C3 and C4. The submatrices Q[I,I] (I=1,2,3,4) then obtain the same structure as Q. The resulting ordering is a nested dissection ordering. The ideas of nested dissection ordering may be applied to other kinds of graphs as well; see [Lipton, Rose and Tarjan 1979].

Assume that Gn is provided with such an ordering. See figure 5 which shows G7 with a nested dissection ordering. LU-decomposition proceeds in the following recursive way. The four subgraphs Ci (i=1,2,3,4) are processed simultaneously. If there are P processors to process the original graph, then there are P/4 processors for each of the subgraphs. After processing those subgraphs a dense (2n-1) x (2n-1) matrix remains, the pivots of which will be processed using an algorithm for P processors as outlined in the preceding section. When processing a subgraph it is split again into four nearly equal subgraphs.

To determine the speed-up we use, just like in section 3, the number of updates of matrix elements as a measure of time. Any number of operations performed simultaneously will be counted only once. The number of timesteps to process the pivots of a dense (2n-1) x (2n-1) matrix equals

$$a n^3 + O(n^2)$$

with a = 8/3; from section 3 we know that the number of timesteps needed by an MIMD processor with P processors is

$$\frac{a n^3}{P} + O\left(\frac{n^2}{P}\right),$$

provided $P < 4 n^2$ holds.

Let gs(n) denote the number of timesteps for the sequential processing of Gn and gp(P,n) the number of timesteps on an MIMD processor with P processors. Assuming for the ease of presentation that n+1 is a power of 2, we have the following relations:

$$gs(n) = 4 \, gs(n/2) + a n^3 + O(n^2)$$

$$gp(P, n) = gp(P/4, n/2) + \frac{a n^3}{P} + O\left(\frac{n^2}{P}\right).$$

As an initial condition we have:

$$gp(1, n) = gs(n).$$

The solutions of the recurrence relations are

$$gs(n) = 2 a n^3 + 0 (n^2 \log n)$$

$$gp(P, n) = \frac{2 a n^3}{P} + 0 (\frac{n^2 \log n}{P}).$$

(Remark concerning initial conditions: Only the coefficient of the n^2 term of gs(n) is affected by initial conditions; see [Peters 1980].)

5. CONCLUDING REMARKS

The analysis of the preceding section is intended to get an impression of possible speed-ups. The result indicates a speed-up factor which more or less equals the number of processors employed. This would imply a 100% utilisation of the processors. So this result is encouraging.

It should, however, be interpreted rather carefully. First of all the analysis is rather crude. If a graph is split into four subgraphs, then those subgraphs are not always precisely equal. Moreover external nodes are not taken into account. (A node of a subgraph S that is connected in the original graph with a node of another subgraph is called an external node of S.) A more extensive analysis is required along the lines of [Peters 1980]. No doubt however, such an analysis would also yield an efficiency of about 100%.

Another point to be made is that the formulae in the preceding section show only the coefficients of the highest order terms. Is it indeed reasonable to ignore for practical values of n the coefficients of the lower order terms? Is the communication overhead indeed negligible compared to the arithmetical computing times? To answer these (and other questions), the best thing to do is to carry out some experiments. Therefore we will code the algorithms and test them on a multiprocessor. The results will be reported in a subsequent paper.

Another interesting research activity is to investigate whether it is worthwhile to design for a multiprocessor a general sparse matrix code for all kind of applications, or whether it is to be preferred to incorporate special LU-decomposition codes in surrounding systems like a finite element package.

References:

Duff,   I.S.   The solution of sparse linear equations on the CRAY-1. Cray
        Channels, Vol. 4 (no. 3), pp. 5-9.
George,   J.A.   Nested dissection of a regular finite element mesh. SIAM J.
        Numer. Anal., Vol. 10 (1973), pp. 345-363.
George,   J.A. and J.W.H. Liu. An automatic nested dissection algorithm for
        irregular finite element problems. SIAM J. Numer. Anal., Vol. 15
        (1978), pp.1053-1069.
George,   J.A. and J.W.H. Liu. Computer solution of large positive definite
        systems. Prentice-Hall, Englewood Cliffs, N.J., 1981.
Lipton, R.J., D.J. Rose and R.E. Tarjan. Generalised nested dissection. SIAM
        J. Numer. Anal., Vol. 16 (1979), pp. 281-285.
O'Leary, D.P. and G.W. Stewart.   Assignment and scheduling in parallel
        matrix factorisation.   Technical Report 1486. Computer Science
        Technical   Report Series. University of Maryland, College Park,
        Maryland. 1985.
Parter,   S.V.   The use of linear graphs in Gauss elimination. SIAM Review,
        Vol. 3 (1961), pp. 119-130.
Peters, F.J. Sparse matrices and substructures. MC Tract 119. Mathematical
        Centre, Amsterdam. 1980.
Peters, F.J. Parallel pivoting algorithms for sparse symmetric matrices.
        Parallel Computing, Vol. 1 (1984), pp. 99-110.
Peters, F.J.   Parallelism and sparse linear equations. Sparsity and its
        applications (D.J. Evans ed.), Cambridge University Press, 1985, pp.
        285-301.
Rose,   D.J.   A graph-theoretic study of the numerical solution of sparse
        positive definite systems of linear equations. Graph Theory and
        Computing (R. Read ed.), New York, Academic Press, 1971, pp. 183-
        217.
Rose,   D.J. and R.E. Tarjan.   Algorithmic aspects of vertex elimination.
        Proc. Seventh Annual Symposium on Theory of Computing, 1975, pp.
        245-254.
Wilkinson, J.H.   The algebraic eigenvalue problem. Oxford University Press,
        Oxford, 1965.

HIGHLY PARALLEL COMPUTERS
G.L. Reijns, M.H. Barton (editors)
Elsevier Science Publishers B.V. (North-Holland)
©IFIP, 1987

A SYSTOLIC SCHEME
FOR FAST PARALLEL COMMUNICATION
IN VLSI MESH-CONNECTED PARALLEL COMPUTERS

Marius V. A. Hâncu and Kenneth C. Smith
University of Toronto
Canada

A systolic bi-dimensional routing scheme is proposed for
solving the communication problem in VLSI mesh-
connected parallel computers. Its main characteristics are:
generality, simplicity, ease of implementation and an
$O(\sqrt{n})$ response time (n being the total number of processing elements). The suggested routing scheme, a deterministic one, is based on the operation of two sets of systolic
carriers (a horizontal and a vertical one), between which
transfers are permitted. The computational results are tran-
sported as packets, first horizontally, until they reach their
final column, then vertically, until they finally reach the appropriate destination processing element. As an example,
the packet permutation case is discussed. Queues are
necessary in the implementation. This communication
scheme is deemed suitable for many "ultracomputer"
configurations.

INTRODUCTION

The problem of redistribution and communication of data resulting from computation
in distributed computer systems is a major one. In this paper, we will focus on regular and modular arrays or ensembles of processing elements (PEs), especially those
suitable for VLSI implementation. In this environment, we propose a systolic communication scheme for the packets (tokens) which serve as vehicles for interprocessor
data communication.

In arrays or ensembles of processing elements cooperating to solve a computational
problem, four operational phases may be identified:
- *input* of instructions and external data to each component of the distributed computational structure (or, equivalently, the setup of proper instruction and external data
flows);
- *computation*, locally in each PE of the ensemble;
- *communication* (routing) of partial results, from source PEs to destination PEs, in
order to provide each processor with the intermediate data necessary to proceed with
the next computational step;
- *output* of results to the external environment.

In a VLSI computing environment, short, regular, neighbour-to-neighbour communication links are a requirement. This constraint has lead to the conclusion that SIMD
(Single-Instruction-Multiple-Data) array structures, with a unique (global) controller,
are to be avoided in VLSI, if possible. Instead, *systolic arrays* [13], characterized by
the use of neighbour-to-neighbour communication, are seen to be a more favorable

implementation for many computational tasks in the VLSI medium.

A major factor in the definition of a distributed computer system is its underlying interconnection network. From this point of view, the *mesh-connected parallel computer* [18], conceived usually as a rectangular array of n PEs ordered in $\sqrt{n}$ rows of $\sqrt{n}$ elements each (Fig.1), has enjoyed considerable attention in the past ([2], [4], [7], [16]) because of its regularity and simplicity. The fact that overlapped interconnections are practically eliminated and that each processor is connected via interconnection links (usually bidirectional) only to its immediate neighbours (or to the I/O interfaces at the boundary), makes this configuration a less wire-intensive one, in comparison with the shuffle-exchange [5], [6], [17], the butterfly or other interconnection schemes [17]. At the same time, the wire-routing and layout problems are considerably less complicated for VLSI-implemented parallel computers using this type of interconnection network. As can be observed, this derives from the fact that the rectangular grid of links (which serves as the conduit along which the packets of information travel) has a local, straightforward, type of connectivity. All the above-mentioned attributes contribute to the obvious appeal that mesh-connected computers possess for VLSI implementation.

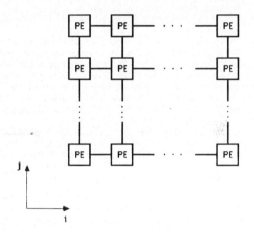

Fig.1. The mesh-connected parallel computer.

This paper addresses the third processing phase, that is communication (or routing) of partial results, seen as packets of information, on such a mesh interconnection network. The packets are labelled by the PE generating them (the source PE) with the coordinates (i,j) of the *destination*, embodied in another PE of the array. To simplify the analysis, we assume that the four phases of the distributed computation mentioned above, (that is input, computation, communication, and output) are separated in time.

The communication problem selected for study is a *permutation*, in which only one packet is generated (at the beginning of the routing phase) and received (at its end) by each PE. As a result , each packet has a unique destination label for a given instance of the communication problem.

The solution proposed to the permutation problem is based on a *two-dimensional systolic distribution (routing)* scheme. The packets are routed according to labels which indicate their final destination. A two-dimensional network of systolic carriers first transports a packet horizontally until it reaches its final column. Then it is carried vertically, until it drops into the appropriate "bin" at the destination cell.

With respect to performance, if we denote by n the total number of processors in the mesh, it is shown that the routing time in the communication network is $O(\sqrt{n})$, the optimal lower bound [2], [16]. The required area is $O(n\sqrt{n})$ for the general permutation case. However, this value can vary depending on whether the number of packets emitted by the source processor at the end of the computational step is strictly greater than one, or zero.

As with any systolic structure, no global controller is required, the routing steps being activated by the clock driving all PEs. This is in contrast with the solutions outlined in [2], [4], where the SIMD model is used in the routing algorithm definition.

THE TWO-DIMENSIONAL SYSTOLIC ROUTING STRUCTURE

As mentioned previously, at the end of a computational step each packet (containing partial results to be used by another processor in the subsequent computational step) is assigned a two-component label (i,j). The two components of the label travel together with the packet throughout the communication step, in which *packet-permutation routing* is to be implemented. After each computational phase, the labels are updated, together with the content of the packets themselves. Such labels are unique, as in a permutation all n destinations are different.

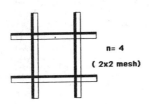

n= 4

(2x2 mesh)

Fig.2. The "cushion" interconnection network.

In the solution proposed, the basic mesh-interconnection network is augmented by a set of wrap-around connections, yielding a "cushion" interconnection network (Fig.2). The original PEs are each augmented with:
• a DR (destination register), where the packets are to be stored upon reaching their final destination;
• four DPs (destination processors), which have the role of moving the packets and checking the index coincidence (Fig.4).

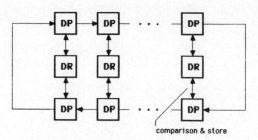

Fig.3. Linear systolic distributor for one
row of processors in the mesh-connected parallel computer.

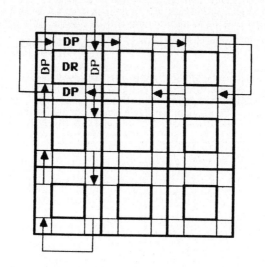

Fig.4. Horizontal and vertical distributor - operation.

The "cushion" interconnection network has the task of implementing, during the communication phase, a multiple replica of a *linear systolic distributor* (Fig.3), which is an extension of the systolic sorters described in [14], [15]. The processing elements used in this linear systolic array are the DPs (destination processors) mentioned above. Within each PE (Fig.4), two of the DPs are allotted to the corresponding horizontal distributor, while the other two form part of the corresponding vertical distributor. The DPs (destination processors) consist mainly of shift- register cells and comparison and transfer circuits.

Each of the linear systolic distributors corresponds to a row or column of the mesh of processors (Fig.4). Their purpose is to implement dynamically the "cushion" interconnection network described in Fig.2. A packet is seen to be moved *as on a conveyor belt*, first on the horizontal systolic distributor until it reaches its proper column, then on the vertical systolic distributor until it reaches its proper row.

While a packet is carried along by the horizontal and vertical distributors, its column (j) and row (i) destination indexes are continuously compared with those of the PE of current residence. Upon coincidence, the packet is seen to have reached its destination and is stored in the corresponding DR (destination register, Fig.4).

As already mentioned, each PE (such as those presented in Fig.1) contains four DPs (destination processors) and a DR (destination register). We could conceptualize this by describing the communication layer as being superimposed over the computational layer. In terms of (planar) layout, a zone assigned to each PE will be used for both the computational and interconnection elements. Since in this paper, we have focused our attention on the communication phase, only the interconnection layer is represented in our illustrations.

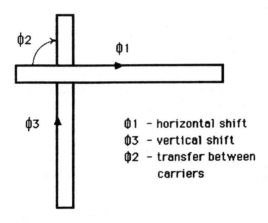

ϕ2 ϕ1

ϕ3 ϕ1 – horizontal shift
ϕ3 – vertical shift
ϕ2 – transfer between
carriers

Fig.5. Clocking scheme.

In terms of implementation, we may assume (Fig.5) that the horizontal distributor shifts its packets on clock phase $\Phi1$, while the vertical distributor shifts its packets on clock phase $\Phi3$. When a packet reaches its appropriate column, but still must be carried to its final row, a packet transfer between the two carriers takes place on $\Phi2$.

AN EXAMPLE ROUTING

A 3x3 (n=9) mesh of processing elements has been chosen for this example. Snapshots of the packet movement are presented in Figs.6a and 6b. To simplify the presentation, a routing case which does not require the use of queues has been represented.

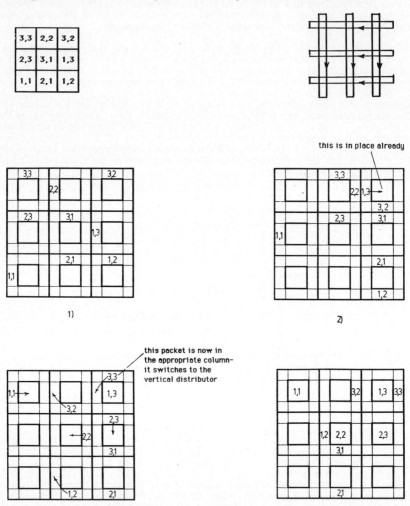

Fig.6a. A sample case.

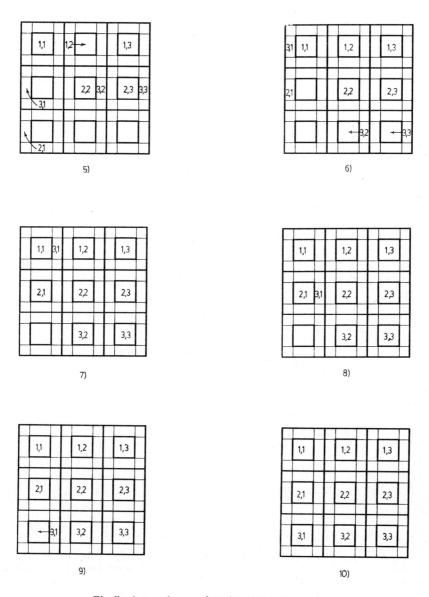

Fig.6b. A sample case (continued from Fig.6a).

In the snapshot 1), we display the initial situation - the location of the result packets at the end of the previous computational phase. If the packets are already in the correct column, they are placed from the very beginning in the DPs (destination processors) of the corresponding vertical systolic distributors (for example, packets (1,1) or (1,3)). If they are not yet in the correct columns, they are placed in the DPs corresponding to the horizontal systolic distributor in their current rows (for example, packets (3,3), (2,3) and (3,1)).

The direction of movement in the two distributors is indicated in Fig.4. To make the operation more explicit, we will follow the displacement of some tokens (Fig.6a&b).
• In snapshot 2), token (1,3) has been carried upwards by the vertical carrier in column 3, to its new DP. Upon destination-index comparison, this DP finds coincidence between the destination label carried by the packet and its own index. This means that the packet has already reached its destination. Accordingly, the next snapshot (3)) shows this packet already stored in the corresponding DR (destination register).
• Following the displacement of another packet (3,3) from snapshot 1) to snapshot 3), one can see that it is shifted two columns to the right by the horizontal distributor. Upon reaching the column of its final destination (3), it is transferred on the vertical distributor (the leftmost DP of PE (3,1) in snapshot 3)). After three more clock periods, it reaches its final destination as shown in snapshot 6).

In order to minimize the number of snapshots necessary to present a full routing process, the tokens have been presented in the positions to which they are brought by the combination of clock phases $\Phi 1$ and $\Phi 3$. The transfers, executed on $\Phi 2$, are merely indicated by slanted arrows. After 9 clock periods, (snapshot 10)), all packets have reached their final destination and the next computational phase can begin.

QUEUES AND RESPONSE TIME

Queues must be incorporated in the PEs in order to provide further storage for the cases when the systolic vertical distributor is already loaded at the crosspoint where a packet transfer (as described above) must take place. As each column contains $\sqrt{n}$ PEs, a simple argument will show that the necessary queue must be $\sqrt{n}$ -1 levels deep to provide for the worst case. This occurs when a packet waits for the longest possible string of $\sqrt{n}$ -1 occupied cells in the vertical distributor to pass, in order to get the right to access that distributor (Fig.7).

However, even when a queue must be used, the routing time (in clock periods) remains $O(\sqrt{n})$. This can be seen to be the combination of the time required for a full diagonal traversal of the array (that is $2\sqrt{n}$) and the waiting time in the queue (at most $\sqrt{n}$ -1), or about $3\sqrt{n}$. If we assume a one-level planar technology, the need for $\sqrt{n}$ -1 level queues at each of the n PEs leads to an $O(n\sqrt{n})$ estimate for the area (a level in the queue being assigned by convention unit area, as is the case for the PEs, too).

The queuing strategy should be of the FIFO (First-In First-Out) type. The queue itself can be managed by a subprogram run by the corresponding PE, which is not encumbered by a computational task as such do not exist in the routing phase. Another type of design could lead to the allotment of a small dedicated PE for queue management, separated from the main resident PE at that mesh location.

An interesting question is how does this distributed system "know" when the communication phase has ended (that is, when all destination PEs have received their corresponding packets), so that the next phase (computation or I/O) can begin. In other words, we require a mechanism by which to appropriately define the duration allotted to the routing interval. In a SIMD architecture, the solution is straightforward, as the central controller being itself fully in charge of the routing process, it is able to keep a clear record of finished transactions.

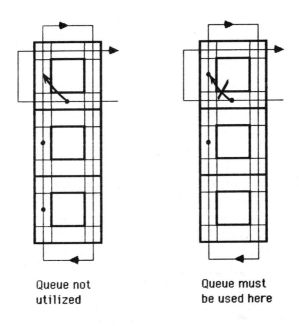

Queue not   Queue must
utilized   be used here

Fig.7. Queues.

However, in the architecture proposed here, of a MIMD type, the global controller does not exist. We suggest two alternative approaches to solving the problem of determining *the end of the communication phase*. In both, the clock to the systolic carriers is disabled when the required time has passed, as the next phase (computation or I/O) is enabled.

In the first approach, a very simple one, the clock to the carriers (distributors) is enabled by a timer set conservatively in such a way as to cover the worst possible case in terms of packet communication delay from source to destination. As noted earlier, this is approximately $3\sqrt{n}$.

In the second approach (Fig.8), upon receiving the correct packet, the respective PE places an ACK (acknowledge) token on the corresponding vertical distributor. These tokens are collected by the horizontal carrier on the top row. The queuing techniques used for these ACK tokens (packets) are similar to those used for the result packets. The top horizontal carrier deposits the ACK tokens with the clock controller (placed in the right corner of the array in Fig.8). Upon receipt of n of them, the clock controller disables the clock to the systolic distributors.

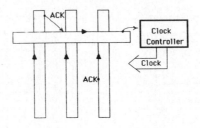

Fig.8. Finding the end of the routing phase.

The reader will have observed by now that both these schemes are synchronous , in accordance with the systolic mechanism employed (which is by definition synchronous [13]. *Asynchronous* schemes, based on similar hardware for packet transportation and for the definition of the communication phase termination are currently under study.

A COMPARISON WITH PREVIOUS SOLUTIONS

Communication (routing) problems in mesh-connected parallel computers have been studied for a number of years. As well, one discovers many cases in which the familiar problem of *sorting* with such structures reduces simply to another particular case of the routing problem. This is especially the case in the treatment of a permutation sort. As a consequence, our references cover works on both routing and sorting.

The solution proposed here *does require waiting queues* in the process of distribution of the packets from the source PEs to the destination PEs, as do the solutions proposed by Valiant and Brebner [7], Valiant [8], and Aleliunas [9], [10]. However, a global controller is not required, as in the work by Thomson and Kung [2], Knuth [3], and Nassimi and Sahni [4], where a SIMD model is used in the routing algorithm definition. The movement of data can be synchronous (for a purely systolic solution - the case on which we focused in this paper), where the existence of a global clock is implied, or asynchronous (for wavefront-type propagation of data - a case still under study).

The above-mentioned solutions by Valiant, Brebner and Aleliunas are based on parallel random communication schemes. In them, on a random path between the source and the final destination, the packets wait temporarily at a predefined number of randomly chosen PEs. In comparison with these randomized routing schemes, our solution has the following advantages:

- *no random sequence generators* (located at each PE) are necessary;
- the routing time is *always* (that is deterministically) $O(\sqrt{n})$, not simply estimated on a probabilistic basis.

The only *systolic sorting* scheme of which we are aware which *might* be used for solving the routing problem in mesh-connected parallel computers, is the one presented by Lang et al. [16]. It is based on shuffle operations and odd-even transposition sorts. In comparison with it, our solution is simpler in terms of data movement (being a direct extension of the linear systolic sorter by Leiserson [14] and Shin et al. [15]). At the same time, the proposed solution *does not require area* outside that occupied by the original n processors. This is in contrast to the systolic structure outlined in Fig. 13 of [16], which needs more than one replica of the $\sqrt{n} \times \sqrt{n}$ array to accommodate the total systolic data flow used for sorting (routing) of items.

CONCLUSIONS

The systolic communication (routing) scheme proposed is applicable, both for the purposes of modelling or implementation, to the rectangular mesh-of-processors configuration or other similar VLSI ultracomputer configurations.

It involves the use of a simple, modular and regular structure and as such is recommended for VLSI or WSI (wafer-scale integration) implementations. It has an $O(\sqrt{n})$ response time, in the range of the optimal.

We believe this solution of the communication problems in the VLSI arrays of computers to be simple and general enough to be applied to a multitude of permutation schemes. However, it does not eliminate the need for queues. Elimination of queues is an open problem for further study.

REFERENCES

[1] Batcher, K.E.,"Sorting Networks and Their Applications", in *Proc. AFIPS 1968 SJCC*, Vol.32, Montvale, N.J., AFIPS Press, pp.307-314.

[2] Thomson, C.D. and Kung, H.T., "Sorting on a Mesh-Connected Parallel Computer", *Comm. ACM*, Vol. 20, pp.263-271, 1977.

[3] Knuth, D.E., *The Art of Computer Programming, Vol. 3: Sorting and Searching*, Addison-Wesley, Reading, Mass., 1973.

[4] Nassimi, D. and Sahni, S., "Bitonic Sort on a Mesh-Connected Computer", *IEEE Trans. Comput.*, Vol.C-28, pp.2-7, Jan.1979.

[5] Schwartz, J.T., "Ultracomputers", *ACM TOPLAS*, 2 (1980), pp.484-521.

[6] Stone, H.S., "Parallel Processing with the Perfect Shuffle", *IEEE Trans. Comput.*, Vol. C-20, pp.153-161, Febr.1971.

[7] Valiant, L.G. and Brebner, G.J., "Universal Schemes for Parallel Communication", *Proc. 13th ACM Symposium on Theory of Computing*, pp.263-277, 1981.

[8] Valiant, L.G., "A Scheme for Fast Parallel Communication", *SIAM J. Comput.*, Vol. 11, No.2, pp.350-361, May 1982.

[9] Aleliunas, R., *Probabilistic Parallel Communication*, Ph.D. Thesis, Dept. of Computer Science, University of Toronto, 1983 (Technical Report No.166/83).

[10] Aleliunas, R., "Randomized Parallel Communication", *Proc.Symp. on Principles of Distributed Computing*, pp.60-72, 1982.

M.V.A. Hâncu and K.C. Smith

[11] Borodin, A. and Hopcroft, J., "Routing, Merging and Sorting on Parallel Models of Computation", *Proc. 14th ACM Symposium on Theory of Computing*, pp.338-343, 1982.

[12] Mead, C.A. and Conway, L.A., *Introduction to VLSI Systems*, Addison-Wesley, Reading, Mass., 1980.

[13] Kung, H.T. and Leiserson, C.E., "Systolic Arrays (for VLSI)", *Sparse Matrix Proc. 1978*, Duff, I.S. and Stewart, G.H., (Eds.), SIAM, 1979, pp.256-282. (An earlier version appears in Chapter 8 of [12]).

[14] Leiserson, C.E., "Systolic Priority Queues", *Proc. Caltech Conf. on VLSI*, pp.200-214, Jan.1979.

[15] Shin, H., Welch, A.J. and Malek,M., "I/O Overlapped Sorting Schemes for VLSI", *Proc. ICCD'83, IEEE International Conference on Computer Design: VLSI in Computers*, pp.731-734, 1983.

[16] Lang, H.W., Schimmler, M., Schmeck, H. and Schroder, H., "Systolic Sorting on a Mesh-Connected Network", *IEEE Trans. Comput.*, Vol. C-34, No.7, pp.652-658, July 1985.

[17] *Special Issue on Sorting, IEEE Trans. Comput.*, Vol. C-34, No.4, April 1985.

[18] Ullman, J.D., *Computational Aspects of VLSI*, Computer Science Press, Rockville, Maryland, Ch. 4-6, 1984.

[19] Barnes, G. et al., "The Illiac IV Computer", *IEEE Trans. Comput.*, Vol. C-17, pp.746-757, Aug. 1968.

HIGHLY PARALLEL COMPUTERS
G.L. Reijns, M.H. Barton (editors)
Elsevier Science Publishers B.V. (North-Holland)
©*IFIP, 1987*

223

HYPERCUBE ARGUMENT FLOW MULTIPROCESSOR ARCHITECTURE
WITH ARBITRARY NUMBER OF LINKS.

RUDY LAUWEREINS AND J.A.PEPERSTRAETE

KATHOLIEKE UNIVERSITEIT LEUVEN
E.S.A.T. LABORATORY
KARD. MERCIERLAAN 94
B-3030 HEVERLEE,
BELGIUM

One important class of data driven multiprocessor systems consists of hypercube architectures. In this paper, three commonly encountered systems of this class are compared. All three of them offer serious problems when modularly increasing the number of processing nodes of an already installed system. Without drastic hardware changes, performance will deviate sharply from the optimum. This work proposes a new architecture which combines a large communication capacity with optimal expandability.

INTRODUCTION

An ever increasing number of applications like weather forecasting, image processing, artificial intelligence, etc. asks for an ever increasing computation power [1]. Citing Neil Lincoln we can say that "supercomputers are just one generation behind computational needs of today". Computer architects can not answer this demands by just implementing technological advances. They try to deviate from the classical sequential von Neumann processor towards highly parallel architectures where several tasks can be executed concurrently. The most powerful computers of today, the vector computers, reach their highest throughput when the same instruction is implemented on a list of data. The next computer generation will be able to perform different computations on different data at the same time [2]. This will be achieved by building up a large network of identical VLSI microcomputers.

The two major problems encountered when interconnecting cooperating microcomputers are the detection of parallelism in the application program and the overload of the communication lines [3]. Data flow systems have already proved [4,5,6,7] to offer a good solution to the parallelism detection problem. They however increase the transmission problem by their excessive amount of communication overhead. In previous papers [8,9], we proposed a different program organization, called "argument flow". The program is divided into procedures which become executable as soon as all arguments are available (cfr. data flow). The procedure itself is then executed on a traditional Von Neumann computer using the control flow mechanism. Argument flow diminishes communication drastically with respect to pure data flow, while the parallelism for most application programs will still be greater than the number of processing nodes. At the same time, the problem of performance loss when executing pure sequential program segments -a problem often encountered in data flow systems [10]- is totally solved by incorporating this sequential segment in one procedure.

After thorough study and extensive simulations [8] we found hypercube networks more valuable than multibus structures. In spite of the intermediate steps needed for message passing between two not-neighbouring processors, the communication capacity of hypercube networks is one or more orders of magnitude greater than for multibus structures with the same cost. Secondly, driving a high speed bus which interconnects 256 processing units causes serious bus driver problems.

The next paragraph will introduce some important performance measurement properties. A two-dimensional fully interconnected mesh will be studied in the third section. The prove is given that it is important to increase the number of dimensions of the network when processing nodes are added to it. Thereafter, three commonly used hypercube architectures are compared: binary hypercube [1,11], generalized nearest neighbour mesh [12,13] and generalized hypercube [13]. It will be shown that increasing the dimension of the network also implies increasing the number of links of each processing node. This obstructs modular expandability. The last section proposes a new hypercube network which is in fact a generalization of the generalized nearest neighbour mesh. It combines modular expandability with a high communication capacity.

IMPORTANT PERFORMANCE MEASUREMENT PROPERTIES

The transmission load or shortly "load" of a link is defined as the average number of messages transmitted by that link when all processing nodes send exactly one message to a randomly chosen destination.

The percentage of use ($\%use_p$) of a processing node is the ratio of effective computation time and total time. "Total time" starts at the beginning of program execution and stops when all procedures assigned to the node, are executed. This $\%use_p$ strongly depends on the parallelism of the application program and on the network structure.

The final parameter is the CCR_{crit}, the critical computation - communication ratio. It indicates the ratio of computation time and transmission time that gives rise to a beginning communication bottleneck. When the CCR of an application program is lower than the CCR_{crit} of the architecture, a violent communication bottleneck occurs, thereby degrading system performance rapidly.

GENERALIZED TWO-DIMENSIONAL NEAREST NEIGHBOUR MESH (fig.1)

This architecture has already thoroughly been studied [12,13]. It is cyclic in both dimensions (i.e. processing node 0 is directly connected with nodes 1,3,4,12). Assuming that the number of processors is the same in both dimensions and equal to W, we can easily prove the average distance a message travels in one dimension equals $W/4$. The average distance ($dist_{av}$) between an arbitrary source node and an arbitrary destination is

$$dist_{av} = \frac{W}{2} = \frac{\sqrt{N}}{2} \qquad (1)$$

The average distance for this two-dimensional structure is proportional to the square root of the number of processing nodes. Since the average load is the ratio of $dist_{av}$ and the number of links per processor, the load too is proportional to this square root.

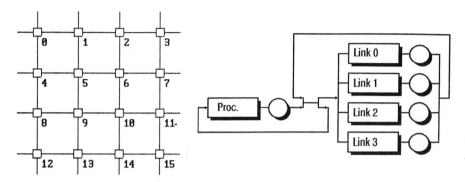

Fig.1 Generalized Two-Dimensional
Nearest Neighbour Mesh

Fig.2 Queueing Model of
one Processing Node

To compute the percentage of use of processor and links, we employ queueing theory [14]. Figure 2 shows the queueing model of one processing node. Detailed computation for this model goes beyond the scope of this article, but can be found in [9,15]. We define the parallelism of the program as the average number of fireable procedures per processing node. Q_P denotes the average number of procedures in the processor waiting queue or during service and Q_L the same for the link system. Since every procedure must be either at the processor either at one of the L links, we obtain relation (2):

$$\text{parallelism} = Q_P + L * Q_L \tag{2}$$

Substituting Q_P and Q_L with their respective formulae, one gets:

$$\text{parallelism} = \frac{\%use_P}{1 - \%use_P} + L * \frac{\dfrac{load * \%use_P}{CCR}}{1 - \dfrac{load * \%use_P}{CCR}} \tag{3}$$

Solving equation (3) towards $\%use_P$, we can compute $\%use_P$ in function of the CCR of the application program with the parallelism as a parameter (fig. 3).

As we can see, the $\%use_P$ strongly depends on the parallelism of the application program. The maximal $\%use_P$ is reached when CCR goes to infinity, since communication is then negligible. Fig. 4 shows the dependency of the maximal $\%use_P$ on the parallelism for randomly distributed procedures. Remark that the $\%use_{P\ max}$ is independent of architectural properties. Defining the critical CCR as the CCR which offers a $\%use_P$ of 90% of the maximal reachable and solving equation (3) towards CCR, one obtains:

OVERVIEW OF THREE EXISTING ARCHITECTURES

1. Binary hypercube [1,11] (fig. 5)

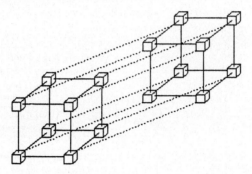

Fig.5 4-Dimensional Binary Hypercube

	Binary Hypercube	Mesh	Generalized Hypercube	Rotating Link
L	L = D	L = 2D	L = D*(W-1)	free
W	W = 2	free	free	free
dist	$\dfrac{D}{2}$	$\dfrac{D*W}{4}$	$D * \dfrac{(W-1)}{W}$	$\dfrac{D*W}{4} + \text{detour}$
load	$\dfrac{1}{2}$	$\dfrac{W}{8}$	$\dfrac{1}{W}$	$\dfrac{D*W}{4*L} + \dfrac{\text{detour}}{L}$

Table 1. Different Hypercube Networks

The number of processing nodes W in each dimension is always equal to 2.   The
number of links L per processor equals dimension D.   Table 1 shows the formulae
for the average distance a message travels from source to destination and for
the average load of the links. Detailled computations can be found in [15].
The major advantage of this architecture is that link load (and consequently
CCR_{crit}) is independent of the number of processing nodes N. It is however
impossible to increase N without increasing the number of links per processor.
Therefore, modular expansion of existing systems without changing the number of
links of the already installed processors is impossible. Since N must always
be a power of 2, only a small amount of different N-values are possible and the
increase between two succeeding N's is great. The last problem is the high
dimension of the architecture. For 1024 processing nodes, the 10-dimensional
structure must be mapped into the three-dimensional physical world.

$$CCR_{crit} = \frac{dist_{av}}{L} * f(parallelism) \qquad (4)$$

Substituting $dist_{av}$ with formula (1), we remark CCR_{crit} too is proportional to the square root of the number of processing nodes for this two-dimensional network. It is obvious we could achieve a lower message distance and a lower critical CCR by increasing the dimension of the architecture. In this way we can arrive at a logarithmical dependency instead of a square root!

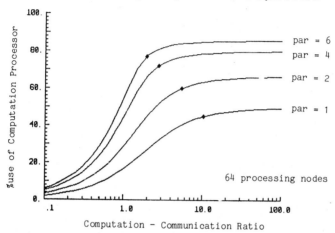

Fig.3 %use$_p$ i.f.o. CCR for Two-Dimensional Nearest Neighbour Mesh

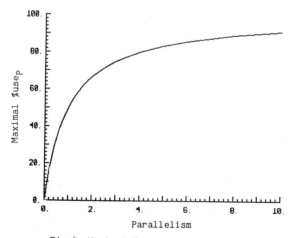

Fig.4 Maximal %use$_p$ i.f.o. Parallelism

2. Generalized nearest neighbour mesh [12,13] (fig. 6)

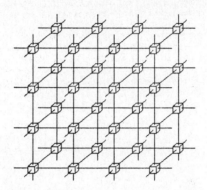

Fig.6   3-Dimensional Generalized Nearest Neighbour Mesh

The number of processors W in each dimension can be chosen arbitrarily. The
number of links per processor is equal to two times the dimension of the
structure. Formulae for average distance and load can be found in table 1.
When W = 4, the load of this architecture equals that of the binary hypercube;
for the same N, both architectures will have the same number of links L and
thus the same cost; the dimension of the mesh system will be half the one of
the binary hypercube. For W < 4, load and CCR_{crit} are less (=better) than for
the binary hypercube. Increasing N, there are two possibilities: increasing D
while not changing W or increasing W without affecting D. In the first case,
load is independent of N, but the number of links must be changed, thereby
obstructing modular expansion. In the latter case, L must not be changed; the
load of the links however will grow proportional to the D-th root of N.

3. Generalized hypercube [13] (fig. 7)

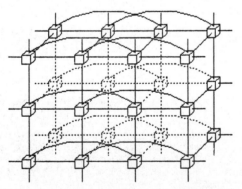

Fig.7 3-Dimensional Generalized Hypercube

Table 1 shows the most important formulae for this network. When W = 2, this
architecture is the binary hypercube and consequently has the same performance
and cost. Since L depends on both D and W, it is completely impossible to
change N without affecting the number of links. Care must be taken when
interpreting the formulae of table 1: it seems better to increase W than D

because the load is inversily proportional to W. In the extremum, D = 1 and W = N will offer the best results, but this means that every processor is directly connected to every other node!

As a general conclusion, we can state that (1) all three architectures offer almost the same performance for the same N and L, (2) the number of links L is directly proportional to the dimension D hindering modular expansion and (3) only for the generalized nearest neighbour mesh N can be increased without affecting L and D, but in that case the load of the links grows too quickly.

In the next section, a new architecture is proposed which offers the same or lower load than the nearest neighbour mesh at the same cost and which can be expanded modularly without needing to change the number of links of already installed processors.

"ROTATING LINK": A MODULAR EXPANDABLE MULTIPROCESSOR WITH AN ARBITRARY NUMBER OF LINKS (fig. 8 and 9)

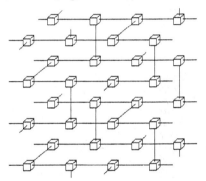 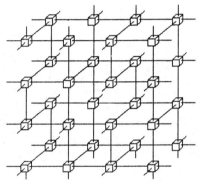

Fig.8 3-Dimensional Rotating Link with 3 Links per Processor   Fig.9 3-Dimensional Rotating Link with 5 Links per Processor

This network can be constructed for any dimension D ≥ 2 and for any number of links L ≥ 3 and ≤ 2D. One dimension is fully interconnected. This means that for each processing node two links are used for transfers in this dimension. The remaining (L-2) links are equally distributed among the (D-1) not fully interconnected dimensions. When L = 2D, this architecture is exactly the same as the generalized nearest neighbour mesh.

Several algorithms to find the shortest path between any source and any destination processor are possible. The following is the easiest one [16]. When source and destination have different coordinates in one of the not fully interconnected dimensions, the message is passed using the link in this direction. Otherwise, a detour must be made: the message is transferred in the fully interconnected dimension until a processor is reached which possesses a link in the wanted direction.

With the help of a small table stored in ROM, this algorithm can be implemented efficiently in hardware. The length of the table will certainly not provide trouble: for a 5-dimensional network with 1024 processing nodes, 96 bytes are sufficient [16].

The number of processing nodes W_i in dimension i must be a multiple of the repeating distance of the interconnection pattern. The architecture has two different repeating distances: one for the fully interconnected dimension (H_d) and one for the others (H_i). They are given by formulae (5) and (6). In formula (5) "LCM" stands for "least common multiplier".

$$H_d = \frac{LCM\left(\; 2*(D-1)\;,\; L-2\;\right)}{L-2} \tag{5}$$

$$H_i = H_d \quad \text{when } H_d \text{ is odd} \tag{6}$$
$$ = 2 \quad\quad \text{when } H_d \text{ is even}$$

Due to the small practical values of H_d and H_i, N can be increased smoothly in little steps, compared with the jerky increases of the binary hypercube. Formulae (7) - (9) give a fair approximation of the load of every link [15].

$$load_{av} = \frac{D*W}{4*L} + \frac{(D-1)*H_d*(W^2-2W+1)}{8*W*L} \quad \text{when } 2L-3\leq D \tag{7}$$

$$load_{av} = \frac{D*W}{4*L} + \frac{(D-1)*(3W-4)}{12*L} \quad \text{when } 2L-3>D \text{ and } L-1<D \tag{8}$$

$$load_{av} = \frac{D*W}{4*L} + \frac{(2D-L)*(W-2)}{4*L} \quad \text{when } L-1\geq D \tag{9}$$

When N increases, there are three possibilities:
- W is constant, L increases proportional to D: $load_{av}$ will be constant. The same was true for the three structures studied above. Modular expandability will be difficult however (cfr. binary hypercube and generalized hypercube)
- D and L are constant, W increases: $load_{av}$ is proportional to the D-th root of N. Modular expansion is possible, but the average load and critical CCR increase too much (cfr. nearest neighbour mesh).
- W and L are constant, D increases: the average load and critical CCR are proportional to $log_W N$ (!) and grow much slower than for the nearest neighbour mesh. Modular expansion is possible because L is constant. This is the most important advantage of rotating link.

Care must be taken when interpreting table 1: comparing the formulae of the average distance for the nearest neighbour mesh and rotating link, one can conclude the latter has a greater $dist_{av}$ because of the detours which must be performed. However, for rotating link the dimension D will only be a little bit greater but W much smaller than for the mesh structure with the same L and cost, favouring the average distance of rotating link.

Fig. 10 shows the critical CCR for a rotating link network with 4 links per processing node and with the number of dimensions as a parameter. Remark that the network with 2 dimensions and 4 links is exactly the same as a generalized two-dimensional nearest neighbour mesh. Especially for the larger number of processors, the rotating link architecture is in favour.

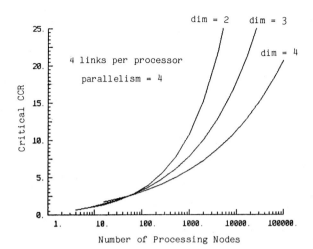

Fig.10 Critical CCR i.f.o. the Number
of Processing Nodes

When designing a multiprocessor configuration, it will be important to determine the optimal dimension. An analytical formula can hardly be derived because of the discrete nature of the optimization problem. Extensive analysis however showed that the optimal structure is obtained when W is about 4. This confirms the conclusions drawn by Bhuyan in [13].

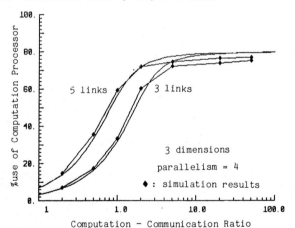

Fig.11 %use$_p$ i.f.o. CCR

Figure 11 compares the computed %use$_p$, with simulation results for 64 processing nodes, 3 dimensions, 3 and 5 links.

In figure 12, which displays the %use$_p$ and %use$_L$ for 64 processing nodes with 4 links each, we remark that the links are used for 50 % at most. This clearly indicates the bottleneck is not caused by overloaded communication channels. A thorough examination of the processes which happen at the occurence of a bottleneck revealed that the absence of work for several processors causes the sharp decrease in %use. Even if the parallelism of the program is greater than N, a processor can become idle due to the random distribution of the procedures. Secondly, a procedure which finishes execution, can not immediately fire another one: it must first travel from source node to destination. A solution to the first problem is the employment of a run-time load balancing algorithm. The important effect such an algorithm has on system performance can easily be seen in figure 12. The load balancing algorithm employed was a very simple one: when a processor has no fireable procedures in memory anymore, it asks its nearest neighbours for work. Each neighbour with more than two fireable procedures, answers the demand. The problem of having too many procedures on the move, can be diminished by decreasing the average distance. At present we are developing a new architecture with the same properties as rotating link but with smaller detours to be made.

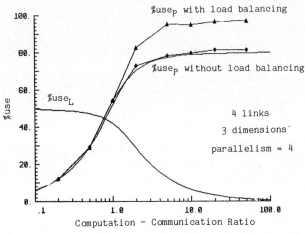

Fig.12 %use$_p$ i.f.o. CCR

CONCLUSIONS

It has been proved that the maximal percentage of use of a hypercube architecture only depends on the parallelism of the application program and not on the architecture itself. On the other hand, the point at which a bottleneck occurs is influenced by the network structure and by the parallelism of the application program. When the number of processing nodes N and the dimension of a hypercube multiprocessor is increased, both the load of the interconnection links and the critical computation – communication ratio increase proportional to the logarithm of N for the architecture proposed in this paper. It is possible to change the dimension of the structure without affecting the number of links per processor. This makes modular expansion feasible. Thorough examination of several hypercube architectures revealed that the bottleneck is not caused by an overload of the communication links, but by the lack of fireable procedures at the processing nodes. This fact indicates the importancy of run-time load balancing.

In the near future, the message routing algorithm will be made fault-tolerant and the run-time load balancing algorithm will be worked out.

REFERENCES

[1] Wain C., "Concurrent Computing: A New Age in Supercomputer Architecture", Solutions, May/June 1985, pp.6-8

[2] Moto-Oka T., "Fifth Generation Computer Systems", North Holland Publishing Company, 1982

[3] Caluwaerts L., "Design and Evaluation of a Data Flow Computer Architecture", Ph.D. diss., KUL-ESAT, Belgium, May 1984

[4] Gurd J. and Watson, "Data Driven System for High Speed Parallel Computing - Part 1 & 2", Computer Design, June-July 1980, pp.91-100, resp. 97-106

[5] Dennis J., "The Varieties of Data Flow Computers", Proc. 1st Int. Conf. on Distr. Comp. Systems, 1979, pp.430-439

[6] Davis A.L., "The Architecture and System Method of DDM1: a Recursively Structured Data Driven Machine", Proc. 5th Ann. Symp. Computer Architecture, Apr. 1978, pp.210-215

[7] Arvind, "The U-interpreter", Computer, Feb. 1982, pp.42-49

[8] Lauwereins R., Peperstraete J., "Influence of the Computation - Communication Ratio on the Efficiency of Argument Flow Multiprocessor Architectures", Proc. 29th Int. Conf. on Mini- and Microcomputers and their Applications, San Feliu, Spain, June 25-28, 1985, pp.128-131

[9] Lauwereins R., Peperstraete J., "Behavioural Level Simulation of a Three-Dimensional Argument Flow Multiprocessor Architecture", Proc. Int. AMSE Conf. on Modelling & Simulation, Monastir, Tunesia, Nov. 25-27, 1985

[10] Amamiya M., "A Data Flow Processor Array System for Solving Partial Differential Equations", Int. Symp. on Applied Math. and Information Science, Kyoto, Japan, March 29-31, 1982

[11] Pradhan D.K., "Fault - Tolerant Multiprocessor Link and Bus Network Architectures", IEEE Trans. on Comp., Vol. C-34, No. 1, Jan. 1985, pp.33-45

[12] Wittie L.D., "Communication Structures for Large Networks of Microcomputers", IEEE Trans. on Comp., Vol. C-30, No. 4, April 1981, pp.264-273

[13] Bhuyan L.M. et al., "Generalized Hypercube and Hyperbus Structures for a Computer Network", IEEE Trans. on Comp., Vol. C-33, No. 4, April 1984, pp.323-333

[14] Allen O., "Queueing Models of Computer Systems", Computer, April 1980, pp.13-24

[15] Lauwereins R., "Hypercube Argument Flow Multiprocessor Architecture with Arbitrary Number of Links: Detailed Computations", Internal report 1985/40, KUL-ESAT, Belgium, Dec. 1985

[16] Lauwereins R., "Hypercube Argument Flow Multiprocessor Architecture with Arbitrary Number of Links: Message Routing Algorithm", Internal report, KUL-ESAT, Heverlee, Belgium, Apr. 1986

HIGHLY PARALLEL COMPUTERS
G.L. Reijns, M.H. Barton (editors)
Elsevier Science Publishers B.V. (North-Holland)
©*IFIP, 1987*

EXPERIMENTS ON A DATA FLOW MACHINE

Masao Iwashita and Tsutomu Temma

C&C Systems Research Laboratories
NEC Corporation, Kawasaki-city 213, Japan

A VLSI data flow chip, the Image Pipelined Processor (ImPP: μPD 7281), which contains 115,000 transistors, has been developed. An experimental image processing system (TIP-3: Template Controlled Image Processing System −3), which includes 8 ImPP chips, has also been developed.

Methods to keep the data stream flow constant and to attain high speed, in the data flow processor, are examined. Schemes to assure effective usage of multiple ImPPs are proposed. A performance upper bound depends on both application and program parallelism. Algorithm improvement for concurrences is discussed and several schemes for using multiple ImPPs effectively, are considered through typical image processing.

The ImPP is characterized by its data flow architecture and a uni-directional pipeline ring bus. Processing performance can be increased by connecting many chips to each other. In this multiple ImPP configuration, an individual ImPP shares different portions of the pipeline programs and different portions of spatial data.

Time independent problems and time dependent problems are considered. Program division, pipeline stream extraction, software algorithm parallelism in view of data dependency, address generation sequence, queue memory size, synchronization, feed back loop insertion for timing control, execution timing, and running efficiency are important for high speed execution.

1. Introduction

Digital image processing and numerical calculation include a huge amount of data and require a relatively long processing time. There is much interest in making processing times short. Fortunately, most of methods contain potential parallelism which can be combined in processing. If we can extract the parallelism from them, the processing time becomes shorter. The authors interest is to extract the parallelism from application maximally and automatically as much as possible.

The authors are concerned about what the maximum speed is to be reached and how to reach it under multiple ImPPs environment. The first step to approach the goal is to clarify which processing portions have the parallelism.

Data dependency is closely related to parallel program execution. Using a data flow graph representation, data dependency is expressed clearly.

However, it is hard to draw a data flow graph for an individual array
element in the array data generally, because the data amount is enormously
large.   In order to simplify, it is necessary to express data dependency
between different array elements. Data dependency within array elements is
expressed by indices.   After that, it is possible to implement the
algorithm on the data flow machine easily.   In implementing the multiple
ImPP chips system, the following several important things must be
considered.

1)   Processing execution sequence
2)   Data flow timing
3)   Open loop control, if necessary

Before discussing the parallelism, the ImPP main features, closely related
to these problems, will be briefly reviewed.

2. ImPP and TIP-3 system

The ImPP consists of nine blocks. (Fig. 1) The input and output controller
exchange data with external circuits.   The link table memory and the
function table memory store programs.   The data memory stores a constant
data for constant operation, queuing data for two operand operation, array
data for buffering, and table data for table look up operation.   The
address generator and flow controller are used for data memory address
generation and flow path modification.   The processing unit has 16 bit
integer operational circuits.

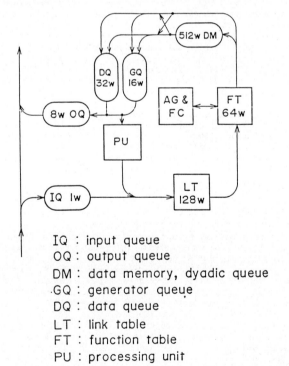

IQ : input queue
OQ : output queue
DM : data memory, dyadic queue
GQ : generator queue
DQ : data queue
LT : link table
FT : function table
PU : processing unit

Fig.I ImPP Chip Block Diagram

2.1 Data flow control

Execution sequence in the ImPP system is controlled by a static data flow control. Operations are fundamentally resolved into sets of two-operand operations. One operand reaches the dyadic queue memory in the ImPP and waits for the other operand. When the latter operand reaches the dyadic queue memory, the former operand is picked up from the dyadic queue memory and both of them flow together to the processing unit.

2.2 Stream processing

In the ImPP, data may not be only a single data value, but a sequence of data, which is called a data stream. One data stream corresponds to an arc in a data flow graph. One data stream includes a number of tokens. An individual data sequence has its own identification number. Data streams which have the same identification number are processed in the same way and flow along the same path. Each element is identified by its location in the sequence.

In the execution process, the data order in the stream should not be changed. Because, data mixes up its paired data when the data order is changed. This means that one element cannot run over the other element in the data stream during processing. The data dependency between data streams is clearly shown on a data stream flow graph. However, data dependency within one data stream cannot be expressed in the data stream flow graph explicitly.

The data in the stream are waiting in the dyadic queue memory. It is necessary to store the formerly reached data stream in the dyadic queue memory. The dyadic queue memory must work fast and is contained in LSI chip, so that the size of the dyadic queue memory is comparatively small. A dyadic queue memory size limitation puts a constraint on the maximum time lag between two paired operands.

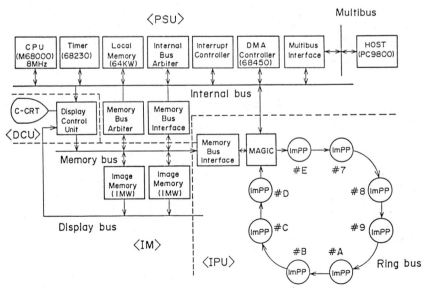

Fig. 2   TIP-3   System

2.3 TIP-3 system (Fig. 2)

TIP-3 system contains an Image Processing Unit as a high speed pipeline image processor, which includes 8 ImPP chips and one interface chip for transferring data among ImPPs, image memory and the host micro processor. ImPPs are connected by a ring shaped pipeline bus.   An image memory functions as a kind of processor chip, which converts an address value into data value in the memory reading process.

3. Parallelism and speeding up

Methods getting high execution speed are data stream division, control loop elimination, scanning address sequence modification, and pipeline staging.

First, data processing loop is discussed. Parallelism between data streams can be estimated from data flow graph representation. However, if the data flow graph has inner loop originated from memory updating, parallelism is restricted by this loop because only one data can be processed simultaneously. Stream division methods can be applied for such case.

Next, generally, synchronization between memory reading and writing can be achieved by using closed feed back control loop.   However, closed loop control bring the processing speed going down.   In order to avoid synchronization between memory reading and writing at the same address, data flow graph modification from closed loop into open loop can be applied. Method to modify the flow graph is proposed.

Third, A dyadic queue problem is discussed.   Address scanning sequence exchange is an efficient method for making the arrival order difference small between two input operand data stream into one function node.

Fourth, pipeline staging is discussed.   Processing, including mutual exclusion, is one of examples of processing sequentiality.   Processing which has both local parallelism and global sequentiality should be, first, divided into pipeline stages.   Parallel portions and sequential synchronization are discriminated. Sub-processing within one stage can be executed in parallel. On the contrary, control among stages is fulfilled sequentially. Using this staging method, total parallelism and execution speed become larger.

3.1 Data processing loop

Working memory is used for long table for table look up operation, long queue during processing, and data rearrangement.   Among these, table look up operation is a reading only operation and can be freely used at random. However, the latter two are reading and writing the same location in the memory.   So, effective and efficient synchronization is necessary between writing and reading.

Histogram and counting are examples.(Fig. 3)   Assume that the original image is represented by A(i, j), where i,j are x-, y- coordinates in the space and A is the density.   Histogram operation is represented by H(A(i, j))=H(A(i,j))+1.   Accumulation is represented by S+S+A(i,j).   counting is expressed by C=C+1.   These operations have an inner state.   State transition is time variant. In these cases, the same memory is accessed at different times.   Apparently, these operations cannot be accomplished independently.

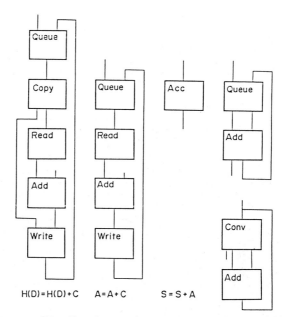

$$H(D)=H(D)+C \qquad A=A+C \qquad S=S+A$$

Fig.3 Data Processing Loop

These operations have a memory updating loop, because the same variable name is used in multiple places. This brings about sequentiality and makes the speed slow. This memory updating loop is discriminated from the feed-back control loop.

The feed-back control loop is necessary when data generation rate is controlled by the processing speed not to make queue memory overflow. This control loop limits the execution speed and parallelism lower than the queue memory size limitation. In the control loop, data value itself has no meaning, only timing is important. The control loop insertion position should not be changed to keep execution timing correct.

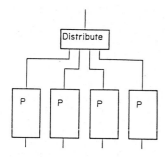

Fig.4 Flow Division

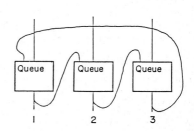

Fig.5 Sequencing Control Loop

But, in the memory updating loop operations, it is better to make the updating loop as short as possible, because the next element cannot enter the loop before preceding data processing has been finished.   In these cases, dividing the data stream into several sub streams is effective.(Fig. 4)   For example, in the histogram operation, individual counters count separately, and finally the values are summed up.

3.2 Changing control loop

Synchronization between memory reading and writing is required when the same   data   is   accessed   from   multiple   places.(Fig.   5)   However, synchronization brings about control loop overhead, irrelevant to intrinsic data processing.   This overhead should be eliminated, if possible.

One way to eliminate the control loop is fulfilled by using the data memory as a buffer.   If data memory reading should be carried out after the previous writing to the same position in the memory updating process, the timing lag between reading and writing is important.   If this lag is constant and small enough, then control is easy and fixed.   However, if it varies according to different data values or due to collision, control is harder.   In this case, the upper bound of the time lag should not be over the queue memory size.

One example is shown in the following.(Fig. 6)   Large image memory address generation is required to handle a large amount of data.   ImPP has only a 16 bit data bus.   The image memory has a 24 bit address in the TIP-3 system.   This address should be sent to image memory in 2 clock cycles. This separation brings about a long transmission time.   When writing into the image memory, 3 data sequential transfer are required.   They are high address, low address, and data value.

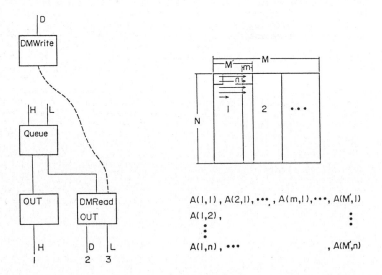

Fig.6 Data Memory Utilization   Fig.7 Scanning Sequence

However, ImPP has a dyadic queue memory for waiting for only two elements. Image memory writing is driven by the low address arrival. Therefore, the low address should be reached last. Image memory circuits have only one level register for storing the high address and the data value. For this reason, the sequence for these three elements should not be mixed. This necessary segregation requires sequence control. This, in turn, brings about a processing speed reduction.

These three sequential data generations are realized swiftly by open control technique. Two succeeding output commands are applied for this purpose. The high address is written into the data memory asynchronously. The high address, which is stored previously, is read out when the data value arrives independently from writing. This allows a time lag between writing and reading, as long as accessing data memory capacity is sufficient to store the data. Using this method, synchronization of three elements can be accomplished efficiently.

3.3 Queuing

A queuing mechanism is necessary, because of the the arrival time lag between two elements, which are waiting for each other. However, the queue memory size is limited to small levels in the ImPP. It is important to judge whether too much time lags can be avoided by the algorithm. The necessary queue size should be estimated in advance.

One method to avoid queue memory overflow is to use cascading queue memories. Using this method, the queue size becomes larger than that for a single queue memory.

The image memory may be used instead of the queue memory. Performance degradation is inevitable, because image memory access time is longer than queue memory access time. This in turn, brings about an increase in the bus transfer.

Data generation sequence exchange can reduce this time lag, in some cases. An address generation scheme should be thoroughly considered. For example, in filtering operation, when a raster scanning is applied to two dimensional filtering, queuing memory size becomes (filter size) × (line length). This amount usually goes over the queue memory size.

Each line should be divided into N small lines, with half filter size overlapping.(Fig. 7) Accordingly, the scanning area is divided into N sub areas. An individual sub area size is (line number) × (sub line length). First, the left most sub area is scanned using two dimensional raster scanning. Next, the right neighboured sub area is scanned. This scanning is continued until the rightmost sub area is reached. Using this method, the required queuing size is small.

3.4 Staging

ImPP adopts a data stream processing. One data stream should be processed in the same way. When data, which are located in different portions of the array, are mutually not independent, some techniques are necessary to isolate the dependency. In the ImPP, staging is a highly efficient means to achieve this purpose.

For one example, FFT uses staging buffer between individual pipeline stages. In this case, the writing sequence is different from the reading sequence between stages. Data sequence in the stream cannot be changed by queuing. Therefore, rearrangement of the data stream should be accomplished by using random access memory reading after writing. Memory reading stage should be separated from memory writing stage.

For the other example, wire routing will be considered.(Fig. 8)   Wire routing is one of the big problems in VLSI design and printed board design. A pin connection path between transistors or ICs should be found.   Metal wires are used without contacting each other. It is assumed that, for each pin pair, a source location and a target location are given.   This processing includes a variety of parallelism, as well as sequentiality which has originated from data dependency and memory updating.   An intersection between wires should be drawn exclusively.   This exclusion control is one reason for sequentiality.   There should not be any two wires passing each other at the same point, nor should any two wires cross each other.

The maze routing method, which is well known and frequently used, although it takes a long processing time, is considered in the following explanation.   In this algorithm, wave expansion processing, used to find path between source point and target point, takes the longest processing time to execute.   The wave expansion phase can be treated generally in the following manner.

Conditions and occupation information are expanded into map data in the image memory in advance.   Map data on the wave front are examined, to determine whether or not maps are already found paths.   Points on the expanding wave, which are presently being processed, are called the cell wave front.   One expansion to the nearest four points from already processed wave front generates a new wave front. each data on the wave front can be processed in parallel because each path finding is independent. But individual wave fronts are processed in different stages.

In this case, however the problem that could appear is that two neighboring cells on the wave front might process identical cell simultaneously during the same stage.(Fig. 9) So, if both the next point address calculation and the map status check are executed simultaneously, the two next addresses will be generated doubly.   This brings about an increase in the same wave front address.   To avoid this, stage separation is needed.   This algorithm works as follows.

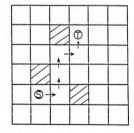
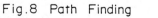

Fig.8 Path Finding

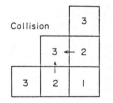
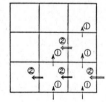

Fig.9 Wave Front Expansion

1)   Condition check
2)   Address calculation
3)   Map data updating
4)   Marking sequence increment

Furthermore, stage 2) is divided into four sub-stages, which are mutually independent. These sub-stages are calculated by using map information in the memory. The double next address generation can be avoided by writing into the map in the memory.

a)   North address
b)   West address
c)   South address
d)   East address

The wave front increases proportionally with the distance from the source point. Parallelism is also increasing proportionally with the pixel number in the wave front. Parallelism grows larger using this method.

4. Consideration

In previous section, main factors, which make influence on high efficiency and high speed execution, are discussed. Among these, loop modification problem can be solved using data dependency represented on a data flow graph. However, the dyadic queue and execution timing problem should be treated as a time varying function. In this section, both idealized case and actual case are considered. Several simple models have been made. Analysis by models is useful for deciding processing execution timing and sequence. Relations between models and performance will be considered.

4.1 Model 1

A simple case is first considered. It has no data queue memory and infinite dyadic queue memory. A copy function, a generation function, and a two output element function cannot be used. No increasing in the inner ring occurs, only decreasing. Moreover, input data, flowing in from outside of the ImPP, should be controlled to prevent it from entering when the processing inner ring is busy. Efficiency is good, as long as input data is continuously sent from the outside. In the ImPP, one data is transferred in two clocks but most processing are executed in one clock. Input and output take twice time comparing with processing. When each fundamental processing consists of N input data, M output data, and L processing node, time required to accomplish the processing are 2N, M, and 2L and data input rate becomes close to the maximum for these three values, on an average.

Data input sequence can be decided freely, because no dyadic queue memory overflow occurs. Any operands can be input at any sequence without the dyadic queue memory overflow.

4.2 Model 2

The data queue memory size is finite, and the dyadic queue memory size is infinite. A copy, a generation, and two-output commands can be available. During these data increasing commands execution, the processor unit cannot allow input from the data queue memory. If these commands are used continuously, then data queue memory overflow occurs.

In order to avoid the data queue memory overflow, data increasing commands should be mixed with data decreasing commands, which are output command, the data memory write command, 2 inputs/1 output commands, etc. The input rate from outside of the ImPP should not go over the maximum processing rate in the ImPP.

Data generation sequence and input sequence are freely chosen.

4.3 Model 3

Both the data queue memory and the dyadic queue memory size are limited. Data increasing commands and data input commands are carefully adjusted in timing, in order to prevent queue memory overflow and queue memory empty which brings about the processor idling state.

One possible way to be chosen is to change flow graph and to make processing as diverse as possible. diversity is measured from various viewing points, such as spatial diversity and timing diversity. spatial diversity can be defined by weighted sum of the distance between individual function nodes and the center-located function node. Timing diversity can be measured from time varying data amount in the data queue memory. When diversity is sufficiently small, the data amount in the data queue memory during execution comes near to the average amount statistically.

In order to realize this, simultaneous data generation number adjustment, feed back control loop inserting location selection, delay insertion, commands mixing are adopted. Commands mixing means that every command that increases the element number is divided into two output data commands and every data increasing command should be mixed with data amount decreasing commands. By this means, data amount does not increase abruptly, and maintains a constant level. High efficiency can be attained by timing adjustment, inserting timing delay at appropriate places and control loops.

In this model, data input rate and output rate should be controlled statistically. Average data input rate should be controlled, considering both output rate and processing speed.

4.4 A complex model

An actual ImPP has a finite queue size and complex instructions. The data queue memory, the generator queue memory reading out, and input data acknowledge signal timing are controlled by hardware. Data value dependent conditional branch and data value dependent flow changing commands are included. The data amount in the queue memory changes irregularly according to time lapse. The necessary queue size depends on algorithm and data values. The number of elements in the queue memory should be lower than 32 levels, which are involved in the actual ImPP. For programming the ImPP, a software simulator is used for analysis. In order to perform simulation efficiently, it is better to execute a small part of the program and to find a fundamental execution cycle. Data queue overflow and executing running ratio can be examined using this simulator.

5. Conclusion

A data flow processor ImPP and an image processing system TIP-3 have been described.   The important factors, which influence the executing speed, were analyzed.   Data dependency, processing execution sequence and data flow timing are main factors.   After improvement on these factors, a higher performance for image processing can be attained.

Acknowledgment

The authors wish to thank Mr. S. Hanaki and Mr. K. Asai for their continuous encouragement and helpful advice.

References

1.   T. Temma, S. Hasegawa, and S. Hanaki, "Data flow processor for image processing", in Proc. Mini and Microcomputers, vol. 5, no.3, 1980.
2.   T. Temma, M. Mizoguchi, and S. Hanaki, "Template-controlled image processor TIP-1 performance evaluation", in Proc. of CVPR, pp.468-473, 1983.
3.   R. Ohta et al., "SAR Data Processing on Data-flow Image Processing System (NEDIPS)", NEC R&D, no.68, pp.61-66, Jan. 1983.
4.   M. Iwashita, T. Temma, K. Matsumoto, and H. Kurokawa, "Modular data flow image processor", in Proc. Spring '83 Compcon, pp.464-467, 1983.
5.   H. Kurokawa, K. Matsumoto, T. Temma, M. Iwashita, and T. Nukiyama, "The architecture and performance of image pipline processor", in Proc. VLSI'83, pp.275-284, 1983.
6.   T. Nukiyama, T. Temma, K. Matsumoto, H. Kurokawa, H. Goto, T. Hoshi, and T. Temma, "A VLSI image pipeline processor", in Proc. ISSCC'84, pp.208-209, 1984.
7.   T. Temma et al., "Chip Oriented Data-flow Image Processor: TIP-3", Proc. of Compcon '84 fall, pp.245-254, 1984.
8.   T. Temma, M. Iwashita, K. Matsumoto, H. Kurokawa, and T. Nukiyama, "Data Flow Processor Chip for Image Processing", IEEE trans. on ED, vol. ED-32, no.9, pp.1784-1791, Sept. 1985.

HIGHLY PARALLEL COMPUTERS
G.L. Reijns, M.H. Barton (editors)
Elsevier Science Publishers B.V. (North-Holland)
©*IFIP, 1987*

A VLSI-ORIENTED ARCHITECTURE
FOR PARALLEL PROCESSING IMAGE GENERATION

Wolfgang Strasser

Technische Hochschule Darmstadt, Informatik,
FG GRIS, Alexanderstr. 24, D-6100 Darmstadt

Real time image generation on raster displays, with a high
degree of realism, can be achieved with reasonable costs
only by distributing the task to a great number of processors.
The many existing alternatives of multiprocessor architectures
are classified with respect to the applied problem partitioning.
The advantages of object space partitioning are described and
a pipeline of identical object processors is proposed. It is
shown that the proposed architecture can be adapted very easily
to various system requirements.

INTRODUCTION

Real-time generation of realistic looking scenes has been a challenge to
computer architects for more than 10 years. The complexity of the computer
image generation (CIG) problem has been tackled so far only by very expensive
special purpose computers of the main frame class or for very simple scenes
not relevant to real tasks. Real time image synthesis has two main problems:

1) Formal description of objects and their environment containing
   enough information to create images closely representing pictures
   of reality.

2) Fast enough generation of images. In the worst case, a totally
   new frame has to be computed with the refresh rate of the screen,
   e.g. 50 Hz.

Quite recently the state-of-the-art in describing most complex, realistic
scenes has made remarkable progress. Even the high demands of the film
and advertising industries can be fulfilled. The second problem, namely fast
image generation is still a hard problem to be solved. Advances in semi-
conductor technology, and more important, the availability of VLSI design
techniques and reliable CAD systems offer new options to solve the problem.
Several proposals have been made recently (Cohen (1980), Roman and Kimura
(1981), Fuchs and Poulton (1981)) to exploit the new technique to solve the
CIG problem by distributing the task to many processors. The way in which
the distribution is done determines to a high degree

- the efficiency of the solution with respect to different
  applications

- the expandability of the system to work on complexer scenes and

- the adaptability to higher resolution displays.

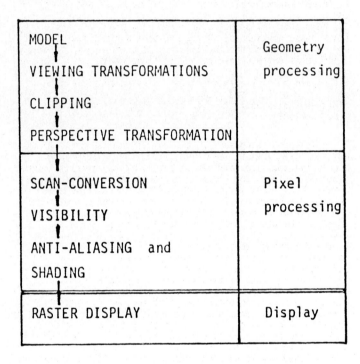

Figure 1: Steps of computer image generation

Figure 1 shows the sequence of operations required to generate a raster display out of the model data. Two main parts can be distinguished:

1) The Geometry Processing section transforms the objects defined in the model from application dependent "world" coordinates into viewing coordinates according to the viewing position and direction. Objects are represented by their boundaries which are

approximated by planar, convex polygons. In this way the
viewing transformation of the objects is reduced to the
transformation of points, namely the vertices of the polygons.
The transformation generally includes rotation, scaling and
translation which is performed by the well-known (4x4)-
vector-matrix-multiplication (e.g. Encarnacao and Strasser,
1986).
The next step (clipping) eliminates on a polygon by polygon
basis those portions of the scene which are outside the field
of view. Then, perspective division is performed to obtain the
illusion of depth. These geometric transformations are carried out
in real time by high-performance calligraphic display systems using
high speed multiplier/accumulator chips. Recently a special
purpose chip set - the geometric engine (Clark 1980) has been
designed and is built in a graphics workstation. (Silicon
Graphics 1983).

2) The pixel processing section has to perform the more time
critical calculations. First of all, the objects have to be
scan-converted, i.e. all pixels belonging to an object must be
identified. Then, the visibility at each pixel has to be
determined (if not yet done before) and finally the greyscale
or color is computed. The task is then to design a system which
is capable of processing a reasonable complex scene within the
time constraints of the frame rate (50 Hz).

In the following, we concentrate on the pixel processing part
and assume an interface to a geometry preprocessor, which stores
and prepares the objects optimally for scan-conversion and
anti-aliasing. Anti-aliasing is necessary to alleviate "stair
cases" and other artifacts present in synthetic digital images
due to the violation of the sampling theorem. Reijns et.al. give
a theoretical explanation of the phenomenons in their paper on
"Parallel Processing of Video Images" in these proceedings.
At the time being objects are approximated by planar, convex
polygons (work on fast rendering of quadrics is in a preliminary
stage). They are tesselated into triangles. This tesselation
has the advantage of being independent of viewing transformations
and therefore has to be done only once.

PARALLEL PROCESSING ARCHITECTURES

Parallel processing with many processors can be successfully applied only
in case that the problem lends itself to partitioning. Considering the
pixel processing part of the CIG problem, at least 3 alternatives can be
found:

Operation Partitioning

Most currently available CIG systems in simulators are based on this
principle. A large scale pipeline system is realized with each processor

performing a special operation on all data of a frame. A great number
of different highly specialized processors is used. Therefore this approach
is not well suited for a VLSI realization.

Image Space Partitioning

Parallel processing may be used by partitioning the image or screen space among
a number of processors. Each of these processors is then responsible
for a region of the screen. This type of partitioning breaks up the
processing among the processors so that each of them operates concurrently,
with a processing task less demanding than computing the entire image.
This solution ultimately leads to one processor per pixel. In this case
all processors work concurrently on the same object (see Fig. 2) which
means that the objects are scan-converted sequentially and the resulting
pixel values are stored in the dedicated refresh buffers corresponding
to the image space partitioning. Pixels are generated in parallel, so that
the obvious choice for the solution of the visibility problem is a
Z-buffer: whenever an object may be visible at a given pixel, this pixel's
Z-buffer content is checked to determine whether the new object is
closer to the viewer than the already stored. If the new object is closer,
its color value and Z-value replace the already stored values.
Because of this operation, anti-aliasing cannot be handled properly:

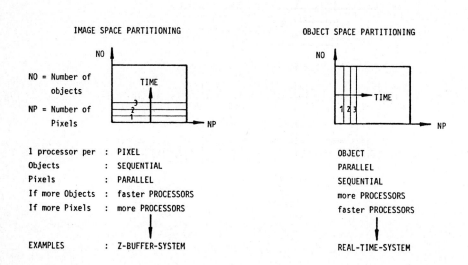

Figure 2: Comparison of two parallel processing approaches

the object nearest to the eye defines the pixel value even in case that
it covers only a small fraction of the overall pixel area. In other words,
the pixel is dealt with as a point instead of an area.For the same
reason transparency cannot be realized, because this would require a
Z-sorting of all contributions to the pixel.

To distribute the objects to the processors and to assemble the results
of their computations to generate the video image requires global communication line (Fig.3). This may cause serious problems for a VLSI realization.

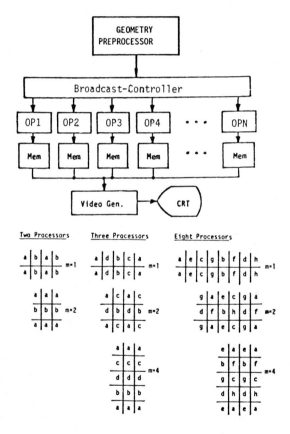

Figure 3: Broadcasting and distributed refresh buffer with interlace patterns

252 W. Strasser

The Pixel-Planes of Fuchs et.al. (1981 ff) is the most consequent
realization of the processor-per-pixel or image space partitioning.
It solves the problems of the great number of processors by reducing
the power of the single processor drastically to one-bit add,
compare and store operations. The global communication is avoided at
the expense of time by transmitting the object information serially.
These compromises make the Pixel-Planes-System too slow with today's
technology.

Object Space Partitioning

In this scheme, objects are assigned to different concurrently operating
processors. Consequently applied this solution requires one processor
per object (see Fig. 2). In this case all processors compute concurrently
on the same pixel. This means that the objects are dealt with in
parallel whereas the pixels are generated sequentially.
This results in the problem to decide the visibility at the single
pixel within a pixel period ($\sim$ 10ns in a 1024 x 1024, 50 Hz,
non-interlaced system). Lindner (1983) describes a solution to this
problem based on a special "Multiple-Write" - Bus. It is attractive
with the assumption that only one object processor fits on a chip
(Fig. 4). Of course the goal is to have many object processors on a chip.

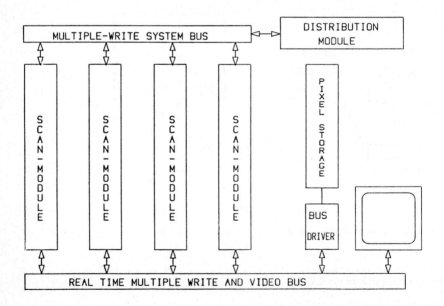

Figure 4: Processor-per-Object Architecture including the "Multiple-Write" -
Bus

In this case this special Bus would be needed on the chip as well as between chips, causing serious timing problems.
Object space partitioning is attractive for real-time-systems, because pixels are computed sequentially in scan line order. But again, the need for global communication for distribution of objects and collection of results may be a problem for VLSI design.
What we are looking for is a systolic system, in which the information flow is passed from one processor to the next.

A PIPELINE FOR SCAN-CONVERSION

The object processors of the object space partitioning scheme can be arranged to a pipeline so that all processors work concurrently but on different pixels. The block diagram and working principle of this design are shown in Figure 5.

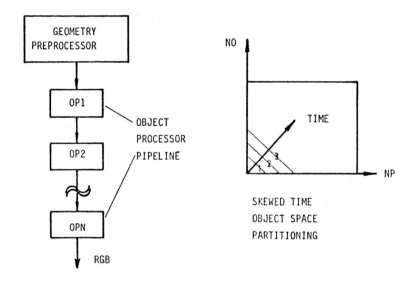

Figure 5: Block diagram and working principle of object processor pipeline

This organization allows for the distribution of the visibility problem: the required minimization operation on N object contributions in one time interval (pixel period) is now executed in N time intervals. In other words, only two Z-values have to be compared within a pixel period in the object processors comparator. This feature is the key to real time visibility computation. Most important, it is independent of the object definition!

In essence, the object processor performs scan-conversion, depth
computation, depth comparison and greyscale or color calculation
and communicates with its predecessor and successor in the pipeline.
To minimize the computations necessary in the object processor, the
geometry preprocessor prepares the object definition in such a way
that from pixel to pixel and from line to line only increments have
to be added or subtracted. The output of the processor pipeline is a
digital video signal which can be passed directly, i.e. without storing
in a refresh buffer, to the digital-to-analog converters of the display.
As expected the generated image shows all the artifacts related to
aliasing. One way to mitigate the errors is to filter the image with
a low-pass before display at the expense of a loss in spatial resolution.
Such a video processing system is described by Reijns et.al. in these
proceedings. Unfortunately effects like blinking of small objects are
not totally suppressed.

Anti-Aliasing

Aliasing can be avoided by correct sampling, which is too expensive
or by area calculations, i.e. weighted averaging of all contributions
that fall within a pixel's area. Correctly realized, this requires the
solution of the visibility at the subpixel level. This again means
that all contributions to a single pixel have to be available. This
second approach is chosen. There exist at least two possibilities for
its realization within the concept of the object processor pipeline:

1) Each object processor computes the sub-pixels covered by its
    object and stores them with the Z-values in a sub-pixel buffer.
    Then a Z-buffer-algorithm between neighboring object processors
    eliminates hidden sub-pixels. Finally the output of the object
    processor pipeline for each pixel is an array of sub-pixel
    values which have to be combined to the pixel value in a filter
    stage following.

2) Each object processor scanconverts its object with respect to
    the pixel area, which is identical to the chosen filter size.
    Then a check is made to found out whether the object covers the
    pixel area totally, partially or is completely outside. It is
    assumed, that the Z-value is constant within the pixel area, that
    is, no change of visibility can occur. The depth comparison with
    the results of the predecessor in the pipeline leads to a
    depth-sorted list of contributing objects for each pixel travelling
    through the processor pipeline. This depth-sorted list is then
    passed to a sub-pixel scan-converter, which fills the pixel area
    with sub-pixel values from front to back. Finally a filter stage
    computes the pixel value.

The first alternative is rejected, because of the increased computing and
communication bandwidth needed in the object processors to calculate and
to transmit subpixel values, which will eventually be thrown away in the
visibility computation.

The second alternative is improved by inserting into the depth-sorted
list only the names of contributing objects. These names are addresses
to a fast random access memory(object table)which is loaded for each frame
by the geometry preprocessor with the object data. The output of the
object table is passed to the sub-pixel scan-converter, which fills the
sub-pixel area line by line. The filter following is organized also
line by line. To be able to work in real-time, i.e. with the pixel rate,
each sub-pixel line has a scan-converter/filterstage, which forms a
pipeline too (Figure 6).

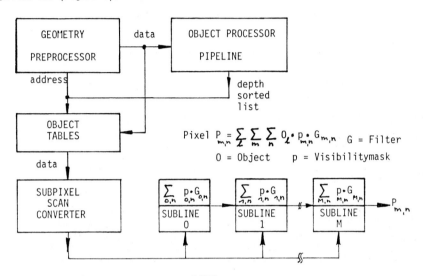

Figure 6: Subpixel - Scanconverter and Filter

Object Processor

The object processor receives from the geometry processor a triangle,
containing all necessary information about location, shape and color or
greyscale. This includes the coordinates of the vertices, the change of the
depth or Z-value in X and Y-direction. The following operations have to
be performed:

> Update of coordinates with respect to the new scanline.
> This means incrementing the depth-value and the intersection
> coordinates of the left and right edge with the scan-line. In
> addition, to be able to compute the intersection of the triangle
> with the square filter region (say 2 x 2), the top and bottom line
> of the "actual" trapezoid is up-dated. This amounts to 5 additions.

For each pixel, the depth or Z-value is incremented.
Then this depth value is compared with the depth value
received from the predecessor in the pipeline. Depending
on this depth comparison and the form of the intersection
with the current pixel region, the object processor rejects
its own contribution and passes the received information to
the successor or rejects the received information and passes
its own contribution or inserts his contribution in depth-
sorted order in the list, which is then transfered to the
next object processor.

This operation requires 1 high resolution addition, 4 comparisons
(the 4 corners of the actual trapezoid are compared with the
current pixel region) at screen resolution and 1 high
resolution depth comparison. Figure 7 shows the block
diagram of the object processor completed with additional
registers to receive, store and send information and the
necessary control logic. A design of the object processor
represents an equivalent gate complexity of about 1500 gates.

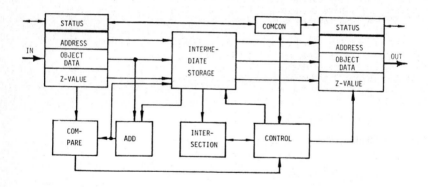

Figure 7: Block diagram of the object processor

If we assume that about 5000 triangles should be handled, depth is needed with 20 bit resolution and some control signals for communicating status information between the processors are necessary, then a chip for this object processor would require about 80 pins. Of course, more than one object processor can be integrated on a chip. Because of the extremely simple inter-connection scheme, external (between chips) and internal interconnection of object processors is the same. Therefore a chip with N object processors needs no more pins than the single processor chip.

System Timing

For each frame, i.e. every 20 ms the object processors have to be loaded and then the objects can be scan-converted. Loading is done by shifting the object description from processor to processor through the pipeline until the last processor received his object or until there are no more objects. This loading time reduces the total time available for scan-conversion.

For example, 5000 objects each defined by 10 values and a shift-delay of 50 ns require a load time of 2,5 ms out of the 20ms available for a frame. After the loading of all objects, scan-conversion and pixel calculation can start. Since objects may be inserted into or deleted from the actual processing, information can be passed from one processor to the next only after ready signals have been exchanged. This indicates that asynchronous timing should be used for the system.

The required processing speed of the object processor can be estimated by comparing the available time per frame with the total number of cycles required. The screen resolution be NxN, S the number of cycles for loading an object processor, O the number of object processors, A the average number of objects per pixel and f the frame rate. Then the number of cycles per second is

$$C = f \times (N \times N \times A + O \times S)$$

Example: $f = 50$ Hz $N \times N = 250000$

$A = 2$ $O = 5000, S = 10$

$C = 27,5 \times 10^6$ per second

This means that the object processor has to perform his tasks within 35 ns which is within the performance range of today's technology.

Conclusions

The presented pipeline system is conceived for high speed generation of computer images with anti-aliasing. Its working principle is independent of the types of objects; even different object processors could be included in the processor pipeline, provided that they meet the system's time constraints. The system can be expanded to complexer scenes by adding more processors. In spite of the fact, that the design of the processor did not include any test circuitry, it seems to be obvious, that a VLSI realization of the system is feasible. For example if we assume a technology with 30000 gates/chip, a 5000 processors system could be built with 250 chips. Compared to conventional systems this is very attractive.

References

Anonymous, The IRIS Graphics System,
Silicon Graphics Inc., April 83

Clark, J., A VLSI geometry processor for graphics,
IEEE Computer, July 80

Cohen, D., A VLSI approach to the CIG problem,
Report of the Information Sciences Institute
University of Southern California, 1980

Encarnacao, J., and Strasser, W., Einführung in die
Graphische Datenverarbeitung,
Oldenbourg Verlag München, 1986

Fuchs, H., and Poulton, J., Pixel-planes: a VLSI-
oriented design for a raster graphics engine,
VLSI-Design, Third Quarter 81

Lindner, R., Introduction to a homogeneous multiprocessor
kernel,
Proceedings of NATO ASI Summer Course 1983

Reijns, G.L., et.al., Parallel Processing of
Video Images,
These Proceedings

Roman, G.-C., and Kimura, F., VLSI perspective of realtime
hidden-surface elimination,
CAD, Vol. 13, No. 2, March 81

HIGHLY PARALLEL COMPUTERS
G.L. Reijns, M.H. Barton (editors)
Elsevier Science Publishers B.V. (North-Holland)
©IFIP, 1987

PARALLEL PROCESSING OF VIDEO IMAGES.

G.L. Reijns*, U.E. Kraus**, G. Kirana*, W.C. Hildering**

* Delft University of Technology
The Netherlands
** Philips TV Laboratories,
Eindhoven, The Netherlands

SUMMARY

This paper describes a parallel processing system for processing TV
video signals in real time. The video computer consists of 16 parallel operating powerful processors, organized in an SIMD arrangement. A
host computer can load the different micro-programs into the connected
video computer. In order to obtain maximum performance, the assembler
level of programming has been avoided in the video computer.
The convolution operation, image expansion and image compression were
implemented. Programs for executing image rotation are under development. Much attention has been paid to the video computer's input and
output memory and its partitioning. The whole system has been implemented and its operation has been demonstrated.

1. INTRODUCTION

Real-time manipulation of digital video images requires extremely fast processing. This is due to the fact that in a 625-line system the line repetition
time is 64μsec., which includes a 12μsec. blanking period during in which the
deflected beam is returned to the left side of the frame. The analog video
signal is usually sampled with a frequency of 13.5 MHz and linearly quantized
into an 8 bit pulse code (PCM). This results in the requirement that one video
line, comprising 702 pixels, must be processed in 64 μsec. However, some ini-
tializations have to be done at the beginning of each video line, resulting in
some 60 μsec. that are available for processing one line. One of the more
complicated processing demands is the capability to execute a 3 x 3 convolution on every pixel. We have designed a processor (see section 3) which is
able to execute a simple convolution in 9 clock cycles, each with a duration
of 125 n.sec. For that reason a convolution takes 1125 n.sec. per pixel and in
order to be able to process 702 pixels in 60 μsec., 13.2 parallel operating
processors are required. In the implementation of our video computer, *16
parallel operating processors* have been used.

2. SYSTEM CONSIDERATIONS

The global block diagram of the architecture is given in fig. 1. The digital
video image processing (DVIP) is carried out by means of 16 processors. One
finds an input memory and an output memory, both containing two memory banks.

The host computer operates as master controller,   which provides the interface with the user.
The architecture is designed to be programmable by means of micro-programs.
These micro-programs are stored in the memory of the host and can be down-
line-loaded to the micro-program memory in the DVIP upon command of the user.

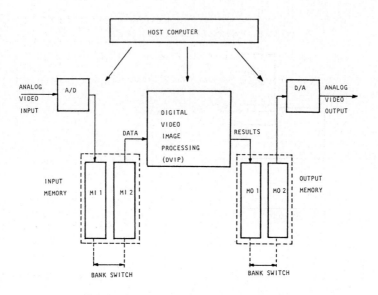

fig. 1   Block-diagram of the system.

A processing job can be split up in various ways. One of these is to split up
a process into a number of sequential steps, each of which are executed by
processors or circuits arranged in series (pipelining). In our design we did
not pipeline processors, although we have applied pipelining at a very low
level, for instance to overlap the fetching of a new pixel value from memory
with the processing of the previous pixel.
Rather than pipelining processors, we designed a system based upon the SIMD
principle (single instruction, multiple data). In the SIMD system, the same
instruction is executed simultaneously in all processors. This architecture
has an advantage over the MIMD system (multiple instruction, multiple data)
since only one program control unit is required for all processors in the system. The SIMD principle can be used very favorably, since every pixel in an
image is usually processed in the same manner. This is reflected in our design
by splitting up the total image into 16 parts, which are independently processed by each of the processors.
One of the potential bottlenecks in parallel processing is the access to the
image memory. If all 16 processors were given one common access to the input
image memory, the processors would suffer long idle times, waiting for memory
access. One solution to this memory contention problem is provided by dividing
the image memory into a number of blocks, which can be independently accessed.

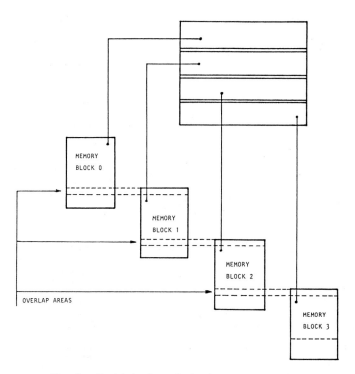

fig. 2   Partitioning of the image memory.

In our design, we divided both the input memory and the output memory into
four blocks, corresponding to the four horizontal parts in the image (see fig.
2). Therefore, the 16 processors have been grouped into four units, which can
independently access the memories. Another solution could have been splitting
up the input and output memories into 16 or 8 independently accessible units.
However, we will see in section 7 that the partitioning of the memory into too
many parts increases the hardware complexity somewhat when expansion of the
image is requested.
On the other hand, a combining of the 16 processors into less than 4 groups is
not very well possible, due to problems of packaging. Moreover, we also wanted
to use the unit of 4 processors in another project, in which each of the 4
groups is capable to process in an independent way a part of the picture (MIMD
arrangement).
In order to ensure that a division of the image memory into four parts meets
the memory access requirements without delaying the processors, a single
access must consist of four bytes of information (four pixels).

The processors of the multiprocessor architecture are controlled by means of a
micro-program. Different micro-program subroutines can be loaded into the
memory of the control unit. The normal assembler level of programming has been
avoided in this machine. The user is able to call the micro-subroutines
directly by means of Pascal statements and link them in the host computer.

Avoiding the assembler level has the advantage of providing a more efficient
machine. A drawback of this directly micro-program driven architecture is the
difficulty of writing micro-programs.

3. DESIGN OF THE DIGITAL VIDEO IMAGE PROCESSING UNIT (DVIP).

3.1 Image memory.

Both the input memory and the output memory contain two memory banks consisting of 256K bytes each. One bank is sufficient to store the information of one
video field of 20 m.sec. The digital signals coming from the A/D converter are
stored sequentially in memory bank M_{11}, while the DVIP simultaneously reads
data from the secondary memory input bank M_{12} in quite a different sequence
(see fig. 1). The operations of M_{11} and M_{12} are interchanged every field
period of 20 m.sec. So in the next field period the signals from the A/D converter are stored in M_{12} and the DVIP reads the data from M_{11}. This arrangement has the advantage that the timing of the processing can be extended to
the blanking periods of the beam. The independence is particularly important
when a part of the image is expanded to the full screen size (zooming).
For the same reasons, the output memory has been duplicated. It is possible to
reduce the number of input and output memory banks from 4 to 3 by combining
the input bank, which is receiving data from the A/D converter, with the output bank, which delivers at that moment data to the D/A converter. In that
case, the operation of the 3 banks needs to be exchanged cyclically. This was
not done because the number of chips required for the additional control
exceeds the number of chips for one memory bank.
The interarrival time between the pixels is 75 n.sec. and a pixel must be
stored in the same time period. In order to cope with this small access time
each of the memory banks has been organized into 64K words of 4 bytes (4 pixels), resulting in a required access time of 300 n.sec.

3.2 Organization of the DVIP unit.

The block diagram of the digital video image processing unit, containing 4
processing units, is given in fig. 3. Each processing unit contains 4 processors, called AU's.
The DVIP has one micro-program memory and one controller. All of the 16 AU's
always receive simultaneously the same micro-instructions. The 4 processing
units in fig. 3 read the image data from the input data memory at the same
time.
The pipeline register in fig. 3 enables the simultaneous fetching of a microinstruction in the micro-program memory and the execution of a microinstruction fetched prior to it. These overlapping operations therefore
inprove the performance.

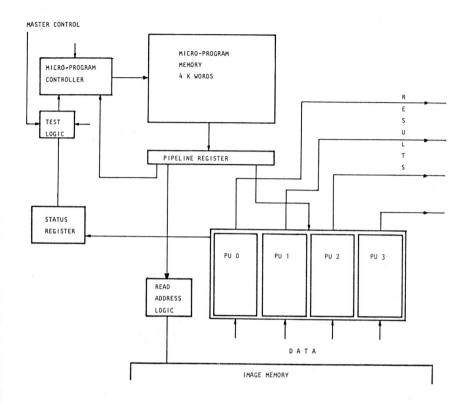

fig. 3   Control of the 4 processing units (PU's).

4.   EXAMPLES OF IMAGE PROCESSING.

As mentioned before, the 16 processors have been grouped into 4 processing
units, with each unit usually takes care of the processing of 1/4 of the
image.

4.1 Convolution
The processing steps of a convolution operation of 3 x 3 pixels is shown
below.

$$A_{-1} \quad B_{-1} \quad C_{-1}$$

$$A_0 \quad B_0 \quad C_0$$

$$A_{+1} \quad B_{+1} \quad C_{+1}$$

fig. 4   Pixel numbering.

A new value of pixel B_0 (in the middle of fig. 4) must be calculated as a function of its own value and those of the 8 pixels around it. Each of the 9 pixel values is multiplied by a certain factor, which can be different for each pixel, and the 9 resulting values are added together.

$P_1 = A_{-1} \cdot \alpha_{-1}$

where A_{-1} is the pixel value of the upper left hand pixel and α_{-1} the multiplication factor. Similarly,

$P_2 = B_{-1} \cdot \beta_{-1}$

$P_3 = C_{-1} \cdot \gamma_{-1}$

$P_4 = A_0 \cdot \alpha_0$

.
.
.

$P_9 = C_{+1} \cdot \gamma_{+1}$

The new value for the pixel in the middle is $P_1 + P_2 + \ldots P_9$. In fig. 5 we again show 3 rows of pixels.

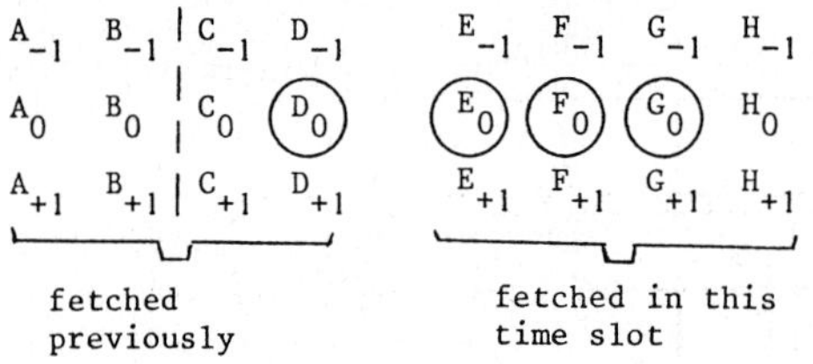

$$
\begin{array}{llll}
A_{-1} & B_{-1} & C_{-1} & D_{-1} \\
A_{0} & B_{0} & C_{0} & (D_{0}) \\
A_{+1} & B_{+1} & C_{+1} & D_{+1}
\end{array}
\qquad
\begin{array}{llll}
E_{-1} & F_{-1} & G_{-1} & H_{-1} \\
(E_{0}) & (F_{0}) & (G_{0}) & H_{0} \\
E_{+1} & F_{+1} & G_{+1} & H_{+1}
\end{array}
$$

fetched   fetched in this
previously   time slot

fig. 5   Method to execute convolution by the 4 processors of one PU.

We assume that the processing unit has arrived at the state in which pixel values D_0, E_0, F_0 and G_0 are going to be calculated in parallel by the 4 processors present in the processing unit. Processor 1 will calculate the new pixel value D, processor 2 the new value E, processor 3 the new value F and processor 4 the new value G.

The original pixel values C_{-1}, C_0, C_{+1} and D_{-1}, D_0, D_{+1} are still present in the processing unit. The first action of the processing unit is the parallel fetching of 4 bytes of information, corresponding to the pixel values E_{-1}, F_{-1}, G_{-1} and H_{-1}, from the input memory into the processing unit. Calculations with C_{-1}, D_{-1}, E_{-1}, F_{-1}, G_{-1}, and H_{-1} can now start.

In one micro-step of 100n.sec. processor 1 multiplies C_{-1} by α_{-1}.
In the same micro-step processor 2 multiplies D_{-1} by α_{-1}.
At the same time processors 3 and 4 carry out multiplications on E_{-1} and F_{-1}, respectively.

In the next micro-step of 100n.sec. processor 1 multiplies D_{-1} by β_{-1} and adds the value it calculated in the previous micro-step to this result. So processor 1 is able to execute a multiplication followed by an addition in a total of 100 n.sec. Processors 2, 3 and 4 execute similar operations in this second micro-step.

In the third micro-step, processor 1 multiplies E_{-1} by γ_{-1} and again adds the previously derived value to it. Processors 2,3 and 4 execute similar operations in this third micro-step. Meanwhile, during these 3 micro-steps, the processing unit has addressed the input memory and fetched the pixel values E_0, F_0, G_0 and H_0. In the subsequent period of 3 micro-steps, calculations are executed with C_0, D_0, E_0, F_0, G_0 and H_0. In the now following third period of 3 micro-steps computations are carried out with C_1, D_1, E_1, F_1, G_1 and H_1. At the end of this total period of 9 micro-steps, the new pixel values of D_0, E_0, F_0 and G_0 have been derived. The whole process is then repeated for the 4 neighboring pixels to the right. The 4 pixel results produced by a processing unit are each provided with an address of the location where it must be stored in the output memory. This write address logic unit also receives its instructions from the micro-instruction memory. Fig. 6 shows some details of a processing unit consisting of 4 processors. The micro-program memory consists of 4K words of 64 bits and has an access time of less than 100 n.sec.

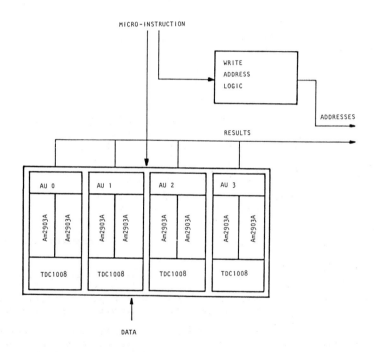

fig. 6   Processing unit consisting of 4 AU's.

5.   CONFIGURATION OF THE PROCESSING UNIT.

As mentioned before, a processing unit consists of 4 processors, called AU_0, AU_1, AU_2, and AU_3, in fig. 7. A processing unit is connected to the input memory via 4 input registers (INR's). Each INR has a direct connection to its corresponding processor. The AU_0 is shown in somewhat more detail than the other AU's. The contents of the 4 INR's can also be transferred to the 4 registers BDR (bi-directional register). These BDR registers are connected with each other to enable a rotation or shifting of data to the left or the right. This operation is needed when a convolution is executed, as explained in section 4. As shown in fig. 6 each AU is equipped with a bit slice processor (two 4 bit slice microprocessors type Am2903A) and a multiplier-accumulator type TDC 1008 of TRW. The block in fig. 7 with input y and outputs A and B represents a RAM in the bit-slice processor. The multiplier/accumulator chip provides an 8x8 bit multiplication including an 8 bit addition in 100 n.sec.

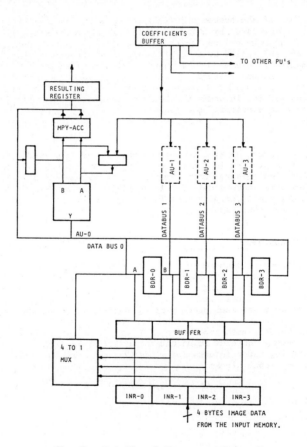

fig. 7   Details of the processing unit.

6. IMAGE COMPRESSION.

Image compression creates the problem of aliasing. In order to explain this problem, let us consider the Fourier transform of a 2-dimensional signal $f(x,y)$:

$$F(h,v) = \int\limits_{-\infty}^{+\infty} \int\limits_{-\infty}^{+\infty} f(x,y)\ e^{-j(hx+vy)}\ dx\,dy$$

where h and v represent horizontal and vertical spatial frequencies. It can be shown that the Fourier transform of a 2-dimensional signal $f(ax,by)$ corresponds to

$$\frac{1}{|a.b|}\ F\left(\frac{h}{a}, \frac{v}{b}\right)$$

This means that if the number of pixels in an image remains the same and the picture is compressed by a factor α in both the horizontal and the vertical direction, the frequency components in both the horizontal and the vertical direction are multiplied by α. If f is the sampling rate or pixel rate of the original image, the system must be bandlimited to a frequency of $f/2$, in order to meet the Shannon criterion. However, after compression the picture would contain frequencies $\alpha f/2$ and the Shannon criterion would no longer be met, causing aliasing. So, in order to suppress aliasing, the original picture must be prefiltered to a cutoff frequency of

$$\frac{f}{2\alpha}$$

Different methods can be applied to implement the required filtering. For instance, if a picture is compressed by a factor of 2 in both horizontal and vertical directions, every other pixel in both these directions can be deleted. However, before deleting these pixels, it is very useful to apply a convolution using all the pixels, but of course calculating only the resulting values for every other pixel.

7. IMAGE EXPANSION.

One of the processing requirements is image expansion. For instance, it must be possible to expand the shaded area A in fig. 8 to the full TV screen. In order to get the 4 processing units to operate in parallel, the video informa-tion between the lines indicated by "start" and "finish" is divided into 4 horizontal strokes and each processing unit processes the information of one stroke.
As indicated before, each processing unit has access to a fixed 1/4 part of the input memory. Special input address logic takes care of distributing the serially incoming video information of the area between the start and finish to the 4 memory input blocks.

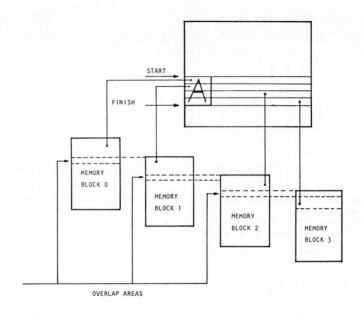

fig. 8   Data partitioning when the image is expanded.

This input address logic contains a few counters and a comparator. As the
expansion ratio is not fixed, the number of horizontal video lines contained
in one stroke is calculated by the host using the relation:

$$\text{SIZE} = \frac{\text{finish-start}+1}{4} \quad \text{(rounded off to the next integer value)}$$

The size value together with the START value is then used by the input address
logic to direct the video information belonging to a stroke to its corresponding input memory block. It will be clear that each input memory block will in
that case only partially be filled with information. The input address logic
also ensures that the last video line of the first stroke is stored in both
the first and the second memory block. This also applies to the first video
line of the second stroke. A similar overlap is created between the other
blocks. This information overlap in the memory blocks provides for the processing of groups of pixels, such as expansion.

```
a  k  b  t  c  u  d
*  _  *  _  *  _  *                    *  pixel of the original
                                          image

n  o  p  q  .  .  .                    -  new pixel

-  -  -  -  -  -  -


A  K  B  T  C  U  D
*  _  *  _  *  _  *
```

fig. 9   Pixels to be processed when the image is expanded.

In the case of expansion, new pixels have to be created among the pixels of
the original image. If a, b, A and B are pixels of the original image (fig. 9)
and the expansion is a factor of 2 in both the horizontal and vertical directions, the new pixels k, n, p and o are found according to

$k = 1/2a + 1/2b$
$n = 1/2a + 1/2A$
$p = 1/2b + 1/2B$
$o = 1/4a + 1/4b + 1/4A + 1/4B.$

8.   CONCLUSIONS.

A real-time black-and-white TV video computer, comprising 16 parallel operating processors, has been designed and implemented. The video computer is
micro-programmable and the micro-programs can be down-line-loaded from a host
computer to the video computer (via a standard VME bus). Microprograms have
been written and their operation demonstrated to execute image expansion,
image compression and convolution.
The 16 processors function in an SIMD arrangement. Special attention has been
given to the design and partitioning of the image input and the image output
memory of the video computer. The processors themselves are able to execute
individually an 8x8 bit multiplication including an addition within 100 n.sec.
The next step in the development will be writing a number of other micro-
programs, to include, for instance, image rotation.

9.   REFERENCES.

- S. Levialdi (editor).
  Integrated Technology for parallel image processing,
  Academia Press, 1985.

- L. Cordella and M.J.B. Duff.
  Comparing sequential and parallel processing of pictures.
  Proc. 3rd International Joint Conf. on Pattern Recognition.
  Coronado, Nov. 8-11, 1976.

- M.J.B. Duff and S. Levialdi (eds.)
  Languages and architectures for image processing.
  Academic Press, London 1981.

- F.A. Gerritsen and L.G. Aardema.
  Design and use of a fast, flexible and dynamically
  micro-programmable pipelined image processor.
  Proc. First Scandinavian Conference on Image Analysis.
  Linkoeping, Jan. 14-16, 1980.

- T. Ito, et al.
  A color picture processing system with firmware facility.
  Proc. 4th International Joint Conference on Pattern Recognition.
  Kyoto, Nov. 7-10, 1978.

- A.P. Reeves.
  Parallel computer architectures for image processing.
  Proc. 1981 International Conference on Parallel Processing.
  Columbus (Ohio), Aug. 25-28, 1981.

AUTHOR INDEX

Auguin, M., 97

Behr, P.M., 1
Bode, A., 19
Boeri, F., 97
Burnett, T.D., 41

Cosnard, M., 127
Cruz, A., 81

Djidjev, H.N., 157

Evans, D.J., 145 175

Fritsch, G., 19

Gao, G.R., 59
Giloi, W.K., 1

Hâncu, M.V.A., 211
Händler, W., 19
Henning, W., 19
Hildering, W.C., 259

Iwashita, M., 235

Jesshope, C., 81

Kirana, G., 259
Kraus, U.E., 259

Lauwereins, R., 223

Maehle, E., 29
McCanny, J.V., 191
Mühlenbein, H., 1

Peperstraete, J.A., 223
Peters, F.J., 201

Reijns, G.L., 259
Robert, Y., 127
Rushton, A., 81

Smith, K.C., 211
Stewart, J., 81
Strasser, W., 247

Tchuente, M., 127
Temma, T., 235
Topham, N.P., 111

Volkert, J., 19

Wirl, K., 29

Date Due

	Returned	Due	Returned
89	AUG 0 7 1989		
89	NOV 1 6 1990		
5 050			